When Soldiers Quit

WHEN SOLDIERS QUIT

Studies in Military Disintegration

BRUCE ALLEN WATSON

Westport, Connecticut
London

Library of Congress Cataloging-in-Publication Data

Watson, Bruce, 1929–
    When soldiers quit : studies in military disintegration / Bruce
Allen Watson.
        p. cm.
    Includes bibliographical references and index.
    ISBN 0–275–95223–1 (alk. paper)
    1. Sociology, Military.   2. Unit cohesion (Military science)—Case
studies.   3. Military discipline—Case studies.   4. Military
offenses—Case studies.   5. War crimes—Case studies.   I. Title.
U21.5.W38   1997
306.2'7—dc20   96–28568

British Library Cataloguing in Publication Data is available.

Library of Congress Catalog Card Number: 96–28568
ISBN: 0–275–95223–1

First published in 1997

Praeger Publishers, 88 Post Road West, Westport, CT 06881
An imprint of Greenwood Publishing Group, Inc.

Printed in the United States of America

The paper used in this book complies with the
Permanent Paper Standard issued by the National
Information Standards Organization (Z39.48–1984).

10 9 8 7 6 5 4 3 2 1

What is too true is that bravery often does not at all exclude cowardice, horrible devices to secure personal safety, [and] infamous conduct.

Colonel Ardant du Picq
Battle Studies, p. 146

Contents

Maps

Preface

In three previous military histories (*The Great Indian Mutiny*, Praeger, 1991; *Sieges: A Comparative Study*, Praeger, 1993; and *Desert Battle: Comparative Perspectives*, Praeger, 1995), I explored the winning and losing of battles. I narrated who did what to whom and when, and I also identified constants and variables of particular types of battle. In doing so, I came across genuine heroes, recited a shamefully long list of military incompetents, and encountered several fools and even some first-rate villains. Yet something was missing. As I moved through various historical periods, many examples of uncharacteristic military behavior surfaced, events benignly dubbed "incidents." These included troop defections, outright mutinies, and riotous behavior of all sorts—wholesale looting, destruction, and violence even to the point of massacre.

A pattern emerged. Seldom are such incidents explained by historians in any depth beyond the occasional and often unnoticed study. Not surprisingly, there is a mountain of literature devoted to gallantry, heroism, and daring deeds, and there is copious literature on why this or that battle was lost. Losing, it seems, is the other half of the military equation called battle. In contrast, military historians have not applied equal vigor to the study of deviant behaviors. Rather, historians, and generals, choose to ignore them.

This attitude is made easy because such awful behavior is often viewed as the fault of individuals. Psycho-medical studies reveal that individual soldiers crack under the stress of war, and legal processes expose rotten soldiers in the ranks. Both responses result in deviants being removed and somehow punished—the World War II "Section 8" discharge for psychological instability or the court-martial. The military establishment is redeemed. The silent bonus is that civilians are kept happy with the sop that "it was the fault of those loonies," because "our boys would never do such things."

This book takes a different approach. Realizing that indeed there are individuals who fall off the edge of acceptable conduct, I offer the notion that aberrant behaviors also result from the social disintegration of the units involved. Disintegration is a group phenomenon that reaches beyond the familiar blame-game. A group orientation forces us to look at the history of military units to trace those processes that take the unit toward disintegration. This approach also forces upon us the appalling realization that perfectly nice people sometimes do unspeakable things to other people.

My intention is not to lay bare secrets, to malign the military, or to bring down heroes. Rather, I offer a historical sociology of a subject that has received far too little attention for far too long.

Acknowledgments

This book could not have been written without the following libraries and their staffs who helped in so many ways: the Doe Library and the Richmond Northern Regional Research Library of the University of California, Berkeley; the Widener Library, Harvard University; the India Office Library and Records, London; and my own college library. But this is not just a library book. I wish I could name all the veterans from World War II through Desert Storm, both long and short service (U.S. Marine Corps, U.S. Army, British Army), who listened to me, answered numerous questions, and read parts or all of the manuscript. A short list must include Bill Perry, Peter Palko, George Potter, Paul Sabatini, Ed Higgins, and the late Bill Plumb and Bill Sparks. I need to thank Richard Risbrough of the psychology department in Diablo Valley College for his enthusiastic reception of the ideas presented here. My wife, Marilyn, read and reread various versions of the manuscript, making invaluable comments and corrections. Linda Fine generously attended to final manuscript corrections. Finally, decades ago Robert Nisbet and Reinhardt Bendix, both at Berkeley, introduced me to historical sociology. Their ideas are not here, but I hope their spirit of inquiry is.

1

Historical Perspectives of Military Disintegration

A great international commemoration heralded the fiftieth anniversary of the Normandy invasion during World War II. Presidents, prime ministers, generals, and even common soldiers gave speeches, while the gravestones in the background recited the sacrifices made in a way words could not capture.

Armies and the nations that spawn them often commemorate wars and great battles. *Ils ne passeront pas* (they shall not pass) still resonates from the ossuary of World War I Verdun. Remembrance Day was added to Waterloo Day in Britain's living history, and Edinburgh Castle's Scottish War Memorial stands as a silent reminder of the thousands killed in the Great War from that one small land. Even major defeats, when transformed into a nation's rallying point, can be honorably remembered. The British evacuation from Dunkirk in 1940 and America's Pearl Harbor disaster are shining examples.

If heroes, sacrifice, and victories represent one side of military memory, then mutinies, mayhem, surrender, and massacre represent the obverse and darker side. Soldiers, often for only a flash point of time, cease to be soldiers as crisis overwhelms an army or some unit within it. These are situations in which military discipline and unit cohesion disappear. Formal rules of conduct are replaced by those that develop within the crisis situation. Formal leadership is replaced by fortuitous leadership as the unit turns into a crowd or mob. Goals cease to be military and become more often related to survival within or escape from the horrible crisis. This is military disintegration.

Along the corridors of power, disintegration may be considered so damaging to the army, the government, or to that most delicate fabric, the national psyche, that the event's documentation is put under lock and key for generations. Even in a more enlightened age, one supposedly inured to shocking events and public disclosures, it does not follow that broad public interest in military disintegration will drive revelations, or that, conversely, revelations will pique public interest. Quite the contrary. Military disintegration is a story that, despite journalistic forays and the occasional historical study, most would prefer to ignore. Typical is the comment by William Seymour, who stated in his narrative of a siege during the Peninsular War that "One must draw a curtain across the horrors of the sack of Badajoz."[1] Certainly the depredations were disgraceful, but to avoid any discussion of this aspect of behavior is to cheat our understanding of events.

I believe it important to understand this other and often darker side of armies. Without it, we not only lack a complete picture but are denied access to a very human side of military behavior. The study of military disintegration is complex, involving some uncommon ways of looking at military history. Therefore, to construct a common starting place, I first present (in thematic rather than chronological order) a few brief historical examples of disintegration, and second, in the next chapter, I introduce some sociological ideas that establish the interpretive tone for the in-depth examples that are developed and that form the substance of this study.

A STARTING POINT: THREE HISTORICAL EXAMPLES

The Battle of Prestonpans, Scotland, 1745

23 July 1745. The plan was absurd from the start. Prince Charles Edward Stuart, 25 years old, son of the pretender to the throne of England and Scotland, landed on Eriskay, an insignificant island in the Outer Hebrides. He brought with him from France only a few followers, a trifling number of small cannons, and practically no money. Yet Charles—Bonnie Prince Charlie, the Young Pretender—sought to wrest the English crown from the Hanoverian George II and restore the House of Stuart.[2]

Charles had never set foot in Scotland. His notions of what to expect, fed by the Irish Catholics in his tiny retinue, were naive. Many Western Highland clans retained strong loyalties to the Stuarts but were taken aback by the prince's arrival. Having endured one failed rebellion in 1715, they dared not risk another. Indeed, Donald Cameron of Lochiel wanted Charles to go back to France. Other clans were loyal to the English crown; others, lukewarm toward the crown, were hostile to another rebellion. Still other clans, such as the Buchanans, remained aloof from any involvement.

The young prince persisted, and, on 19 August, having spread his charm and sense of purpose throughout the sounds and lochs of Morven and western Inverness, he arrived at Glenfinnen. He was met by about 1,200 men, mostly of Lochiel,[3] including a converted Donald Cameron, and the MacDonalds of Keppoch. The banner of King James III was raised and Charles named his regent. With great enthusiasm, the prince led his band of warriors, not yet nor really ever an army, in search of battle.

The Royal Army garrisoned in Scotland, about 3,000 men under the command of Lieutenant General Sir John Cope, was only the strength of a full brigade. The force was organized into three regiments, plus extra infantry companies, and two regiments of dragoons. They suffered a severe artillery shortage.

Cope's plan to suppress the emerging rebellion involved concentrating all his troops at Stirling Castle. Then they would march to Fort Augustus at the south end of Loch Ness, engaging Prince Charles in battle. He wanted to defeat the rebels before they gathered much momentum. The plan received unanimous approval from the so-called King's Servants (crown legal officers in Edinburgh) and from the Lords Justices in London, acting on behalf of the absent king.

From paper to reality is a big jump. Cope's plan fell apart with each step his army took to Fort Augustus. His men were ill-equipped, poorly trained, lacked discipline, and were led by incompetent officers. The baggage train continually broke down. He still lacked artillery. Moreover, he was very disappointed that clans loyal to the crown did not spring to his side. Were all these problems not enough, he was subjected to a persistent and false rumor that a French force had landed somewhere in Scotland. Cope did receive reliable but unwelcome information that Charles intended to attack him at Corryarrach Pass near Fort August. Knowing his men were not suited for battle and convinced that Charles' force outnumbered his own, Cope bypassed Fort Augustus and headed for Inverness.

Cope's maneuver gave Charles the option of turning south into England, but he wanted to take Edinburgh, the Scottish capital, and once again raise his father's banner. On 4 September, the rebel army occupied Perth, their ranks swelled by recent adherents to the cause. Many of these so-called volunteers were actually dragged from the land by their lairds' threats to burn their cottages and kill their cattle if they did not join. On 17 September, the rebels marched into Edinburgh, avoiding Edinburgh Castle and its garrison that remained aloof and impregnable atop its massive rock. Charles performed his act of self-anointment in front of Hollyrood House to the cheers of the assembled. The rebel army now numbered about 2,400 men.

Cope, realizing something must be done, decided to rescue Edinburgh. He marched his force to Aberdeen, put them on ships, and sailed south, landing at Dunbar on the shoulder of the Firth of Forth, 17 September. His force numbered around 2,500 and included five infantry regiments (the 6th, 43rd, 44th, 46th, and 47th) and the 13th and 14th Dragoons. His optimism about a march against Edinburgh was aided by the addition of cannons he commandeered from the navy ships along with some gunners.

Cope led his men inland to Haddington. The next day they marched toward Tranent, about 10 miles east of Edinburgh. Cope halted his men on flat, low ground. Flanked by the Firth of Forth on the north side and by a marsh and ditch to the south, the general believed it was the best battle-ground between Dunbar and Edinburgh. Whether this was a calculated decision or an explanation after the fact is unclear.

Prince Charles, meantime, receiving news of Cope's landing, was deter-mined to engage in battle as soon as possible. He took his rebel force east toward the Tranent-Haddington road. Lord George Murray, at the head of the column, received a report that Royalist dragoons were headed for high ground near Tranent. Murray rushed his troops forward, not only to deny the Royals the high ground but to give his Scots the advantage of a downhill charge. Cresting a hill south of the Tranent-Haddington road, Murray found Cope's force already deployed. It was 20 September.

The prince and other leaders soon joined Murray, and none liked what they saw (Map 1). Cope's right flank was protected by the village of Preston and secured by a 10-foot-high wall at Preston House Park. To the rear were the coastal villages of Prestonpans and Cockenzie. To Cope's front, on the south, was a ditch 8 feet wide and 4 feet deep, with a marsh running its full length. Only Cope's left or eastern flank was relatively open. Murray and his fellow officers concluded that a frontal attack was out of the question.

During the night, the rebel leaders held a meeting. Murray outlined a plan by which his force would march around Cope's left flank and attack him from behind. The leaders agreed to the plan. In the predawn darkness, the rebels started their flanking maneuver. But outriders alerted Cope to the rebel's movements. He ordered his men to arms and marched them north and then parallel to the rebel movement. The Royals halted and faced right, or east, in three ranks. Their left flank to the north was covered by the 14th

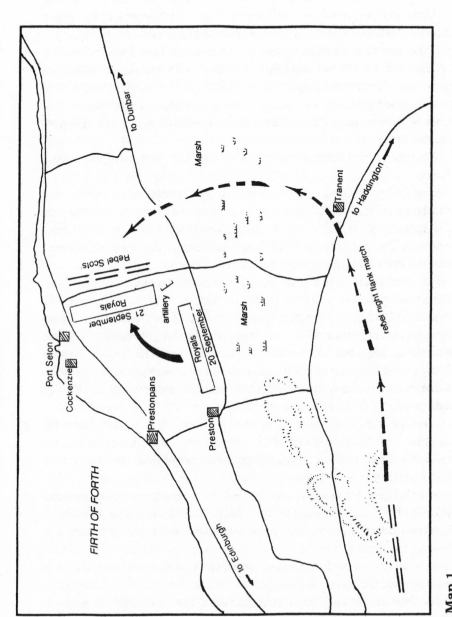

Map 1
Battle of Prestonpans

Dragoons. Then in line were nine companies of the 46th Regiment, two companies of the 6th, and five of the 44th. Two squadrons of the 13th Dragoons covered the right flank. Just beyond the dragoons, in an unconventional placement, was the artillery, consisting of mortars and 1½-pound cannons. Not only was the artillery undersized, but, as events transpired, it was also unreliable. The sailor-gunners were drunk, and civilians handled the horses. The artillery's unreliability was immediately demonstrated when the rebels fired some musket shots in their direction. The sailors and civilians bolted, leaving only an aged gunner and another man to handle the artillery. They managed to fire six mortars and five cannons, but the effect was minimal.

The rebels advanced in bunches, first firing their muskets, then throwing them down. Drawing swords and daggers, brandishing axes and poles with scythes tied to the ends, they sprang forward, their Highland battle cries sounding over the skirl of the bagpipes. The Royals could not believe what was happening. The Highlander charge was not the kind of battle they expected. This was an unremitting, savage attack by tribesmen who showed little inclination to take prisoners.

Fear swelled up in the Royal ranks. The dragoons galloped from the field. The Royal infantry wavered at first, uncertain what to do. Cope gallantly rode along his line, ordering his men to stand and fight. Then panic seized the soldiers as their regiments disintegrated. Throwing away their muskets and packs, they fled. Some managed to clamber over the wall at Preston House. Others squeezed through narrow openings. Many more were caught by the Scots. Blades flashed. Mutilated bodies littered the battlefield. The battle was over in ten minutes.

Cope, the fate of his infantry sealed—some 300 were killed, 500 wounded, and 1,500 taken prisoner—managed to lead the surviving dragoons east to Coldstream. On 22 September, he reached Berwick, where Lord Mark Kerr allegedly observed that Cope was the first general to bring news of his own defeat.[4] That caustic remark, its authenticity now in doubt, spread throughout Britain as derision heaped on the hapless commander. Accused of ineptness and even cowardice, Cope was scorned in song and verse.

An inquiry was held by a Board of Generals. When asked why his men ran away, Cope offered little beyond saying that they were seized by panic before the unexpectedly fierce Scots charge. Cope was rightly exonerated, the explanation of his men's conduct actually correct. His cavalry were poorly trained and lacked discipline, and they rode unseasoned horses that bolted with the first shots. The infantry regiments may have carried battle honors from the Flemish wars two years before, but the men in those regiments were raw recruits whose scant training did not prepare them for what they were to face in Scotland. The officers, having purchased their commissions, were dandies who knew nothing of war.

Ironically, Prince Charles' success at Prestonpans was a prelude to defeat. Encouraged by another victory over Royalist forces at Falkirk in January 1746, and urged on by his Irish advisers who were certain of massive English revolt against King George, Charles took his army south to Derby. He found that the English were not in revolt. With dissension between his officers worsening and desertions mounting, Charles retreated into Scotland. In April 1746, the Duke of Cumberland, the new Royalist commander, forced Charles into battle at Culloden, near Inverness. The Highlanders were slaughtered. The union between England and Scotland was preserved.

The British Retreat to Corunna, Spain, Winter 1808–1809

In 1808, Napoleon Bonaparte deposed the Bourbon king of Spain and replaced him with his own brother Joseph. Spain would be the springboard for an invasion of Portugal to punish that small country for not allying its interests with Bonaparte. But at Vimeiro, Portugal, the French forces under Marshal Andoche Junot ran into a British expeditionary force commanded by Sir Arthur Wellesley (later the Duke of Wellington). Junot brokered a generous armistice, so generous in fact that Wellesley was recalled to explain to an angry Parliament just what he thought he was doing. Sir John Moore replaced Wellesley in Spain.

By December, the French were ready to have another go at Portugal. One army corps under Jean Soult would take a northern route through Palencia and León. The main attack, thrusting due west from Madrid, would be commanded by Napoleon himself.

Lord Castlereagh, British secretary for war, ordered a countercampaign into northern Spain, taking the war to the French rather than waiting in Lisbon for them to attack. He envisioned a campaign that would be near the coast, simplifying logistical support, for never had a British army so dependent on seaborne supplies fought so far from home.

But Sir John Moore developed his own plan for a Spanish campaign. His army, numbering about 30,000 men—with British reinforcements on the way from England and a Spanish force waiting to join him—would plunge into Galicia, across León, toward Palencia and Burgos, and perhaps as far south as Valladolid (Map 2). The British would harry Soult's corps, cut

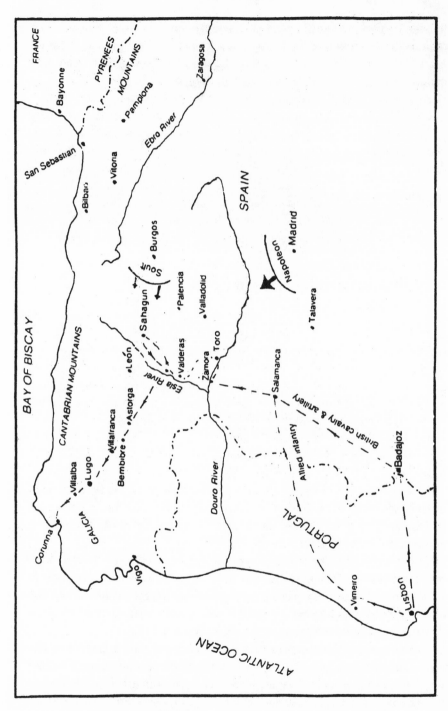

Map 2
Northern Spain: Moor's Campaign

Bonaparte's main communications route to France, and, it was hoped, distract the main French force from its strike west.[5] An invasion of Spain did not really appeal to Moore, who decried the lack of supplies, maps, and information. He thought his masters in London put no more thought into ordering the campaign than they would a walk into Hyde Park.

Castlereagh was taken aback by Moore's plan to campaign away from the coast. He found an ally in William Eden, Lord Auckland, who portentously recognized the inherent problems. Moore's force would enter Spain at the end of October, just when heavy rains, the first snows, and freezing temperatures hit the region. The army would have to march literally 550 miles from Lisbon to Burgos along roads that would be mud wallows and that traversed territory lacking suitable quarters and sufficient provisions. Auckland concluded that the campaign was excessive.

That assessment was unfortunately correct. The British marched in two columns from one wretched town to another. Those who recorded their experiences tell of a dreadful, filthy, and impoverished country. Wolves attacked sleeping soldiers near Montesalgueiro. The towns, in ruination, were uncultivated, cold, wet, and nasty. Officers used their own money to purchase pack animals for their luggage, but there was never enough money sent from England to obtain sufficient transport for the entire army. Moore complained of a chronic money shortage. Unable to forage off the land, the commissariat had to buy what supplies they could. Most of the commissariat could not speak Spanish, leading to misunderstandings and a legacy of resentment among the townspeople. Worse, carts broke down and animals suffered terribly in the rough and cold terrain. The 7th Hussars lost sixty horses in only nine days. By the first week in November, Moore knew he was in trouble and expected the worst was yet to come.

His expectations were fulfilled in December as his troops entered Salamanca just as Marshal Soult's French corps, to the east, defeated a Spanish force. The beaten Spanish regiments hastened to León and waited for Moore to arrive. Bonaparte, at the head of 50,000 men, and not knowing where Moore was, marched north after taking Madrid. The danger to the British of being caught in a pincer movement, Soult from the east and Bonaparte from the south, suddenly was very real. But Moore's constant maneuvering kept the French off balance. He left Salamanca, joined David Baird's column of reinforcements at Benavente, then marched east to Sahagun. Food supplies were critical, and the weather worsened. With his intelligence sources only slightly better than the French, and realizing his army was in bad shape, Moore decided on 24 December to retreat west.

The northern Spanish winter ripped the little army. Torrential rains soaked the troops and turned the roads into swamps, the mud sucking the men's boots from their feet. They heaved against stuck carts and gun carriages. Animals floundered, and many were shot. Ice and snow increased the agony as the troops entered the Galician mountains. Typhus, dysentery, and exposure dropped men in their tracks. Forty miles night or day, the army struggled northwest toward Corunna.

Compounding the agony was the plight of the women marching with the army. Six wives per company were usually permitted to accompany their husbands on active duty. In return, the women cooked, sewed, and performed nursing duties, however minimal their skills. The reasons remain unclear, but the ratio of women in Moore's force was higher than allowed, exceeding the standard ratio by two and even five. Babies were born and died alongside the road. Many women had brought children with them who lacked the strength to endure. Bundling their children as best they could, many mothers collapsed into snowdrifts to await their fate. The survivors trudged on. None looked back.

The impact of the march on subalterns was also very hard. Most were only boys who did not possess the strength and stamina of the older enlisted men, many of whom were veterans of past campaigns. Lieutenant Colin Campbell, age 16, of the 9th Regiment, huddled in his coat, a scarf tied around his head, shivering against the cold. His boots were worn through, and the tops fused with his skin. What could he tell the men that they did not already know? Better to let the sergeants keep the men together. His job was to watch and learn and, by keeping silent, set an example of fortitude.

Rifleman Harris, 71st Regiment, remembered that a soldier's greatest enemy was his backpack.[6] Sixty pounds dug into the shoulders. Musket and bayonet weighed another 13 pounds. Carrying that load along a dusty road in balmy weather could exhaust a man in 20 miles. Marching in mud and snow, having already walked more than 500 miles, men became exhausted in a few hours. They cast aside their equipment. Better to lose a pack than a life.

Tempers shortened and morale dropped. Except for the excellent work done by Edward Paget's cavalry division and the German Legion's dragoons in keeping the French away from the column, hardly a shot had been fired against Soult's troops. Many men considered the retreat a disgrace and a strain on their regimental honor. And where were the Spanish? It was their country after all. The British soldiers could not vent their anger and frustration at the Spanish Army, nor could they lash out at Moore directly. Instead, they turned on the Spanish civilians. Violence built slowly. The soldiers started by foraging and soon escalated to rampant pillaging. At Mayoraga, at Valderos, and at Benavente they hammered in doors and windows, even of private houses, storming inside and taking everything they wanted. Entire buildings were torn down for firewood. Hundreds of soldiers found illusory relief in wine and brandy casks.

On 31 December, Baird's division entered Bembibre. When ordered to move on the next day, a thousand men lay dead drunk and were left behind. French dragoons entered the town the next morning. They were not met by the determined fire of British infantry but by a howling, hung-over mob who were incapable of firing their weapons, much less of running away. A few bloodsoaked survivors, sabre cuts the dripping testimony of their stupidity, managed to rejoin the division. They were paraded before the troops as examples of what happened to stragglers. Soult could have had the whole lot, but, four days earlier on the 27th, thinking Baird's division was 50 miles away, he broke off pursuit and marched south to join Bonaparte. Actually, the British were only 9 miles distant.

Moore, never known as a disciplinarian, neared despair. His army was disintegrating. He blamed the regimental officers for not keeping discipline and, in a notice issued 6 January 1809, lamented that he was tired of giving orders that were not obeyed and told his officers to restore discipline, without which the army would never reach Corunna and escape by sea. Robert Craufurd, commanding a light infantry brigade, set an example of what could be done to keep discipline. He shared the hardships of his men and never let his officers take advantage of rank. He hired Spanish peasants to bring in stragglers, and he galloped about, herding his men like cattle. Above all, he was a flogger. As Rifleman Harris noted, Private Dan Howans made an insubordinate remark about Craufurd taking time to punish men even though the French were near. Craufurd arrested Howans and sentenced him to three hundred lashes, a punishment witnessed by the private's wife.

The army somehow found itself. Rumors of impending battle may have brought them to their senses as much as the lash. Just west of Lugo, Soult's corps, once more in the chase, ran into concentrated British artillery and infantry fire. Soult hesitated and broke off the action. Moore continued to retreat for three more days, reaching Corunna on 11 January. Five days later, he won a stunning victory over the French. The British Army, amid much confusion, was evacuated by the Royal Navy and returned to England. They left behind the body of Sir John Moore, killed in action at Corunna.

The London *Times*, 26 January 1809, took a dim view of the whole campaign: "Our victory [at Corunna] was as useless as our retreat; and neither in flying nor in fighting, do we appear to have any other object in view than that of saving ourselves and deserting the cause we sent the troops to sustain." Nearly a year later, on 5 January 1810, the *Morning Chronicle* was still bemoaning the campaign: "The consequences of our rash and desperate expedition now begin to be felt . . . for the finest army that England ever equipped is now reduced and melted away. What an account Ministers have to render to Parliament." What the two papers overlooked was that Moore's campaign was a desperate gamble, nearly lost, whose flash point, if it had to be, came and went at the most convenient moment. Moore saved the Spanish cause, and Bonaparte was deflected from his march on Lisbon.

The Siege of Jerusalem, 1099

27 November 1095. Pope Urban II, addressing a large gathering outside the city gates of Clermont, France, called for a holy war to save Byzantium and the Eastern Christian Church from the Muslims. The call was not a sudden militant burst by Urban. Quite the contrary. The previous March, Alexius I, emperor of Byzantium, sent envoys to Urban, seeking his help. Urban spent the next several months traveling about France, garnering the support of various lords. He wanted an experienced army of knights and men-at-arms, but so widespread was the appeal of a holy war, that he unintentionally launched a social movement that included not only soldiers but also people of all sorts—men, women, and children of all ages, the healthy and the infirm, the wealthy and the poor. They came from Scandinavia, Britain, Germany, the Low Countries, Italy, Bohemia, and Spain. Most, however, were French. They responded to visions of adventure, loot, land, and a release from the boredom imposed by the routines of medieval life. Many, perhaps most, sought redemption. The First Crusade was launched.

Raymond IV, Count of Toulouse, put together an army of 10,000 men. He led his force across the Alps and down the Dalmation coast to Dyrrachium. There the Crusaders were met by imperial envoys and police to escort them to Constantinople. But weakened by the long march, their supplies dwindling, Raymond's men sacked the countryside near Constantinople, an activity that became common among the western armies. Only intervention by Alexius' troops restored order.

Another lord to join the Crusade was Godfrey of Bouillon, Duke of Lorraine. He packed his belongings, his wife, and his children and marched south in search of new land. Bohemund of Taranto, his future in southern Italy and Sicily turning bleak, also marched east. Robert of Normandy, his cousin Robert of Flanders, and his brother-in-law Stephen of Blois joined. So, too, did Godfrey's brother Baldwin, and Hugh of Vermandois, son of King Henry I of France. Peter the Hermit, a charismatic preacher gathered 20,000 peasants and marched uninvited south from Cologne.

Between 60,000 and 100,000 Crusaders of all sorts marched to Constantinople. Of these, about 25 percent were noncombatants.[7] The problem inherent in the army was that it reflected its feudal origins. Each lord was independent of the others, and each lord had his own agenda. Urban, for what reasons are not clear, did not appoint an overall leader. Nor did Alexius. Bohemund and Raymond both wanted the job. Lacking any presumptive rights, the two lords eyed each other suspiciously. Alexius was even more suspicious. He needed these barbaric Franks, as they were generally called, but he wanted them out of Constantinople as soon as possible. Before shipping them across the Bosphorus, he exacted from each a vow that any imperial lands they freed would be returned to Byzantium.

Camped at Pelacanum on the Sea of Marmara, the Crusaders faced a 1,100-mile march across the Anatolian highlands, through snow and rain, down to the desert lands of Syria, Lebanon, and Judea. They fought Muslim armies most of the way and besieged cities to obtain needed supplies. In May 1097, the Crusaders reached Nicaea, laying siege to the ancient fortress that was surrounded by a wall 4 miles long and reinforced by 240 towers. By mid-July, the defenders surrendered but not to the Crusaders. They negotiated a deal with the Byzantine general Manuel Bustimites, who promptly put imperial guards at the city gates. The Crusaders marched on, heat, disease, and defections cutting their numbers. They reached Antioch on 20 October. The city walls bristled with 450 towers, and, being on a fertile plain with ample water, Antioch was too well supplied to starve into submission. Bohemund decided he had enough crusading and wanted the city for himself. After bribing a tower captain, Bohemund sent some men past the defenders to open the gates. The rest of his army rushed in, butchering the inhabitants. Bohemund claimed Antioch as his own.

The Crusade was nearly undone. The lords argued among themselves, Stephen of Blois so disenchanted that he gathered his men, turned around, and went home. The common soldiers and camp followers, urged on by charismatic peasant-priests, swore that if the lords did not reach some agreement, they would burn Antioch and march to Jerusalem without them. Raymond, barefoot and looking more pilgrim that knight, started walking toward the Holy City. His men gradually fell in behind. Shamed by Raymond's example, the remaining lords joined the column.

On 7 June 1099, the Crusaders reached Jerusalem (Map 3). After nearly three years on the road, the available fighting army had melted away to a dismal 13,500.[8] On 12 June, all enthusiasm and no planning, having abandoned their siege equipment at Antioch, the Crusaders literally hurled themselves at Jerusalem's walls. Their foolishness only produced heavy casualties and great disappointment. Five days later, ships arrived at the coast with supplies, siege matériel, and some men skilled at constructing the needed machines. The Crusaders toiled for a month under the hot summer sun. Quarrels erupted, disease and heat took their toll, desertions increased, and the movement hovered on the edge of self-destruction.

Priests, claiming visions and declaring prophesies, brought the Crusaders to a revival meeting on the Mount of Olives. Peter the Hermit and others sermonized. Everyone prayed and sang songs. Enthusiasm restored, the Crusaders, barefoot, carrying palm leaves and icons, chanting and sounding trumpets, marched around the city walls.

The lords planned an attack for the night of 13 July. At great risk, the ditch surrounding the city walls was selectively filled and tamped. Three siege towers were rolled into place. Raymond's men scaled the tower on Mount Sion but could not escalate the defenses. Godfrey's men, using a tower positioned near the Jaffa gate, cleared the wall to position scaling ladders. More men topped the wall and descended into the city. Another column followed them led by Tancred, nephew of Bohemund. This penetration of the defenses forced the Muslims fighting Raymond to retreat. Iftikhar-ad-Dawala, the Egyptian governor of Jerusalem, sought refuge with his bodyguards in David's Tower and negotiated safe passage out of the city. They were the only survivors.

A flash point was reached as the Crusaders, running amok, swept through the city. Heads rolled in the streets. Children were dashed against walls. Crusaders broke into houses, killing every man, woman, and child they could find. When Tancred first entered town, he accepted the surrender of Muslims hiding in the Masjid-al-Aqsa—in return, of course, for a ransom. He put his banner on the roof to guarantee their safety. But the next morning, other Crusaders broke into the mosque and killed everyone there. Ibn-al-Athir, an Arab chronicler, claimed that 70,000 people, including priests and scholars, were slain.[9] The figure is doubtlessly exaggerated; numbers of that sort are taken to mean, by modern historians, that a lot of people were killed. Tancred's men looted the mosque and the Dome of the Rock. Another mass slaughter took place at the Temple of Solomon. Muslims on the roof were shot with arrows as the Crusaders burst into the temple, beheading 10,000, according to Fulcher of Chartres, a chronicler in Raymond's entourage.

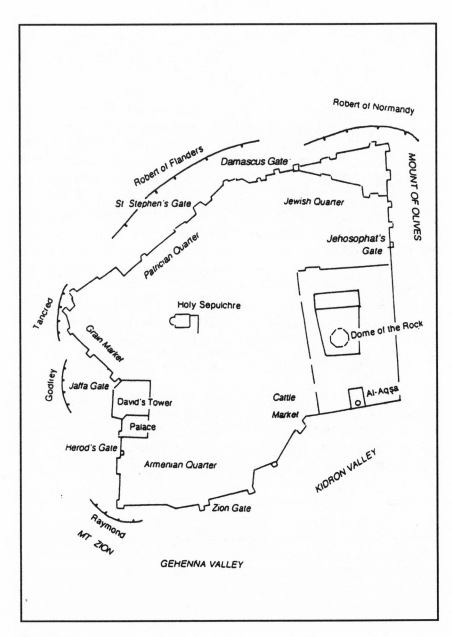

Map 3
Jerusalem, 1099

"None was left alive," he glowed. "Neither women nor children were spared."[10] Many other Muslims were either tortured to death or thrown alive into fires. Not even the Jews were spared. They crowded into their synagogue for safety, but the Crusaders locked and bolted the doors and burned down the building. Within two days the entire population was dead.

The massacre horrified many who participated in it and stunned the western world as news filtered back. Of course, similar massacres had been perpetrated before, but Jerusalem was after all the Holy City. As Steven Runciman concluded, what happened in Jerusalem during those two days in July 1099 affected all future Arab dealings with the west, stirring the depths of Muslim fanaticism as a response to Christian fanaticism.

AN INVITATION

At Prestonpans, the Royal troops broke ranks and ran away despite their commander's orders to stand and fight. Had the battle ended differently, the troops could have been arrested for mutiny, tried, and executed. The march to Corunna was a retreat during which entire regiments lost control, the troops turning into drunken, undisciplined, and sometimes violent mobs. The French killed many of these men at Bembibre, but others who returned to their units were punished as examples of bad soldiering. The Crusaders battled their way into Jerusalem, the aftermath of their clear victory a two-day massacre that, to them, was God's wrath visited on the faithless.

Conventional wisdom would have us believe that these incidents just happened, excessive responses to the peculiarities of each situation, the fault of deviants within the ranks who led their fellow soldiers astray. Not so. But the path to this abrupt, if not brash, conclusion is rather complicated, involving an understanding of some sociological processes. The first task, taken up in the following chapter, is to define the nature of regimental behavior—the recruitment and training of soldiers, and the transmission to them of the military ideology.

2

Sociological Perspectives: Regimental Behavior

The preference for thinking of the mutiny, mayhem, and massacre described in the foregoing historical examples as aberrations or, at least, exceptions to military authority, is rooted in the notion that they are bound to happen, the natural and inevitable accompaniment to war. This allows us to mumble a little moral indignation and move to the next war. If, however, we look carefully at military history, we find similar incidents repeated again and again, more often than random—even if inevitable—occurrence suggests. Their repetitive character has led me to conclude that military disintegration does not just happen. External elements, such as the brutal winter during the Corunna retreat, for example, or religious fanaticism during the Crusades, may set the stage for disintegration. But the social prerequisites to military disintegration are, as with other human groups, carried within the military unit involved. To understand what causes some armies or units within them to disintegrate and, by implication, to understand why others do not, we must first have some insights into regimental behavior.[1]

RECRUITMENT AND TRAINING

Every society confronts situations requiring immediate response. Many of these situations are expected, even though their precise timing is usually unpredictable. Dangers to social stability, if not to the very existence of the society, may be so profound that the society will create organizations in anticipation of crisis. Fires, earthquakes, and floods are repetitious disasters that necessitate specially organized, well-trained, and disciplined response teams. When a society is repeatedly threatened by another, when war lurks as a perpetual threat, the society justifies the organization of an army.

The function of an army, regardless of what other rationales are given, is to prepare for war. At a practical level, the ability of an army to defeat an enemy quickly and massively is directly related to the number and lethality of the weapons at their disposal and the efficiency of their use. Even more basic, but less obvious to the equation, is the efficiency with which men and women who become soldiers submit to the authority of the army and the regimentation necessary to fulfill its function.

The process of submission begins with recruitment. This was an automatic process in many tribal and ancient societies, for to be a male was to be a warrior. In the European Bronze Age, for example, warriors were elevated to a privileged class as the elements of hierarchical societies were created based on skill at arms, a process that later found fruition in medieval knighthood. Another way to develop an army is through conscription. This was used at times from ancient Greece into the Middle Ages, but it was usually local or regional in scope. Modern systems were instituted as a response to the growth of nationalistic wars. Sweden's King Gustavus Adolphus used national conscription in 1600. The French and Prussians soon followed his example. But massive conscription, involving millions of men, became a necessity in World War I and World War II because of the multiple theaters of operations and high casualty rates.

Professional soldiers traditionally view conscription as a necessary but unwanted process. It pulls into the military an undifferentiated mass, varying in physical and intellectual skills and in levels of commitment to military service. The ideal soldier is thought to be the volunteer.[2] Thus the Victorian-era British publicly boasted of their volunteer army. Richard Cannon, for example, wrote a series of British regimental histories in the 1840s, commenting in one of them that "The British soldier is distinguished for . . . [an] unconquerable spirit and resolution,—patience in fatigue and privation, and cheerful obedience to his superiors."[3] This glow was dimmed by reality.

Actually, soldiering was generally despised by the Victorian population, at least in England, and, as Colonel H. de Watteville concluded, putting on a scarlet coat "was the mark of a lost soul."[4] To draw men to the colors, recruiting sergeants lurked about pubs, showing off their colorful uniforms, enticing young men with promises of adventure, camaraderie, a comfortable barracks life—an outright fraud—and, of course, an enlistment bonus. The men recruited were frequently dispossessed Irishmen, sullen and destitute youths from the rookeries of England's industrial towns, and those seeking escape from the tedium and poverty of rural life. During the 1850s, fully 60 percent of them were illiterate. Even though many reforms were instituted beginning in the 1870s, soldiering was not a popular career choice in Britain, even though it developed an excellent small army. World War I slowly convinced the British that their little volunteer force was inadequate to the task of fighting the horrendous battles being waged in France. Conscription was invoked, as it had been already in France and Germany. The United States soon followed.

With peace, war-weariness emerged, coupled with a widespread realization that war was not a glorious enterprise. Recruitment declined as both the United States and Britain returned to volunteer forces. But the Great Depression forced many youths to consider the military life. In Britain, not surprisingly, recruiting sergeants once again appeared in their bright uniforms, chests covered with medals, attracting men into service.

Thus recruitment fluctuated back and forth in the nineteenth and twentieth centuries between voluntary enlistment and conscription. Toward the end of the twentieth century, with fear of world conflagration subsiding, and with the extraordinary success of British and American volunteer forces in the 1991 Gulf War, the debate between conscription and voluntary enlistment ended momentarily in favor of the latter.

But armies still clung to many traditional recruitment lures. These included appeals to patriotism, camaraderie, the wholesomeness of barracks life, adventure, and travel. Education was added to the list earlier in the twentieth century, but this goal was subsequently elevated from the remediation of basic skills to college preparation. The non-college-bound recruitment was promised job training. All these enticements paled before another that was consistently offered by armies, especially in the western world: joining the army was and remains a way to be a man.[5] How easily the appeals to physical strength and endurance, to being part of a team, to measuring up to the idealized warriors seen on recruitment posters and videotapes were informed by boyhood experience. Being strong and uncomplaining, toughing it out, denying pain—"walking it off"—being "one of the guys," emulating older boys who became, consciously or not, willingly or not, role models, are experiences that translated into another opportunity (for it is never too late) to "be all you can be," to be selected as one of "the few, the proud."

Training follows recruitment. Learning to be a warrior was an integral part of the maturation process in many tribal societies. The child learned to handle weapons as hunting tools, then, at an older age, extended those skills toward warfare. Marching off to war in a modern industrialized world does not guarantee competency at arms. Sometimes training is hasty and incomplete, a response to political exigencies. In Spain, 1936 to 1939, Republican militias were thrown together and into battle with little or no training. In the 1980s and 1990s, many eastern European ethnic groups formed militias as they sought national identities separate from such parent states as the Soviet Union and Yugoslavia. These militias had little training beyond how to find their way to the front and fire their weapons.

But most armies rely on lengthy formal training, a practice formed in Europe during the sixteenth century from the realization that the more complicated black powder weaponry just invented and the increasingly sophisticated battlefield maneuvering by large mass troop formations demanded disciplined instruction. Muzzle-loading muskets were notoriously inaccurate, short-range, and unreliable. Consequently, large numbers of soldiers in column or line were required to close on each other to make their firepower effective. Marching across a rough battleground, maintaining order, and closing on the enemy to stand and deliver or receive musket volleys required iron discipline. The men were trained from dawn to dusk in mind-numbing, close-order marching and weapons drills until they became automatons. Obviously the example of Prestonpans demonstrated that the system could fail. It worked at Waterloo and beyond as Britain's Thin Red Lines, their crashing volleys delivered around the world, won many victories, established many proud regimental histories, and created an empire. In the United States, the system created the horrors of the Civil War.

Rapid-fire, long-range weapons necessitated newer training techniques. But many armies retained traditions that thwarted full-scale change. Britain's so-called "contemptible little army" of pre–World War I years was a proud volunteer long-service corps that enjoyed remarkably high morale steeped in the regimental traditions of the past and, by any measure of that time, was well trained and disciplined. Men enlisted in specific regiments that were responsible for their training. Sergeants were the taskmasters. Cleanliness of self, weapons, and barracks were at the center of training, the final expectations of which were to create soldiers that looked smart on parade, who could march long distances, and who could shoot accurately.[6] Yet those fine regiments, unable to cope with German machine gun fire, were cut to pieces during 1914 and 1915 at Mons, Loos, Neuve Chapelle, and Aubers Ridge. They were replaced in 1916 by Lord Kitchener's New Army, that mass of eager volunteers who were shot to pieces at Ypres and the Somme.

The tactical and strategic failures of 1914–1918 motivated the Germans in the 1930s to develop the blitzkrieg, the highly mobile integration of infantry, armor, and air units. Even though the level of mechanization has been overstated, the Nazi war machine, in a series of short campaigns, overran the European continent in 1939 and 1940.

The British and American armies had to change to meet new battlefield challenges; nevertheless they clung to established training systems for long months into World War II. Close-order drill, frequent inspections, endless marching, and myriad small and meaningless tasks were the standard curriculum. Correlatively, U.S. combat veterans complained that training was needed in anti-tank tactics, familiarity with enemy weapons, and small unit tactics that reflected the realities of the battlefield. One service branch that adapted very rapidly to changing conditions was the United States Marine Corps. Their Pacific Ocean island-hopping mission, based on short, combat-intensive, amphibious campaigns, drove their change. Thus replacement battalions were familiarized with enemy weapons, learned about jungle survival, small unit fighting, and about the integration of weapons systems.[7]

REGIMENTAL IDEOLOGY AND MILITARY STRUCTURE

There is more to training than learning soldierly skills. Those are usually easily taught and easily learned, especially in a volunteer force. More difficult to transmit is the military ideology, the raison d'être of the army. All armies must instill in their recruits a desire for combat, a willingness to risk wounds or death in order to kill others. The absorption of that ideology is exemplified by a comment from a U.S. Marine Corps sergeant during the Guadalcanal campaign against the Japanese in 1942: "Be mean and kill 'em. Kill 'em dead. Our motto in this Platoon is 'No prisoners.' "[8] In a more contemporary example, Philip Caputo, a Marine lieutenant, wrote in *A Rumor of War* that when he was undergoing jungle training for Vietnam, a sergeant burst into the room where he and his fellow officers were waiting, buried a hatchet in the wall, let out a terrible scream, and yelled at them, "Ambushes are murder and murder is fun." The class yelled back in unison, "Ambushes are murder and murder is fun."

The creation of a will to combat begins with separating the recruits from civilian life. A recruit comes into the armed services carrying his culture's general values. These can include, traditionally among many American recruits, such elements as sharing and being kind, a certain value on intellectual development and accompanying skills, freedom of expression, a taboo against killing, and freedom of movement both social and physical. But the recruit enters a world that is rigidly hierarchical and authoritarian, one generally not much interested, until recent high-technology wars, in things intellectual, one that teaches soldiers how to kill, a world that generally lacks compassion and is filled with threats and humiliation. The transition, as John Keegan noted, can be a profound culture shock.[9]

The constant psychological hammering and often outright denegration of the recruits that has characterized so many training programs focus their attention on immediate military goals. Anything beyond the program's parameters has secondary importance. As one U.S. Army colonel stated in about 1970, "It only takes a year to take the average man out of civilian life . . . and really mold him into a very effective soldier. . . . [The] mission becomes your job. Nothing else but that."[10] To get through the program, to survive the training to be a man and not a wimp, not to let one's buddies down, to do the job—these become central concerns for the recruit. Nothing else but that. And the ultimate job is to kill the enemy as efficiently as possible.

The evidence regarding the enduring impact of basic military training is contradictory. Eliot Cohen cites evidence that many men considered basic training a rewarding experience.[11] A U.S. Army veteran of three years' fighting in the Pacific during World War II told me that, "Unless all that civilian crap is knocked out of you, you don't have a chance of survival." Similarly, Eugene Sledge, a Marine combat veteran, thought that learning to respond to orders under the stresses of basic training made the difference between living and dying in combat.[12] In contrast, Paul Fussell, an infantry officer in Europe during World War II, dismissed much of basic training as so much abusive nonsense perpetrated by small minds or, to use a common military phrase, so much "chickenshit."[13] Interestingly, both Sledge and Fussell come to the same conclusion, however different the routes: combat was the place where the lessons learned were fully utilized and upon which survival depended, or, from the other direction, combat was the only place in the army where the soldier could escape the chickenshit. Either way, the military won.

That soldiers can even think that training and ideology are a lot of nonsense is a reflection of the dual reality of military life. One dimension of that life is the formal system into which he is indoctrinated, consisting of ideological commitment, skill acquisition, rank, and organization by regiment, battalion, company, platoon, and squad. The other dimension is the system of interpersonal relationships, of informal roles and social statuses—the substrata culture of the enlisted man—that emerges within a unit and binds it together as a social as well as a military group. The military can encourage such relationships in the name of camaraderie. What the military cannot control or put on their line-staff charts is the generation by these informal groups of their own values, beliefs, and ideologies that may have little to do with the formal military system. Whether a soldier survives the training cycles may depend less on what his drill sergeants think of him than upon the support he receives from his informal group—from his buddies, to use a common phrase. The army occupies a soldier's time with onerous, low-grade work assignments: dig latrines, dig a hole and then fill it up, put up a flagpole, guard a bench in a parking lot, and other minor nightmares thought up by sergeants. How often a soldier is picked for such work may have less to do with a rational selection method than his status in the informal substrata grouping. That status, even though it lacks official blessing, is often recognized at the company and platoon levels by noncommissioned officers when convenient, and it helps them co-opt the enlistees into the formal structure. The ultimate test of the integration of the formal and informal systems is battle, during which the value of survival may replace all others.

INTO THE ENVIRONMENT OF THE UNEXPECTED

When compared to training, battle shifts military life to another order of reality. The vast unbroken plain of a desert battlefield may be just as unexpectedly disorienting as the fetid darkness of a jungle. Smoke and dust, rain and mist obscure vision. Men charge about seemingly without any purpose, forward, backward, in a jumble of movement. The sickly sweet odor of the unburied mixes with the stench of burning oil and spent ammunition. A cauldron of noise engulfs everything and everyone. Death is absurdly arbitrary. In most battles there occurs what Barrie Pitt described as that "most searing experience that comes to a soldier . . . when he realizes that out there is another man intent on killing him."[14]

That kind of experience reduces battle from a vast and impersonal arena to a very small space, making combat, particularly infantry combat, per- sonal, cold, destructive, and physically and emotionally exhausting. The soldiers' survival becomes doubtful. If the men succumb to despair, the processes of disintegration can undermine all their formal military training. Worse, the system of informal relationships within the unit is also threat- ened. If the processes of disintegration reach finality, new forms of association emerge that frequently lead to crowd formation. The ensuing behaviors leap beyond the bonds forged within the formal and informal systems.

Contrary to public, political, and even military expectations, training and previous battle experience sometimes do not adequately prepare a soldier for crisis. For the real test of a military unit may not be facing a foreign invader in battle but confronting their own terrors. Thus, as Pitt illustrated the point, Erwin Rommel's well-honed desert advance across Cyrenaica in April 1941 rolled back the British defenders with awesome certainty. For the German Africa Corps, the advance was business-as-usual, another blitzkrieg offensive as practiced across Europe but now transferred to the North African desert. But, within a week, the Germans were at Tobruk engaging in the slow death dance of a siege. In one salient, the Australian defenders used the ground to their own advantage, were better than the Germans at small unit fighting, were deadly in bayonet charges, and could shoot more accurately at longer ranges. Rommel's men were profoundly unnerved, not only because the Australians proved better soldiers in the situation but also because neither German training nor previous battles prepared them for what they experienced at Tobruk.

Crisis, that which threatens group survival—in past or future tenses, in either real or imagined terms—is the final and most abrupt change for any soldier. Crisis is the environment in which the last gentle expectations of civilian life are completely shed, and in which a world filled with the terrors of the unexpected engulfs the men.

Crisis behaviors are often associated with moments of defeat. Objectives are reached ahead of schedule or not reached at all. The unit that achieves its objective may exist only as a number on a chart. During a 1916 Mesopotamian battle, the 2nd Battalion of the Black Watch reached the Turkish trenches following their advance across hundreds of yards of open desert, but only 25 men were left of an original 850. Despair loomed among the survivors. Or the enemy may spring a new weapon on unsuspecting troops. The mutinous sepoys defending Lucknow in 1857, for example, panicked by British rocket fire, broke ranks and fled. What else to do? Leaders are killed with regularity, the life expectancy of infantry lieutenants reduced to minutes. What to do? An order is given: advance from one meaningless point to another. An order is given: fall back and hold one meaningless position after another. More men die. Fall back again. The soldier asks why he should bother to hold? What is he doing here? Can he run away? Someone wants to kill him, but he sees no one. What to do? Many British and Australian units defending Singapore in early 1942 rejected their soldiers' role, sat down in the jungle, and waited to be captured. Others threw away their equipment, opted out in small groups, and tried to make it to the sea, seeking escape from the stupid campaign and its defense of worthless positions. What else to do?

The promise of success also breeds crisis behaviors. The troops of the French King Charles VIII invaded Italy in 1494, reducing by cannon fire in only eight hours the great fortress of San Giovanni. The French infantry rushed forward into the fort and butchered all the survivors for no other reason than they were available. In 1858, the 4th Punjabis and the British 93rd Regiment (later the Argyll and Sutherland Highlanders) burst into the Kaisarbagh, a fortified palace, during the battle for the Indian city of Lucknow. Killing all the defenders—even pulling wounded mutineers from the stacks of dead and bayoneting them—they then fell to an orgy of looting and destruction. Fires burned, furniture was heaved through windows, every room was looted, and every corpse picked clean. One observer commented that the men were "wild with plunder," and there were scenes "worthy of the Inferno."[15] On the Salerno beaches during World War II, 200 British soldiers were arrested and later convicted of mutiny because they refused to accept reassignment to units other than their own. If I may, a friend who served as a captain in the Indian Army told the tale of a regiment just out from Britain that refused transport to the Burma front to fight the Japanese. This was palpable mutiny. Their officers, drawn from the ranks and sent to quick-study officer training schools, were men just like themselves—the equivalent of American "ninety-day wonders." The regiment simply wanted "gentlemen" to lead them.

Military disintegration, thus far, is quite unpredictable. Two units subjected to nearly equivalent crises can exhibit very different behaviors. Thus the Royal troops at Prestonpans ran away under the savage Scottish attack. At Neuve Chapelle in 1915, the 2nd Scottish Rifles lost 70 percent of its men in six days attacking German positions but continued on as a fighting unit under a lieutenant, the remaining officer. Such variations can be explained only in relation to group processes, and that in turn necessitates a reorientation of thinking away from individual aberrations and culpability.

AN ORGANIZATIONAL NOTE

The discussion so far has been intentionally preliminary, designed to stimulate interest rather than definitively answer questions. Because military disintegration is historically and sociologically complex, involving a variety of sources that lead to different and usually unanticipated behaviors, the field is quite broad and is rich with possibilities. But I do not want to offer a survey that merely nibbles at all the bits and pieces. I have chosen instead to narrow the focus to six historical examples that tell some important things about the social institution we call "army" and what happens when that institution or some part of it fractures under stress. Thus the background to disintegration is as important as the flash point. The six examples are the Great Mutiny in India, 1857; the 1917 French Army mutinies; the mayhem that took place at the close of the British siege of San Sebastian, 1813; the surrender of the U.S. 106th Infantry Division in December 1944; the Sand Creek Indian massacre, 1864; and the My Lai massacre during the Vietnam War, 1968. However, rather than just revisiting the agonies once again, I sketch in at the end of each example some sociological interpretations suggested by the evidence. The final chapter connects the examples and the sociological interpretations within a more systematic framework. There I more formally explore in greater detail the foundations of military disintegration—failure of leadership, the collapse of primary groups, despair among the troops, and alienation—and the types of collective behavior that arise from it and that are expressed through crowd formation. With this preliminary groundwork in place, we can now proceed in depth.

3

The Great Indian Mutiny, 1857

In 1857, native troops—the sepoys—of the East India Company's army mutinied against what they believed were British attempts to undermine their culture. The mutiny developed into a three-year war during which the British Army conducted a series of punitive campaigns.

THE HURRICANE BREAKS

Lieutenant Colonel George Carmichael-Smyth, commanding the 3rd Light Cavalry of the East India Company's Army (the Indian Army for short), returned to Meerut from a brief leave on a hot and dusty April day. He brought disturbing news of disaffection among native troops, the sepoys, at other garrisons.[1] The issue giving life to the disturbances surfaced in January 1857, when the army received new Enfield rifles from England. These required the soldiers to bite off the ends of cartridges specially lubricated to fit the tighter rifled bores. Rumors quickly spread that the lubricants were made of beef and pig fat, anathema to Hindus and Muslims respectively.

Carmichael-Smyth might have discounted the news except that Meerut was an important garrison in British India (Map 4). Located on a plain about 40 miles northeast of Delhi, the garrison provided troops to fight along the Northwest Frontier, protected the Great Trunk Road that connected the Punjab in the west with Bengal in the east, and supported the Delhi garrison.

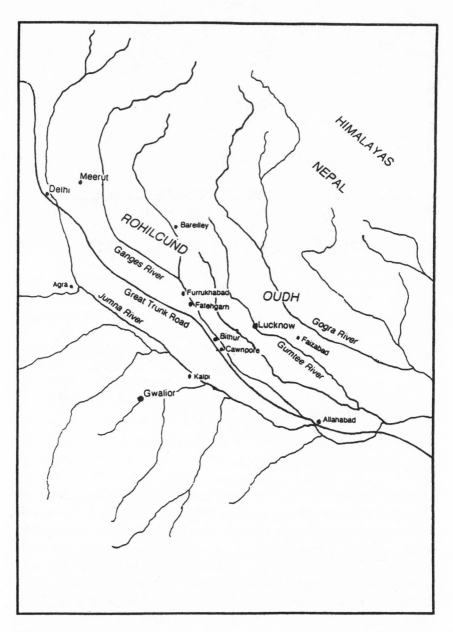

Map 4
Northern India

He determined to end the nonsense before it consumed his regiment, ordering a firing-parade of the regiment's skirmishers to teach the new loading drill. The men would tear off the cartridge tips and load their guns, demonstrating the absurdity of the rumor and salving discontent. The unit petitioned him to delay the parade, but he persisted. Thus, on 24 April, 90 skirmishers marched onto the parade ground. The regiment's acting adjutant ordered them to take three cartridges each. Only five noncommissioned officers accepted the new ammunition. The 85 men who did not obey were relieved of duty and confined to quarters. The next day, a board of inquiry consisting of five native officers and two British officers court-martialed the offending sepoys. Rather than handling the affair within the regiment, Carmichael-Smyth thrust it into the machinery of military bureaucracy and law. All the convicted men were sentenced to hard labor, most for ten years, at the Adaman Islands penal colony. Before transportation of the prisoners, the Meerut garrison was marched out to the parade ground, forming three sides of a square. Then the prisoners were brought forward on the fourth side. They were stripped of their uniforms and their boots, and their ankles were shackled. They marched or rather shuffled off to the garrison prison to await departure. They cursed aloud Carmichael-Smyth as they passed by him.

Later that same day, Lieutenant Hugh Gough, also of the 3rd Light Cavalry, was at his quarters, having returned from visiting the imprisoned men. One of his native officers came to him with the warning that sepoys were planning to release the prisoners the next day. Gough reported the conversation to Carmichael-Smyth, who was surprised that Gough would bother him with such a preposterous tale. Gough then went to Brigadier Archdale Wilson, who also dismissed the story. Gough persisted, going over the heads of his immediate superiors, telling the story to Major General W. H. Hewitt, area commander. Hewitt refused to believe him. After all, the sepoys were loyal men devoted to their British officers. Such outrageous behavior was unthinkable.

Yet, at 6 A.M., Sunday, 10 May 1857, several hundred sepoys set fire to their barrack huts. British officers of the 20th Native Infantry who rushed to the area found the sepoys running about in a frenzy. Troublemakers from the town's bazaars, already agitated by the sentences handed down, had gathered about the 20th's ammunition magazine. Suddenly a cavalryman from the 3rd Light galloped toward the crowd, shouting that British soldiers were coming to disarm the sepoys. The crowd broke into the magazine, looted it for weapons, and discharged them into the air. Others killed any British soldier they could see, shooting the commander of the 11th Native

Infantry. A young subaltern of the 3rd Light Cavalry was cut to pieces, identifiable only by some unusual frills on his uniform. The veterinary surgeon was shot in his bungalow while trying to protect his wife. She was cut down and the bungalow set afire. The wife of the 11th's adjutant was caught by the mob and hacked to death. The wife and children of an officer of the 21st, disguised as natives in an attempt to escape the town, were caught and killed. Those Britons not in hiding tried to reach the relative safety of the Queen's 60th Regiment, a regular British Army unit. Not all made it. The slaughter, the butchery, continued into the evening.

By midnight, the gunfire subsided, and, fires still burning, the hurricane of hate, revenge, and murder passed from Meerut as the mutineers abandoned the town and marched south to Delhi. "[They] were not fleeing the scene of their mutinous crimes; rather they sought blessing from the one man who could stamp their actions with the sign of legitimacy. That man was Bahadur Shah II, the last legitimate Mogul ruler," the so-called King of Delhi.[2] Bahadur Shah was an enfeebled old man, a British puppet ruler supported by a healthy subsidy over which his greedy and self-serving relatives constantly quarreled.

The Meerut mutineers reached Delhi at 7 A.M., Monday, 11 May. Bahadur was bewildered by their presence, but, once their intentions became obvious, and seeing himself powerless to do anything about emerging mutiny in Delhi, he became a captive of events, revered by millions as the new emperor, in fact nothing more than a puppet ruler once again. By noon, Delhi was in confusion. Great crowds were in the streets, ebbing and flowing, not knowing what to do or where to go, aware only that the city had become, in the short space of one morning, a very violent place.

Captain C.R.G. Douglas, palace guard commander, escaped from an angry crowd and reached his quarters above the Lahore Gate. Meanwhile, Simon Fraser, Delhi commissioner, struggling through hostile crowds, arrived at Douglas' front steps. But two swordsmen killed him. Fraser's decapitated head was skewered on a sword's point and carried joyously through the streets. A small party did find sanctuary in Douglas' quarters. This group included the Reverend M. J. Jennings, his daughter, and a Miss Clifford. Crowds pounded on the doors and shutters. The terror of those trapped inside must have been overwhelming. Reverend Jennings, believing he could calm the crowd with some pious platitudes, naively opened the door. The natives burst through, killing Captain Douglas immediately. The two girls, hiding in a wardrobe, were dragged out and butchered. Jennings managed to grab a sword, but, in a moment, he too was hacked to death by a dozen blades.

Across town, fifty British and Eurasian women were captured and imprisoned in a dark room. Soon all the Christian women in the group were called outside, leaving only five Muslim women behind. The Christians were roped together and pulled en masse into a courtyard where the king's personal servants murdered them all with swords.

Two miles beyond Delhi a military camp known as The Ridge was occupied by the 54th Native Infantry. Lieutenant Colonel J. P. Ripley, commanding, received orders to enter Delhi and put down the disturbances caused by the entry of Meerut mutineers. The 54th marched to the Kashmir Gate which was guarded by fifty men of the 38th Native Infantry. As the 54th passed through the gate, their officers were fired on by 3rd Light Cavalry mutineers. The 54th's officers ordered their sepoys to return fire, but the men discharged their weapons into the air and attacked their own remaining officers with bayonets. Colonel Ripley, shot and barely alive, was attacked by swordsmen and dismembered. The gate guard did nothing.

Mutineers ran rampant through the city. Both the Delhi Bank and the offices of the Delhi *Gazette* were overrun, and everyone inside the buildings killed. Then the structures were set afire. St. James church was looted. But the biggest prize awaited the mutineers: the Dum Dum arsenal. Lieutenant George Willoughby was responsible for the arsenal. His security force consisted of two other lieutenants, a couple of sergeants, four civilian clerks, and a detachment of sepoys. The sepoys bolted at the approach of mutineers. Willoughby realized that any defense he mounted would be short-lived, so he set a powder trail to blow up the arsenal. With mutineers pounding on the gate and climbing ladders propped against the surrounding walls, Willoughby ordered the trail lighted. The explosion, heard in Meerut, blew the arsenal flat, burying hundreds of mutineers. Willoughby and most of his comrades miraculously escaped.

The Delhi mutiny harbored an even darker side, no less vicious for being commonplace. Those rioting through the streets used the mutiny as an excuse to loot and murder their own. As James Leasor noted, shops and homes were plundered for what could be carried away, all in great haste because the perpetrators believed the Queen's troops—the regular British Army—would soon arrive and exact a terrible vengeance.[3]

Other garrisons mutinied throughout the late spring and summer of 1857—Aligarh, Gwalior, Indore, Allahabad, Fatehgarh, Bareilly, Shahja-hanpur, Kalpi, Bithur, to name but some stations and towns. Mostly the sepoys mutinied first, encouraging known troublemakers and hooligans (called *badmashes* in Hindi) to follow them. In a few instances, as at Agra, the civilian population rose first, burning British schools, churches, offices, and factories. Christopher Hibbert notes that there was no definite pattern to the mutiny.[4] Yet, despite the rapidly changing configuration of power across northern India, many sepoys, both individuals and entire units, remained loyal to the British.

Among the most infamous of the early mutinies was that at Cawnpore,[5] a city of 60,000 between the Ganges River and the Great Trunk Road. Cawnpore was rich and relatively new. Founded in the early nineteenth century as a station for the Indian Army, it rapidly grew into an important commercial center for Oudh province. The Ganges was navigable to the east all the way to Calcutta and west for another 300 miles. In May 1857, the Cawnpore garrison numbered 3,000 native troops representing three infantry regiments, one of cavalry, and some gunners. Two hundred of the Queen's troops were also stationed at Cawnpore. This included one company of the 32nd Regiment; the remainder were invalids. Major General Sir Hugh Wheeler commanded the garrison. He had been commissioned in the East India Company's army at age 14, spoke various native dialects fluently, and married a native woman. Wheeler was confident his native troops would remain loyal, or, if by some odd stroke they did mutiny, the local disturbance would be brief because the mutineers would march away to Delhi.

Wheeler's confidence and his contingency plan in the event a mutiny erupted did nothing to allay the anxieties of the city's European population. He believed everyone would be safe in the British military barracks, the two principal buildings of which were covered by dangerously flammable roofs and proved too small by half for the crowd that eventually populated them. Built on barren ground, they were surrounded by a 4-foot mud wall and a shallow trench. Although Wheeler brought in extra supplies, they proved inadequate in the long term.

Even the best military plans can be undercut by the unanticipated: enter Dhondu Pant, better known in history as Nana Sahib, the maharaja of Bithur. Nana was the adopted son of Baji Rao II, a Mahratta ruler whom Lord Dalhousie, India's governor general, deposed when he annexed Oudh to British India in 1856. Nonetheless, the British granted Baji an annual subsidy of £80,000. With his death, the subsidy stopped. Nana appealed to Lord Dalhousie for continuance, but his claim was refused. A London appellate court also refused the claim. Nana never forgave Dalhousie. Yet, despite his enmity and loss of revenue, Nana maintained a sumptuous court, entertaining British guests with a certain Oriental splendor. Even though Nana was considered an opportunist by many British residents, and a man not to be trusted, General Wheeler named Nana Sahib guardian of the city treasury.

On 5 June, all Wheeler's optimism came crashing down as mutiny, murderous and incendiary, burst forth in Cawnpore. The 2nd Native Cavalry rode to the city treasury. Helped by Nana and his guard, they broke it open and carried away the treasure. They then released all those in the local prison. Joined by the 1st Native Infantry, they stormed the local munitions depot. *Badmashes* from the local bazaars joined the mutineers, and together they turned to looting and burning the city. They were quickly joined by two more regiments, one of which—the 53rd Native Infantry—was initially reluctant to mutiny. But after Wheeler ordered three cannon shots fired over their heads as a warning, all but 80 men of the regiment defected. The mutineers, meantime, offered Nana a choice. He could be king of the Mahratta territories formerly ruled by Baji Rao II, or he could die where he stood. "What have I to do with the British?" he responded. "I am totally yours."[6]

Wheeler's so-called safe barracks rapidly filled beyond capacity with Europeans escaping the mutiny. The occupants included the British invalid soldiers and the 32nd's company, about 100 British officers from mutinous native regiments, another hundred civilians (others escaped into the coun-tryside, and still others hid in the city where they were soon discovered and killed), and those Indian officers, enlisted men, and servants who remained loyal.

The mutineers attacked Wheeler's entrenchments on 6 June, beginning a nineteen-day siege. Although outnumbering the defenders ten-to-one, the mutineers did not want to attack the entrenchments directly. They manned their cannons and sniper posts, pounding away at the thin defenses. Yet Wheeler's small band would not yield. And that took an unanticipated toll on the sepoys. As one day passed to the next, day in and day out, many of the mutineers grew bored and undisciplined. They showed less respect for their own elected officers than for the British they replaced. Many mutineers simply wandered away, going back to their villages, or sought their fortunes in other mutinous cities. For the defenders, life became a matter of chance as cannon balls crashed through walls, decapitating someone here, shred-ding legs and arms there, or cutting someone else in two. Snipers took a deadly toll, especially among the defending artillerymen who were exposed to enemy fire as they manned their guns. The only water was from a well in an unprotected area of the barracks. Anyone approaching was an easy target. The dead piled up, the living unable to bury their comrades lest they risk joining them. A dry well became their tomb as corpses were unceremoni-ously dropped down the shaft. Animal carcasses, bloated and rotted in the heat, added to the wretched atmosphere.

By 25 June, all the army gunners were either dead or wounded, the remaining cannon manned by civilians. Food was critically short, medical supplies nonexistent. Exhaustion, heat prostration, thirst, shock, exposure, infection, and disease knocked down those the sepoy gunners missed.

Nana Sahib, through a spy, knew of Wheeler's plight. He sent a message to the beleaguered British, guaranteeing safe passage to Allahabad for all those who were not connected with any of Lord Dalhousie's actions in Oudh. Wheeler agreed, providing Nana supply transportation downriver to Allahabad.

On 27 June, arrangements made, the siege survivors wearily made their way out of the stinking trenches and barracks to the Satichaura Ghat, a grubby dock with steps leading from the Ganges to a temple. The women, their skeletal children, and the wounded were handed onto the boat decks where they found some relief under thatch shading. Then the able-bodied men started to clamber aboard. At that moment, Nana's hidden cannons opened fire with grape shot. Musket volleys crashed into the boats. Several of the boats were already on fire, the parting gift of mutineers who, after helping load the craft, left hot coals in the thatch. A cavalry squadron charged into the water, cutting and slashing those trying to escape. Finally, club-wielding townspeople dispatched other survivors struggling in the water. The men who survived the onslaught were gathered together and shot. The remaining women and children, about 125 of them, were sent to a house in Cawnpore known as the Bibighar. They were soon joined by 75 women and children who had escaped from other mutinees and thought Cawnpore would be safe. Disease quickly found its way into the house and twenty-five died. They were the lucky ones.

Meanwhile, Brigadier General Henry Havelock, leading a column of European volunteers and Sikhs, was headed for Cawnpore from Allahabad. Nana Sahib and his army withdrew to the south where, if necessary, they would make a stand. But first they had to deal with the captives. Killing them all, the reasoning went, might forestall a battle because the British would be less eager to fight once they found the dead women and children; furthermore, the dead could not testify to the Satichaura Ghat massacre.

The sepoys assigned to kill the women and children refused to obey, firing their weapons into the air. So five men were brought to the Bibighar, including two butchers. They waded into the captives, wielding *tulwars*, or curved swords, axes, and knives. The next morning, the bodies were dragged from the house and pitched down a well or into the Ganges. What Nana Sahib and his cohorts underestimated was the legacy of hate they left for the British to discover.

Lucknow, on the Gumtee River, was the capital of wealthy Oudh province. William Howard Russell of the *Times* considered Lucknow the Paris of India. The population numbered 600,000. Toward the north end of the city was a collection of government buildings collectively known as the Residency. To the south were palaces, mosques, and royal tombs. A little further south were Dilkusha Park, featuring peacocks and deer, and a modified classical pile called the Martinière, built by a French adventurer as a college. Henry Lawrence, a man with deep sympathies for native problems, was commissioner of Oudh, recently appointed to the post after a long career in the Punjab.

Lawrence's sympathy for native problems and his conciliatory maneuvering could not diminish widespread native resentment over the Dalhousie annexation, which the Indians saw as a major disruption of their traditional lifestyle. Furthermore, the annexation robbed the Oudh sepoys of a previously envied position because they had been better able to get their petitions heard by the king of Oudh and his ministers than by their civilian relatives.[7] Under British rule, the sepoys faced an often disinterested and cantankerous civil service. And certainly the sepoys resented the new Enfield cartridges. Lawrence was warned that mutiny was imminent but, like Wheeler at Cawnpore, he did not believe Lucknow was in any danger.

On the night of 30 May, the sounds of Mutiny rolled over the city. Those in the Residency heard gunshots from the sepoy regimental lines 3 miles away, and the sky turned red from the burning camps. By morning, mutiny had spread through the Lucknow garrison. Only about 500 sepoys and the city police, the latter standing firm another 11 days, remained immediately loyal to the British. Beyond that pitifully small number, only the Queen's 32nd Regiment, short the company stationed at Cawnpore, was available to stem the crowds. By 1 June, thousands of civilians filled the city streets, many to loot and murder, their rapacity nearly a replica of the first mutinous days in Delhi.

Just as suddenly, a calm settled into Lucknow as the police restored a semblance of control. British and Europeans shopped safely in the bazaars, laying in supplies they believed would eventually be necessary. Those seeking safety or eschewing mutiny gradually found their way to the Residency. Lawrence rushed the building of defenses. An old fort, the Machi Bhawan, was strengthened with equally old cannons. The able-bodied men dug trenches, strengthened walls with fascines (bundles of sticks), and bricked or boarded windows. A 5-foot berm was constructed with a ditch on both sides, the outer one lined with sharpened stakes. Lawrence and his force, short of necessities, were surrounded by mutineers and under siege.

The mutineers pounded the Residency with artillery fire—round and grape shot, chains, nails, coins, scrap metal, wire, and wood blocks.[8] Every wall was soon chipped or holed. Musket fire and even arrows, the latter shot with considerable accuracy, pelted the defenders. Twenty men, women, and children fell dead or wounded every day.

While the men in the Residency, civilians and soldiers alike, manned the cannons and trenches, the proper Victorian ladies gradually accepted their plight. They tended the wounded, took care of the children, cooked, sewed, gathered wood, and carried water. This was quite an adjustment because these were tasks done by Indian servants prior to the mutiny.

The force of 7,000 that besieged the Residency was comprised of sepoys from several irregular native infantry regiments, 800 cavalrymen, the 22nd Native Infantry, artillerymen, and, after 11 June, two native city police regiments. These men were constantly reinforced by rural levies, officered by *talukdars* (local landowners) and bureaucrats from the Indian civil service.[9] Despite the number of soldiers from the East India Company's army, the organization of the mutineer force was fractious. Their British officers dead or in the Residency, the sepoys from the city garrison elected as leaders men possessing little military distinction and even less knowledge of warfare. The officers were obeyed and not obeyed. Discipline slackened. Many sepoys, as at Delhi and Cawnpore, grew bored with the whole affair and went home. Thus attacks against the Residency, sporadic at best, were usually poorly planned and poorly executed. Artillery fire, devastating to those on the receiving end, lacked focus. A lot of guns fired a lot of shot in the hope something or someone would be hit.

The city of 600,000 needed governing. The mutineers elected a council, half Hindu, half Muslim, and accepted a boy prince as their ruler. His mother, a feisty and ambitious woman named Birjis Qudr, a royal concubine of the deposed king, was named regent. No military men were given cabinet-level responsibilities. Nepotism, corruption, incessant quarreling, and timidity were rampant. Only the energy and ambitions of Birjis Qudr maintained the momentum of the city's mutiny. But the quarreling persisted, and so too did the incompetency. Birjis wondered why the Residency had not been taken and why no one knew what to do about it.

Then a self-declared holy man named Ahmad Allah Shah, the *maulvi* of Faizabad, appeared on the scene. He was known as a Muslim scholar and a maker of seditious speeches for which the British had imprisoned him. Freed by the mutineers in Faizabad, he traveled to Lucknow where he preached cooperation between Hindus and Muslims and exuded an enthusiasm for and knowledge of military affairs. The *maulvi* was eventually made commander-in-chief of the Lucknow forces.

Meanwhile the Residency siege ground on, the cannon and musket fire a steady and lethal din to those trapped inside. The possessions of the dead were auctioned. Those among the living with money bought necessities from those who arrived well provisioned. Thus, while Martin Gubbins, the Oudh financial commissioner, set an elegant dining table replete with French wine, many others neared starvation. Scurvy was common. Children died of malnutrition. Cholera and dysentery spread. No one thought of commandeering all the food and rationing it equally among the occupants. Yet most endured the squalor, disease, and deprivation with seeming equanimity. Inevitably, as exhaustion triumphed, hope of relief faded.

At midnight, 21 September, a loyal sepoy named Angad Tewari made it through the mutineer lines and into the Residency. Six days before, he had volunteered to carry a message to Brigadier General Henry Havelock, informing him of conditions in the Residency. Havelock sent back a message that he led 3,000 men and expected to be in Lucknow within a few days. With him was Major General Sir James Outram, long detached from the army for political duties. Even though senior to Havelock, he nominally relinquished command to the brigadier.

Havelock's march to Lucknow began on 21 September. He first battled his way through a mutineer force awaiting him at Mangalwar, then continued his advance toward Lucknow, running into a strong rebel force at the Alambagh, a suburban garden and palace. A surprise British attack against the mutineer's right flank forced them to withdraw to a new line along a canal at Lucknow's south end. That line was reinforced by the complex of fortified royal tombs, mosques, and palaces leading north to the Residency. Given the two-to-one odds favoring the mutineers, Havelock's prospects of reaching the Residency looked dim.

Outram exercised his authority as senior general and ordered a push directly across the canal into the city, fighting past the fortified tombs and palaces to the Residency. A determined infantry charge secured a bridge across the canal and entrance into the city where the British found themselves in a maze of streets and alleys, not knowing which way to turn. Mutineers stood atop walls and on roofs, showering the advancing troops with musket fire, arrows, and even rocks. Scottish Highlanders and loyal Sikhs surged forward in a desperate gamble, tumbling across ditches and rubble, until they at last reached the Residency. Five hundred men were lost in that dash, but the so-called First Relief of the Lucknow Residency was accomplished.

As the Residency gate shut behind the last British soldier, the mutineers resumed the siege. Doubtless, the guns and men of the relief column strengthened the Residency force, and fortunately a large grain cache was discovered hidden beneath a pool. Yet a major problem remained: once the column was in the Residency, no one gave any thought about how to get out. Someone from somewhere would have to mount a second relief.

THE BRITISH RESPONSE TO MUTINY: THE DELHI EXAMPLE

Russell, the *Times* correspondent, clearly and for once succinctly captured the emotion of the mutiny when he wrote, "Here we had . . . a war of religion, a war of race, and a war of revenge, of hate, of some national promptings to shake off the yoke of a stranger."[10] Revenge partly explains the carnage wrought by the mutineers and their followers. That same passion partly explains the carnage wrought by the British and their allies upon the Indians. Fanny Duberly, wife of a hussar officer and chronicler of the Crimean War, followed her husband to India and wrote a narrative of the mutiny. She held back nothing:

When I think of this terrible insurrection and recollect how deeply the rebels stained themselves with English blood, the blood of English women and little helpless children, I can only look forward with awe to the day of vengeance, when our hands shall be dipped in the blood of our enemies, and the tongues of our dogs shall be red with the same.[11]

Suspected mutineers were executed across northern India. Some were strapped to the muzzles of cannon and blown apart, and others shot like jackrabbits as they attempted to run away. A few were thrown into bonfires. Colonel James Neill, 1st Madras Fusiliers, marched to Benares and Allahabad, burned and pillaged the towns, then hanged everyone thought to be mutineer. At Cawnpore, suspects were rounded up, made to lick blood from the floor of the Bibighar, flogged, and hanged.

The British response was not merely an orgy of vengeful killing. They also organized military campaigns to end the mutiny. Lord Canning, replacing Dalhousie as India's governor general, believed that Delhi must be retaken. The city was not only the residence of Bahadur Shah II and the rallying point for thousands of mutineers, but was also the most important military post in northern India. Allowing the mutineers to keep the city only fomented more mutinies. As a result, a British column under the command of Sir Henry Barnard was organized in mid-May at Ambala to march on Delhi. The force consisted of a few loyal native infantry regiments and a hurriedly organized irregular cavalry detachment. A siege train slowly made its way from Phillour to Delhi. Another column from Meerut, put together through the energy of Brigadier Archdale Wilson, rather than the befuddled Hewitt, merged with Barnard's force. The evening of 8 June, the combined columns camped on The Ridge above Delhi. They were few in number: 2,300 infantry, 600 cavalry, 22 field guns, a couple of 24-pounders, and a few howitzers.[12]

In Delhi, the rule of Bahadur Shah proved more symbolic than substantive. He was reduced to a minor player in the mutiny, issuing proclamations that everyone ignored. He also appointed his eldest son, Mirza Moghul, commander-in-chief. Reluctant to lead and wanting to avoid battle, Mirza earned the contempt of the mutineers. For their part in the drama, the mutineers looted the bazaars, argued over the spoils, complained about not getting paid, and killed many civilians without consequence. Thousands of other sepoys, discouraged and disappointed, impatient with the ignorance of military affairs shown by their leadership, packed their belongings and disappeared into the hinterland.

Even though rampant desertions infected the mutineers' ranks, there were always enough sepoys to keep the cannons pounding the British on The Ridge and to mount an occasional attack. Soon there was little to distinguish between the British siege of Delhi and the Delhi siege of The Ridge. Both sides suffered appalling casualties. No exact figures exist, but for every 1,000 sepoys charging The Ridge, about 400 were killed. The British lost 30 to 40 men a day. Delhi, as with most sieges, became a battle of attrition.

By 7 September, the number of active troops on The Ridge numbered 6,000, to include seven cavalry regiments, units from various Queen's infantry regiments, a Punjabi infantry brigade, men from a half dozen loyal native infantry regiments, six horse artillery batteries, and the siege train. The time had come to attack Delhi.

With great difficulty and under constant fire from Delhi, siege guns were dragged forward to batter the city walls. At 8 A.M., 11 September, the British guns opened fire, ripping apart the 13-foot thick walls. Huge chunks of the city's Kashmir Gate turned to dust. The bombardment continued until shortly before dawn on the fourteenth. As the guns fell silent, the infantry attacked. Three assault columns, a fourth in reserve, converged on Delhi's strong points. The defenders, awakening to their common plight, fought back ferociously. But the British breached the walls, and the attacking columns made their way into the city, pushing the defenders further and further back.

No prisoners! That was the British command. With relentless fury born of hate, they bayoneted or shot everyone they found. Bodies choked the streets, and the stench of death spread over Delhi. So great was their emotional drive that the attacking forces lost formation. The attack stalled, churned forward, and stalled again. Soldiers complained that their officers were incompetent to direct fighting in the streets and houses. And no wonder! None had ever been trained for such fighting. There was talk of withdrawing in the face of stiffening resistance. But the order was never given. The attack persisted, or muddled along, until the last of the enemy strongholds collapsed. The battle in Delhi lasted six days.

The triumphant soldiers went on a rampage of looting and wanton destruction. Just as wanton were the death sentences given surviving mutineers. William Hodson, leading a contingent of irregular cavalry, captured three royal princes and was taking them back to Delhi, trailed by a few thousand Muslims. The situation turned ugly as the crowd closed in on the little column. Hodson had the princes stripped to their loin cloths, announcing to the crowd that these men were responsible for the deaths of innocent women and children. He then took a carbine from one of his troopers and calmly shot each of the princes dead. The crowd dispersed. The Delhi mutiny was over, the dead beyond count.

Many Delhi veterans claimed that the victory broke the back of the Great Mutiny. That conceit did not extend into the provinces of Rohilcund and Oudh. In the latter, the Lucknow Residency was still beseiged. Lord Canning urged that the Residency be relieved and that Lucknow be retaken. He wrote his new commander-in-chief, General Sir Colin Campbell (whom we last encountered as a young subaltern on the iced roads to Corunna): "It is difficult to exaggerate the importance of showing ourselves to be masters of Lucknow. . . . I believe it to be impossible to foresee the consequences of leaving that city unsubdued. I believe that we should see [the Indians] rise up all around us."[13]

Campbell marched to Lucknow in November with a force of 3,000, battled his way to the Residency, gathered the survivors, and marched practically unmolested out of the city. His troops then defeated Tantya Tope, the most gifted rebel leader, at Cawnpore. In March 1858, Campbell returned to Lucknow with a force of more than 30,000 and conquered the city. He then embarked on a highly mobile campaign, securing successive victories until, in April 1859, the Great Mutiny was declared officially over.

THE ROOTS OF MUTINY

To better pursue a central thesis of this study, that the causes of disintegration are found within the given military unit, we must examine more closely the character of the Bengal Army and its social context.

The Bengal Army, like the Madras and Bombay armies, was a part of the East India Company's army used to police the subcontinent. Both Hindus and Muslims served side by side. They were literally mercenaries, supplementing regiments of the regular British Army, which was too small to do the job by itself. Most of the Bengal Army's men were from the north central province of Oudh (now Uttar Pradesh), its approximate boundaries running from the Jumna River northeast to the Himalayas, and from around Furrukhabad east to Allahabad. Three-quarters of the enlistees were either Hindu high caste Brahmins or Rajputs, a caste of landowners originating on the Ganges plain. These were important people within Hindu society, and their military service gave them an added luster. They were also physically very fit—tall, well muscled, well fed, and often in better condition than their British counterparts. The sepoys lived in barracks sometimes, but more often in huts they were allowed to build for themselves. They brought along their families, cooked their own food, mostly rice and vegetables, and enjoyed a kind of village life within the army compounds. The sepoys trained in the British fashion, wore European-designed uniforms, used British weapons, and were organized into British-style regimental units. As was characteristic of the Indian Army as a whole, the men were promoted by seniority, but very few became *jemadars* or lieutenants, and fewer still became *subahdars* or company officers—somewhat like captains. Regardless of experience or time of service, all were junior to the youngest, most inexperienced British subalterns. Yet serving in the Company's army was considered an honorable profession, and most sepoys took great pride in that service.

Gradually, however, discontent arose, rooted in increasing suspicion of British motives toward India, creating conditions that made many sepoys feel increasingly alienated from the values, beliefs, and meanings that shaped the character and quality of their lives as soldiers. I should like to emphasize four conditions.

1. From their arrival in India and through the campaigns of Arthur Wellesley, the British appeared invincible to the Indians. Other foreign powers were driven away with a ruthless efficiency, often with the help of native troops, that quickly established British dominance over the subcontinent. Subsequent events diminished that aura. In the 1840s, the British

were savaged in the First Afghan War during which a column of 15,000 soldiers and civilians, including women and children, withdrew from Kabul to Jelalabad. Only one man survived. The others died of exposure or were killed by Muslim warriors. Just a handful were captured. Then the Punjab rebelled, momentarily put down by the First Sikh War. But the Second Sikh War in 1849 was fought by the British with an incompetence not lost on the sepoys. At the Battle of Chillianwallah, for example, the Sikh commander Shere Singh forced Sir Hugh Gough, the British commander, into battle on ground unfavorable to the British. Thus the Queen's 24th Regiment advanced into a jungle and were cut down by masked batteries of Sikh artillery. Of 800 men, 231 were killed and another 236 wounded. Brigadier Pope, aged, fat, and nearsighted, trotted into the jungle at the head of his cavalry, got lost, went in the wrong direct, and, panicked, led his troops into his own advancing horse artillery battery, knocking over the guns. British leadership slipped badly, and the sepoys knew it.

That decline of confidence was reinforced by the Crimean War (1854–1856). A handful of British regular officers serving in India rejoined their regiments going to the Crimea, but most Indian Army officers were bypassed as second-raters. However, the Queen's regiments in India, seldom more than one-eighth the total strength of the Company's army, were drawn away to the Crimea. So too were cannons, gunners, engineers, munitions, the machinery for making bullets, medical supplies, tents, blankets—all went. Already certain the British Army was diminutive, the sepoys convinced themselves that Britain had reached the end of its resources.

2. Circumstances in Oudh province fomented mutiny. Lord Dalhousie's annexation was precipitous, even though he thought good reasons existed. The king of Oudh led a luxurious life, even one of excess, showing little inclination to rule effectively. Corruption thrived. Annexation saw the king deposed, an action not viewed by the native population as a release from incompetence but as an invasion of their culture. When Dalhousie disbanded three-quarters of the king's private army, he created a pool of unemployed and angry soldiers, men stripped of an important status within the province. The Company's sepoys were also adversely affected when Dalhousie seized the lands of anyone unable to prove ownership. Sepoys routinely set aside what savings they could to purchase land for their retirement. But title was often a handshake or a verbal understanding, good enough within a village but not before a British court. Thus many sepoys found themselves dispossessed of their futures.

A sepoy could serve honorably for thirty or forty years. There were even those who hung on longer, awarded the last promotion, eking out the last few years that would secure their pensions. Burned-out, often half-crippled by wounds or injuries, they bumbled along, revering past glories and looking forward to being invalided out. But under Dalhousie the Enlistment Act of 1856 was passed by which men considered unfit for service would be retained by the army to do menial tasks around the cantonments. Another path to security in retirement was cut, replaced by humiliation.

3. The interpersonal relationships between the sepoys and their British officers had been quite close into the first decades of the nineteenth century. Officers learned native dialects, lived with and married native women, and appeared to sincerely care about their men. The sepoys, in turn, became trusted members of British households and on the battlefield earned the respect and admiration of their officers. Thus a gentle paternalism emerged. As early as the 1830s, however, officers coming to India distanced themselves from the Indian population and from their men. Intermarriage was openly derided. Few bothered to learn dialects. Having reported to their regiments, officers with enough money often absented themselves by going on hunting trips, traveling, or taking up sports, such as polo. Others sought positions in civil affairs. For example, Lieutenant Colonel Frederick Mackeson was commissioner in Peshawar and Captain H. R. James was his deputy commissioner, a quite common situation. So great was the turnover that one Bengal Army regiment, within only a year, had four commanders, three adjutants, and two quartermasters.

British attitudes toward the sepoys also changed from respect or at least decency to outright antagonism and occasional cruelty. Many officers, as *Subahdar* Sita Ram noted in his memoirs, were always impatient or angry with their men, calling them names like "pig" and "nigger." Sepoy orderlies or those in domestic situations were hit, knocked down, and even flogged for minor transgressions. Sita Ram noted that some officers apparently thought it was all very funny. The sepoys were stunned.

4. The onslaught of Christianity was seen by the sepoys as a calculated British maneuver not only to convert them to a new faith but to tear the entire fabric of Indian society. Russell, in his mutiny diary, noted on 20 March 1858 that a Reverend McKay gave a sermon stating that the British Empire, unlike others, was Christian and invincible because it carried the Ark of the Covenant. This statement might be dismissed as so much flummery but for the fact that it accurately reflected the sentiments of many British in India. For example, Herbert Edwardes, a commissioner in the Punjab, believed that God gave India to the British so they could convert it to Christianity. Christian evangelism was well established by 1810. Chapels were built, Bibles distributed, and public prayer meetings held. The task, I am per-

suaded, was not attended by much Christian charity, attested to by a report of the Society for the Promotion of Christian Knowledge appearing in the *Times*, 1 September 1813: "The [Indian] converts," it stated, "are comprised of the dregs of the people, discarded from their society, and a disgrace to ours."

Christian evangelism found easy access to the Indian Army. As T. A. Heathcote demonstrated in his study, *The Indian Army*, 307 British officers in the Bengal Army during the 1820s and 1830s had fathers in clerical orders. This represented 15.7 percent of all officers. Only those with military fathers exceeded that figure. Some openly proselytized the sepoys; others gave evangelists access to their troops. Getting the army involved in evangelism was a mistake. Indian civilians could ignore the attempts to convert them; unfortunately the closed society of the army gave the evangelists a more captive audience, for ignoring the wishes of one's officers often had bleak consequences.

The sepoys lived in an increasingly ambiguous world. Everything the army expected of them was British in origin. In most instances, the sepoys modified their behavior sufficiently to match those expectations, resulting in a system that was initially comfortable for both. Then the British crossed an invisible barrier between what they could fairly expect from their men as soldiers and intrusion into their private lives. Perhaps it was naive to assume that two such diverse cultures could ever coexist. Perhaps the relative harmony achieved early on was a fool's paradise, disguising very real discontinuities. Thus the men who refused the new cartridges at the Meerut firing-parade thought they were engaging in a traditional behavior—withdrawing their services as a means of conveying dissatisfaction. The humiliation of being arrested, court-martialed, and chained was beyond their comprehension. The incident quickly emerged as a symbol of all grievances against the British. Mutiny, bloody and destructive, overtook Meerut.

The perception of many sepoys, it may be speculated, was that the British did not provide the Indian Army with the means of resolving their discontent, nor did the British officers, some sensitive individuals notwithstanding, even recognize that such discontent existed. Consequently, as discontent changed to despair, the mutinous behavior that emerged was the attempt by the sepoys "to escape from intolerable social circumstances by attacking a person, a class of persons, or a class of objects rather than attempting to change the social system which . . . generated those circumstances."[14] The sepoys could hardly strike at Britain, nor could they really do harm to the Indian Army as a whole. But events such as the abortive firing-parade provided a specific context within which the sepoys and inflamed civilians became aware of common grievances and frustrations, and within which agitators stirred their collective anger. In the end, the real leaders of the mutiny were not the Nana Sahibs. They were instead the fortuitous and anonymous voices in the crowds who shouted above the din of dissatisfaction "Let's get the British!" or "Shoot all the officers!" or "There's one—let's get him!" or "Kill, kill!" or "Burn, burn!"

The commonly shared fear that their native culture was at risk created social and psychological separation from a system within which the sepoys once felt welcome, giving rise to feelings of alienation. Four types of alienation were primarily at work.[15] Meaninglessness, the first form of alienation, found its way into Indian Army ranks as the British flouted traditional expectations and long-established values. The name-calling, the contempt for native culture, and brutal conduct toward the sepoys created bewilderment because no matter what the sepoys did, it seemed to be wrong. Native officers and noncoms of the 3rd Cavalry not only warned Carmichael-Smyth not to hold a firing-parade, but they formally petitioned him. They finally withdrew their labor at the parade by politely but firmly refusing the new cartridges. The response by the British was arrest, trial, conviction, and punishment. That confusion about what to believe fed a growing sense of powerlessness, the second form of alienation—the expectation by the individual that his behavior would not influence the outcome of his actions. The sepoys became pawns of the British in an uncaring, often faceless system that used them remorselessly until they were discarded at the system's pleasure. Officers no longer cared about their welfare. Traditional means of protest were not respected but were looked upon as court-martial offenses. Nothing worked anymore. Powerlessness gave rise to accompanying feelings of normlessness, the third form of alienation. The sepoys felt that since the system ignored or degraded their native values and beliefs, their only recourse to attaining their goals was in unapproved, often illegal, behaviors. Thus, perceiving that formal means of rectifying the crisis were closed to them, and when military and social controls deteriorated during periods of increasing agitation, the pathways to crowd formation were opened. The sepoys, now functioning in a more volatile environment, turned verbal aggressions into overt physical violence and destruction as a means of rescuing native Indian culture. Isolation was the fourth form of alienation. The sepoys assigned low value to goals and beliefs that were typically highly valued by the army. The sepoys, feeling betrayed, rejected the old paternalisms as a fraud, allowing them to shed loyalties to their officers, the officers' families, and to the regiments in which they served.

This sense of isolation gave the ensuing violence a disturbingly impersonal character.

The mutiny ultimately failed because the participants could not overcome built-in problems. As the mutiny was reshaped into outright war, engaging in formal battles necessitated replacing the crowd behaviors of urban riot with some kind of military organization. Unfortunately for the sepoys, they could not shake that mutinous heritage, with the result that many of their formations lacked internal cohesion. Their military leadership, with some notable exceptions such as Tantya Tope, lacked the skills and knowledge necessary to battle the British. The result was that a smaller but more disciplined British army consistently defeated larger undisciplined mutineer formations. The mutineers anointed civil leaders whom they believed could govern the cities and provinces. Even though some led well enough, a coordinated national movement never emerged—despite the efforts of Marxist historians to rewrite the mutiny's history—because those leaders, such as Nana Sahib, carried forward agendas quite apart from what the mutineers wanted, and often wallowed in ineptitude and corruption. They did not communicate much with each other if at all, and they failed to coordinate their military movements.

The mutiny remained provincial and often localistic. The British reacted to those circumstances by isolating targets for reconquest, such as Delhi, Cawnpore, and Lucknow, while keeping other regional mutineer armies at bay. That continuously forced the Indians into defensive postures, fighting battles in which disciplined British firepower overcame them. Campbell could hunt down their leaders without much interference and eventually smash the mutiny.

4

The French Army Mutinies, 1917

Fifty-four French Army divisions experienced some form of mutiny during mid-1917. The French soldiers despaired of dying in massive battles that accomplished nothing. Isolated at the front, they felt that no one cared what happened to them.

YEARS OF PAIN: 1914, 1915, 1916

August 1914.[1] A great German offensive slammed into the French and Belgian frontiers. The German Army, like an enormous door hinged on the Swiss border, its leading edge toward the English Channel, struck west and south. British and French forces rolled back under the shock. The British retreated from Belgium to Mons, past Cambrai, across the Oise River, south toward the Marne River east of Paris. The French 5th Army retreated west toward St. Quentin, south past Laon and Reims, and across the Marne. The French 4th Army offered a feeble offense in the Ardennes, then retreated south to Chalons-sur-Marne.

The Germans vigorously pursued the Allies, exacting terrible casualties. But General Alexander von Kluck, commanding the German right wing, thought he could deliver a death blow to the British if he kept after them. Rather than enveloping Paris from the west as originally planned, his wing of the German Army pulled east of Paris, exposing their flank to the city's garrison. The Allies counterattacked. The Germans retreated across the

Marne River on 9 September and, a few days later, were forced to retreat further across the Aisne River to the north. British and French forces raced the German right wing to the channel coast, forcing them back into Belgium.

Even though the Allied victory at the Marne robbed the German advance of its momentum, the French and British did not possess the resources to force a complete German retreat from France. October brought cold weather rain, and mud. Movement ground to a standstill because, in 1914, most men still marched to war. The armies dug trenches, each side trying to consolidate gains and, at the same time, recuperate from already staggering losses. Eventually the trenches wound their way from the channel coast in Belgium across northwest France to the Vosges Mountains of eastern France. From there to the Swiss border, because of the mountains, the line was comprised of strong points, guard posts, and garrisons. This great scar across the land was known as the Western Front (Map 5).

The first trenches were crude affairs, mere scratches in the ground, featuring an occasional artillery spotting post, some machine gun emplacements, some well-spaced dugouts, and sandbags on top of the ground. As the winter of 1914 passed, and as the battles of Neuve Chapelle, Aubers Ridge, and Vimy Ridge demonstrated that no one was going anywhere, a siege mentality took hold of the opposing generals. Trenches were constructed in earnest and with increasing sophistication.

Most noticeable along the front was the open space between the opposing forces, a shell-blasted, twisted no-man's land. Barbed wire barricades, varying in depth from 10 yards to 200 yards, defined the front lines. For behind the wire—whether French, British, or German—was a firing trench. The front wall of the firing trench was faced with sandbags. More sandbags across the top of the front wall formed a parapet. This was loopholed for rifles and machine guns. The trench itself was between 6 and 8 feet deep, with a firing step about 2 feet from the bottom. Wood duckboards covered the trench bottom. The back wall contained niches for ammunition, tools, and some dugouts for officers and signalmen. The top of the back wall was also lined with sandbags. Fifty to 100 yards to the rear was an identical trench for support troops. About 200 yards further back was a third trench for more support troops. Behind that line the French typically built a redoubt, a position completely surrounded by barbed wire and manned by a platoon. The final trench for the battalion command post was a few hundred yards further back. Fresh troops theoretically occupied this line. All the parallel trenches were dug with frequent traverses, or jogs, in the line to prevent penetrating enemy troops from firing the whole length of the trench. The firing trenches were connected to each other by communications

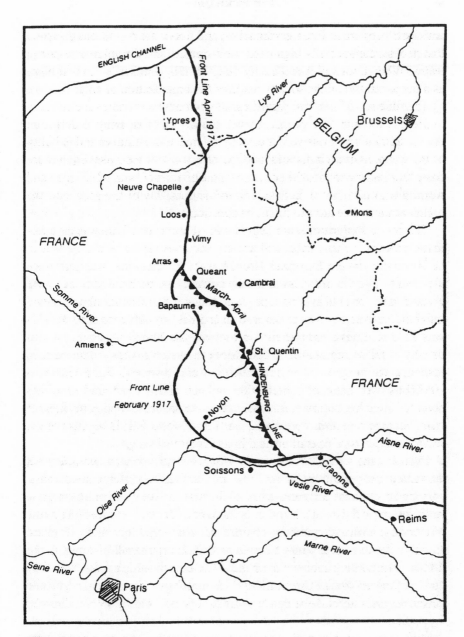

Map 5
Western Front, 1917

trenches, perpendicular cuts that supposedly became deeper as the firing trench was approached. In reality, they were often not much more than water-filled mud wallows. Paul Fussel, in *The Great War and Modern Memory*, estimates that by 1918 the Allies and the Germans on the Western Front dug a combined 25,000 linear miles of trenches.[2]

The French rotated their infantry companies, 200 men plus officers, into the firing trench every week to ten days. The men took positions on the firing step at dawn in expectation of an enemy attack. If none developed, they ate their rations and went to work carrying supplies, filling sandbags, and digging. At night, patrols crawled forward into their wire screen to repair or extend it, recover wounded men, or conduct trench raids against the enemy in the hope of capturing someone or seeing what was happening on the other side.

The men lived in a two-dimensional linear world, a world defined by two dirt walls and the sky above. Little could be seen from the trenches. Hundreds of thousands of men lived in close proximity but almost never saw each other. Exposure meant death. Enemy snipers looked for the slightest movement, sighting in on a loophole for hours. Machine gun fire randomly raked the parapets. Harassing fire from artillery and mortars landed in the trenches, bringing death by long distance. The British had 20,000 men killed and other 30,000 wounded on the first morning of the Somme offensive, but, as Martin Gilbert points out, that number, a slaughter by any human standard, represented the average death toll among the French and British for four days of ordinary passive trench duty.[3]

Occasionally a great offensive was ordered by the generals who worked up to 25 miles behind the lines. They operated on the principle that if they collected more men for an attack than German artillery and machine guns could kill, then they would achieve a breakthrough of the enemy lines. Most attacks began with ferocious bombardments, some lasting a week, to cut the enemy wire and flatten their trench lines. When the shelling stopped, the French officers blew their whistles and clambered over the parapet followed by their men. Typically two assault platoons charged forward first. Most of the men were bombers—grenade throwers—supported by some riflemen. Successive platoons from the same company followed, passing through the exhausted and casualty-ridden assault troops. With luck, they penetrated the German wire and might even take the first and second trenches. Theoretically, another assault wave caught up with them, passed through, and went on to take successive trenches.

That seldom happened because the concept contained several flaws. The generals and their obsequious staff officers, sitting far removed from the lines in their splendid chateaux, seldom had any idea of conditions in the trenches. The attacking infantry first had to get through their own wire, a slow process even with paths cut the night before. Crossing no-man's land was not the energetic charge conceived by the generals but a slow, even arduous, picking across a landscape filled with shellholes, disinterred bodies from previous attacks, litter, and mud. Frequently the German wire, barbs like sharks' teeth, was not cut because the famous French 75s, their principal artillery, was too light for the task. Meanwhile the Germans rose from dugouts 30 feet deep, barely shaken by the bombardment, and re-mounted their machine guns. Waves of French soldiers were cut down. German artillery blanketed the front of their wire with shrapnel shells. Whole French battalions disappeared. Then the German fire swept across no-man's land, finally hitting the French trenches crowded with support troops who could not go over the top because of the relentless enemy fire. Such offensives went on and on, each one the promised "big push," the anticipated big breakthrough.

The urge to continue these attacks against the Germans was based on two unquestioned premises. First, the French general staff developed a philoso-phy, really a dogma, of attack following the disastrous Franco-Prussian War of 1870. French soldiers, the dogma held, were innately endowed with *élan*, an eagerness to attack, the crowning glory of which was the bayonet charge. Thus the machine gun was seen as a defensive weapon, inappropriate for infantry companies. Heavy artillery, unable to keep up with rapid advances, was considered an impediment. Instead, the 75mm gun was developed. Easily maneuvered and rapid fire, the gun was ideal for infantry support. Attack! The philosophy was so mesmerizing that alternatives were not considered. Second, despite the Allied success at the Marne, the Germans still held substantial areas of French territory, making offensives necessary to drive them out. Moreover, offensives gave the impression that the French were winning, that the siege would be broken. Unfortunately for the French (and the British), the Germans realized in early 1915 that the war had nothing to do with territory but, instead, would be attritional. They bided their time, picking the date and place for their offensives with care. In the interim, they would let the French Army bleed to death trying to crack their defenses.

And bleed is just what the French Army did. Richard Watt states in *Dare Call It Treason* that the French suffered total casualties of 754,000 in 1914, another 1,549,000 in 1915, and through October 1916 they experienced 861,000 casualties. When the war ended, French dead numbered 1,368,000, and another 3,600,000 were wounded. Watt concluded that "the real horror

of World War I . . . was in the fact that so many men died and achieved
nothing for it."[4] Edmund Taylor wrote that "The trench warfare of 1914–
1918 was perhaps the cruelest large-scale ordeal that the flesh and spirit of
man have endured since the beginning of the Ice Age."[5] These bleak
assessments stem from the realization that the few times a breakthrough did
occur, the Germans willingly retreated, often surrendering several miles of
ground. Then they reestablished a new and stronger defensive line, and
waited for the Allies to attack again.

Attritional war was also expensive to the defender. The Germans, knowing they could not sustain an indefinite defensive war, made plans to literally
bleed the French Army to death in one great offensive of their own. General
Erich von Falkenhayn, chief of the German general staff, proposed a massive
assault on the fortress complex at Verdun,[6] which the Germans had captured
in both 1792 and 1870. The French dared not let that happen again because
the defeat would devastate their morale. Falkenhayn was convinced the
French would be forced to defend the historic fortress city, and reasoned
that if the Germans took Verdun, the French would pour more and more
resources into its recapture, leading to their exhaustion in the bloody battle.
As Werner Beumelburg said, "We must apply a suction-pump to the body
of France."[7]

Headed by Joseph Joffre, hero of the Marne, the French general staff at
first showed little concern for Verdun. When attacked in 1914, Joffre ordered
the fortress complex be abandoned, but the local commander refused to
obey. The garrison held out, forcing a bulge or salient in the front line.
Nevertheless, the staff concluded that, in an epoch *élan*, fortresses were
anachronisms. They reduced the garrison and dismounted the heavy fortress
guns for use elsewhere.

Denuded though it may have been, Verdun remained a formidable site, a
consequence of its topographical features. The Meuse River runs north
through a limestone escarpment that is cut on its eastern fringes by endless
ridges and ravines, and is run through by caves and rock shelters. Not only
would the Germans have to surmount the ridges, but they would also have
to cross and recross the river in its flat meandering bed.

Falkenhayn put a 6-mile arc of 850 artillery pieces around the salient—
everything from light 77mm guns to heavier 380cm and 405cm siege guns.
Thousands upon thousands of men, including the entire 7th Reserve Corps,
were stuffed into an 8-square mile area already piled high with supplies,
especially ammunition. Falkenhayn wanted his initial attack to be monumental.

At dawn, 21 February 1916, the German artillery opened fire. Whole sections of French trench line disappeared, men disintegrated or buried alive. Great sections of forest were obliterated. The bombardment lasted nine hours. German assault infantry advanced from the north. They shot and bayoneted survivors, pitched hand grenades into remaining trenches and dugouts and, for the first time in warfare, utilized flame throwers. Three thousand French soldiers were captured. The next day eighteen German infantry divisions advanced, capturing another 10,000 men and smashing a mile into the defensive perimeter.

The French responded as Falkenhayn predicted, reinforcing Verdun with a massive infusion of men, artillery, and supplies. General Henri-Philippe Pétain was made sector commander, pronouncing "They shall not pass!" He had a road built, an automotive conveyor belt hauling in reinforcements and taking out the wounded. Men, guns, and machines poured into the front week after week. And more men, more guns, and more machines were destroyed as fighting was reduced to vicious contests for unimportant plots of ground. Fort Vaux, for example, reaching an importance beyond its tactical significance, changed hands thirteen times at enormous cost to both armies. The German suction-pump was working, and no one knew how to turn it off.

Joffre grew dissatisfied with Pétain's lengthy and blood-soaked defense of Verdun, promoted him to another command, and put General Robert Nivelle in his place. Nivelle audaciously changed the fighting scheme. In recapturing Fort Douaumont, for example, he first took his assault divisions out of the line, rested and refitted them, and trained them in small unit attacks against a model of the target. Then he brought forward his heaviest guns and pounded the fort. This was followed by a creeping barrage meant to support the usual French infantry attack. Masked German guns opened fire, but the French barrage was only a ruse to locate the German artillery. Other French artillery destroyed them. This enabled the infantry assault units to move forward supported by trench mortar fire. Douaumont was captured in two hours. Verdun remained in French hands. In December, the Germans, exhausted and reeling from their own monumental half million dead, ordered their troops to assume defensive positions. Despite Nivelle's innovations, the cost of defending Verdun was 650,000 French dead.

Verdun was celebrated as a great victory. Pétain was a hero; Nivelle was catapulted into stardom. Yet the men in the trenches were increasingly morose. To help relieve pressure on the Verdun front, the French demanded a British offensive—the Somme. The French supported that campaign, losing another 50,729 Frenchmen killed; the British killed in the four-month fight numbered 95,675. The Germans did not go away. They retreated into stronger positions, regrouped, and waited for the next attack.

1917: THE NIVELLE OFFENSIVE ON THE AISNE

Joffre was another casualty of Verdun. The taciturn old man, given extraordinary powers in 1914, persuaded the government to establish the Zone of the Army—the area of the Western Front—within which he created his own fiefdom. He forbade journalists at the front. He communicated very little with the government and then in the most obscure terms. His war strategy and plans were his own. But with the war dragging on, Joffre became more vulnerable to criticism. The butcher's bill of his offensive strategy increased each year with no appreciable results. At the end of 1916, with the Germans still firmly entrenched on French soil, Joffre was passed into retirement.

Who else but Robert Nivelle was capable of replacing him? He was the hero of the hour. Handsome, vain, impetuous, self-promoting, mercurial, Nivelle eagerly accepted responsibility for formulating a new offensive for early 1917.[8] He believed that the application of his Verdun tactics to a larger field of combat would win the war. The plan was simple enough. The German withdrawal at the Somme left a salient projecting into the French lines from Péronne to a point west of Noyon, and then east, past Soissons, to Craonne. Nivelle's plan called for a British diversionary attack 70 miles north in the region of Arras, thrusting past Cambrai. The French would mount the main attack from the south between Reims and Soissons, moving north of the Aisne River, over the ridge known as the Chemin des Dames, and beyond into open country (Map 6). The French attack would use twenty divisions, 1,200,000 men, all trained in the so-called Nivelle system. They would be supported by a massive artillery bombardment along the full length of the front. Extra weight of attack, guaranteeing that the German wire would be knocked down, was provided by 128 tanks. The plan called for a 6-mile penetration of the German positions. *Élan*, speed, and brutality of attack were the offense's slogans. Hope spread among the French from officers down to the enlisted men. So many troops, so much artillery, so much ammunition—and tanks! Special training. New equipment. This was the Big Push all had hoped for. They could not lose. Optimism soared among the line officers as they saw the tangible results of new training techniques. Optimism soared among the troops who found in the careful plan a general's concern for their survival.

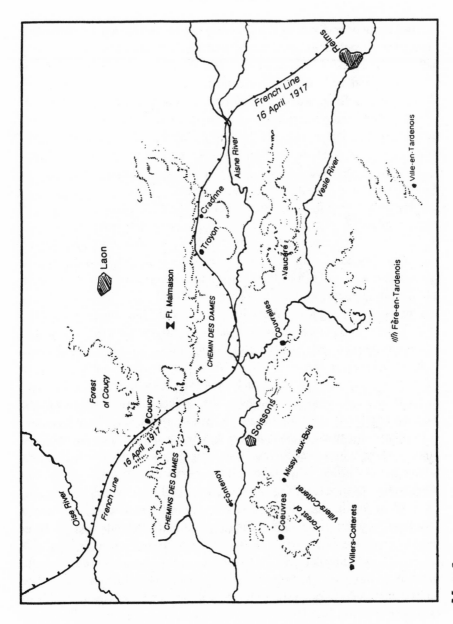

Map 6
Chemin des Dames, April 1917

The Germans realized an offensive was in the making. All the movement behind the French lines could not be disguised, and, besides, they captured a plan of the attack. As a countermaneuver, the Germans withdrew between 9 February and 19 March to new defensive positions variously called the Hindenburg or Siegfried Line. The repositioning shortened the German lines 25 miles, enabling them to redeploy several divisions, making their defenses more dense. The new defenses featured concrete dugouts and pill-boxes for machine guns. Artillery was carefully positioned to support the front trenches. Most important, this repositioning meant that the salient, the whole point of the attack, no longer existed.

Despite the obvious conclusion that the French would be attacking into the strength of the German defenses, Nivelle saw no reason to alter any part of his plan. Opposition grew. Paul Painlevé, the war minister, begged President Raymond Poincaré to let him resign because he did not trust Nivelle and had no faith in the strategy. On 6 April, a meeting was held attended by Poincaré, Painlevé, Pétain, and Nivelle. But the president and war minister only suggested that Nivelle modify his thinking, not cancel the assault. Pétain was more outspoken: the army did not possess the means to carry out the plan and, if successful, could not exploit any gains. Nivelle was furious and threatened to resign. Since that would be political suicide for Painlevé and Poincaré, the attack went forward unmodified.

15 April. Rain, sleet, and cold swept the battlefield. At 6 A.M., the French went over the top into a mud wallow that was no-man's land. The goo pulled at the boots and stuck to their uniforms. Their heavy packs weighed them down. The tanks lumbered forward and immediately bogged down. The men arrived at the German wire and found it uncut by the artillery. So slow was the infantry advance that the rolling barrage established to protect them was far in advance, allowing the German artillery to respond by laying down a counterbarrage the full width of their front. Although gains were made in the center of the line, taking most of the Chemin des Dames, Nivelle's expected 6-mile advance averaged only 600 yards,[9] especially from Craonne to Reims. He expected 15,000 casualties. The total was almost 100,000. The tanks were targets of opportunity for the German artillery, a quarter of them destroyed the first day. There was no great breakthrough.

Nivelle did make a concession during the 6 April meeting, agreeing to cancel the offensive if no significant progress was made within the first 48 hours. Despite the evidence of complete failure, and eager for victory at any price, Nivelle refused to quit. The fighting ground into a third day and a fourth, into a week and beyond. The roads were impossible, the front was a confused jumble as assault wave after assault wave stacked up in the trenches, unable to launch into no-man's land because of the German bombardment. Communications broke down, and coordination ceased to exist. Nivelle, moreover, possessed neither the wit nor the means to bring the growing tragedy to an end. The sheer inertia created by the weight of attack could not be stopped with the wave of a hand. Nivelle's offensive system, successful on the small stage of Verdun but transmogrified by its application to the larger arena of the Chemin des Dames, stalled, shuddered to a sickening halt, and collapsed.

MUTINY

Some assault divisions were stuck at the front and ordered to attack again and again. Luckier units were rotated out to rest camps in nearby towns and villages. The men were strangely silent, even sullen, as they marched or were trucked along the rutted roads. Their faces showed their exhaustion, shock, bitterness, and despair. Many wondered if the war would ever end. Others wondered if their generals knew what they were doing. They wondered how the government, after so many promises and such glowing optimism about the offensive, could let it degenerate into another bloodbath. But some men, as they passed fresh troops headed for the front, shouted, "*Vous êtes bouteilles vides!*" You are dead soldiers! (in the jargon of the troops empty bottles were known as dead soldiers). "*À bas la guerre!*" Down with the war! "*À bas l'armée!*" Down with the army!

The rest camps were bitter places, many as unappealing as sectors of the front. Some men were fortunate enough to be billeted in abandoned barns or houses, but most were consigned to wet tents in muddy fields. Others simply hunkered down in the mud and made the best of it. Endless rounds of training started. Company and battalion officers reported that more and more men shirked their duty, or were too drunk to report, or took their time obeying orders. Others even insulted their officers and noncoms. The stolid *poilus* (the common soldiers) were acting strangely. Their usual fortitude, even under the worst conditions, was giving way to disrespect, anger, and indifference.

The 2nd Battalion, 18th Infantry Regiment had been in the first assault. Of 800 men, there were only 200 shocked survivors. They were assigned to a rest camp. Replacements fleshed out the empty ranks, and it was rumored that the regiment was going to the Alsace front where things were quiet. On 29 April, the regiment was ordered back to the Chemin front. Many of the men got drunk, refused to obey orders, and shouted "*À bas la guerre!*" Later, having sobered, the men grudgingly formed ranks and marched to the front. A few men were arrested in camp for mutiny. The police randomly scooped up several more off the streets. They were tried and convicted of mutiny. Four were shot. One managed to escape.[10]

On 3 May, the 2nd Colonial Infantry Division, camped outside of Soissons after being bled to death in the first assault, was ordered back into the line. Many men were too drunk to march, and others waved pacifist leaflets that had found their way into camp. "We're not going!" they shouted. Those who did fall in left their rifles on the ground. Officers who were known to be well liked circulated among the men, preying on their guilt—they were going back to relieve a division already too long on the line; and those men, who never let down the Colonials, were waiting. The division formed ranks and went back to the front. But, as Richard Watt significantly notes, a lesson was learned by the troops and those in authority. There were too many men involved in the division's mutiny for all of them to be punished.[11]

Typical of the mutinies was that of the 301st Infantry Regiment, in camp at Coeuvers, 2 June. Joseph Jolinon, an eyewitness to the events, wrote an impressionistic memoir.[12] The stirrings of mutiny began when the troops of another regiment passed the 301st's camp on 30 May. Men in the passing trucks yelled, waved red flags, and sang the *Internationale*, the communist revolutionary song. Many men threw away their equipment. They shouted the now-familiar slogan, "*À bas la guerre!*" "Be like us," they called out. "The whole corps has refused to march. Be like us and we can end the war tomorrow." The men scattered pacifist leaflets and sang more revolutionary songs. "Down with the army!" They spat out the words with anger. "Throw down your guns. Death to the government. Death to the police. Liberty or death! Follow us, brothers."

Men of the 301st quietly watched the spectacle. They watched, questioning, wondering. They walked back to their camps in barns, orchards, and fields. The group that included Jolinon welcomed some officers and noncoms. They sat and talked, agreeing they would go back to the trenches to defend them but would refuse to attack. After all, most of the damned army staff were safe enough during the first assault, tucked away far behind the lines, unable to see the terrible losses. They should be shot, someone said, but no one volunteered to pull the trigger. The men talked on, sharing their thoughts and feelings. Then a "little machine gunner" said, "Think about this: if we attack Fort Malmaison [a German strong point] many men will be killed; if we refuse, there will be fifteen firing squads for us." The talk went on for three days.

On 2 June, orders came to return to the front. The men stirred themselves into a frenzy, fixing their bayonets, firing guns into the air, cursing the war, the army, and the government. A large crowd, not the entire regiment, marched to a wood near Villers-Cotterets. They established a puritanical, revolutionary discipline that forbade all wine drinking. They elected leaders and posted sentinels to watch for the cavalry that blocked the road further south. They stayed in their makeshift camps for four days, subsisting on a Spartan diet of bad water, bread, bully-beef, kidney beans, and nettle soup.

Finally, weary of their ordeal, not having any clear idea of what to do, they washed, shaved, and cleaned their uniforms. They then formed columns of four and, by companies, marched from their camp and surrendered. The rest of the regiment went back into the line between Laffaux and Filain.

The mutineers of the 301st were accused of instigating rebellion, a crime punishable by death. Of the 400 men arrested, only 32 were actually brought to trial. Fifteen were sentenced to hard labor, and 17 were to be executed. Of those awaiting execution, a review board in Paris pardoned all but one. He was shot. The mutiny of the 301st was over.

Mutinies, in fits and starts, occurred all along the Chemin des Dames front. At Fère-en-Tardenois the mutineers tried to get to Paris, but the trains were blocked from leaving the station. At Missy-aux-Bois a regiment took over the village and elected an anti-war council. They were blockaded in the village by cavalry and forced to surrender. The 128th Regiment was in rest camp near Reims. Replacements to the regiment distributed anti-war leaflets picked up in Paris and told tales of rioting in railway stations. When ordered to return to the front, the regiment mutinied, refusing to board their trucks. Instead, they gathered to hear soldier-speakers denounce the army and the government. Only after a personal appeal by the corps commander did the men straggle back to duty.[13] At the front itself, XXI Corps refused the order to attack and stayed in their trenches. Thus, as mutiny was stemmed in one unit, it surfaced in another. Of the 100 French divisions at the front, 54 experienced some form of mutinous behavior. The general staff and the government agreed that something had to be done.

SUPPRESSION OF MUTINY

Pétain succeeded the disgraced Nivelle as commander of the army on 29 April. Thrust into yet another unenviable command, his orders were straightforward: stop the mutinies; restore discipline. Pétain took steps both draconian and humanitarian to rescue the deteriorating situation.

He convinced Painlevé to grant him powers never given a commander-in-chief. The government was to keep out of the Zone of the Army. There was to be no interference in Pétain's interpretation of military justice—swift trials and severe punishment. All avenues of appeal were cut (although Painlevé was allowed to review some verdicts related to politically sensitive cases), and President Poincaré would not be allowed to pardon anyone. Instead of formal courts-martial, war councils were created by which any officer could, in response to a mutinous act, form a group of fellow officers for the immediate trial, conviction, and sentencing of the perpetrators. If the death sentence was given, a firing squad waited around the corner. In a 5 June directive, Pétain stated that he would protect all those officers who displayed "vigor and energy in the suppression [of mutiny]."[14] If officers did not display those characteristics in the face of mutiny, they would find themselves before a council of war.

This drumhead justice was applied to a mutinous battalion of XXXVII Corps. Seven hundred men took refuge in a cave, refusing to go back to the front. General Émile Taufflieb, corps commander, arrived at the scene and to everyone's surprise entered the cave unarmed. The men were sullen, disrespectful, and refused to leave. Taufflieb ordered that if the men were not out by morning, the cave was to be sealed. The men came out and formed ranks. Taufflieb then had five men from each company selected for execution as examples to the rest of the corps. The men selected were quickly marched away and shot. The general turned to the battalion and told them that they would return to the trenches that night.

No one knows precisely how many men in the Zone of the Army were sentenced to hard labor in penal colonies, or ordered to hazardous duty in lieu of execution, or were actually shot. The government was precluded from keeping records, and those records the army kept—if indeed they did—were destroyed with other army papers in 1940. As a whole, the army kept silent about the mutinies. So too did Pétain to the day he died.

Pétain knew that harsh means needed to be tempered with concern for the soldiers. Their complaints were often legitimate. For example, under existing policy, a seven-day leave was granted every four months. However, no one with any authority bothered about getting the men home. Once they left the trenches, they were on their own. They walked, burdened by rifles and full packs, to railway stations behind the lines and waited for their trains. But there were too few trains. No provisions were made for feeding or housing the men. There were no sanitary facilities. A man could spend his entire leave trying to get out of the miserable town.

Pétain kept the ratio of men on leave at the established 13 percent, but hinted that a unit being reformed because of a high casualty rate might allow up to 50 percent to take leave. Trucks were made available for getting from the front to the railway stations. Cafés were built at or near the stations, as were bathhouses, laundries, and simple barracks. Canteens run by the Red Cross and the YMCA were allowed in the Zone of the Army.

Pétain ordered that rest camps be resituated on drier ground. He gave strict orders that the men in the camps were to be left alone for four days. After that, retraining could begin but only by progressive stages. Pétain visited the rest camps and areas near the front on a regular basis, giving the men a little speech explaining his concept of limited offensives supported by heavy artillery. He promised an end to the "butcher's bill" war by emphasizing defense. Within hearing of the enlisted troops, he enjoined his field officers to take interest in their men. He also told them in a voice that was easily overheard by the soldiers that the officers needed to be pitiless against mutiny for he, the commander-in-chief, did not have time for legal niceties. Then Pétain listened to the soldiers, noting their complaints, and ordered instant remedies where feasible. The soldiers, awed by his presence, saw in Pétain the end or, certainly, the beginning of the end of their worst nightmares. Tangible, visible change was coming.

THE ROOTS OF MUTINY

Pétain searched for causes of the mutinies. In late May 1917, he wrote a report in which he listed several.[15] These can be conveniently divided into two categories. First were those causes indigenous to the Zone of the Army and second were those related to the homefront.

As early as April and May, soldiers within the Zone realized that mutinous behavior would probably go unpunished. The number of mutineers notwithstanding, the government had a policy of severely restricted courts-martial, and a long appellate road was open to anyone convicted. The soldiers knew this. Pétain established the war councils as a countermeasure. But a major source of undisciplined behavior was excessive drinking. Far too many men used their leaves or time in rest camps to get drunk and to stay drunk as long as possible. In that condition, they not only exhibited disrespectful and undisciplined behavior but were open to the mutinous influences of the radicals in the wine-soaked ranks. Consequently the amount of wine in the Zone was reduced.

In Paris, pacifists and radicals, socialists and Russia sympathizers, held anti-war rallies, published their own newspapers extolling the principles of Russian revolutionaries, and even sent provocateurs among the troops. The anti-war demonstrators frequently abetted Paris strikes. When dressmakers walked out, supported by students and by soldiers (who it seems only wanted to get close to the pretty girls), political radicals and disaffected soldiers often attended the workers' rallies, giving inflammatory speeches. Government treasury workers struck for higher pay. Thousands of workers in war-related factories walked out. Stop-the-war meetings were held seemingly everywhere at once. According to Pétain, the officers and soldiers who attended these meetings did so knowing they would seldom be punished. That had to stop.

Pétain's condemnation of homefront anti-war activities, their impact in the Zone notwithstanding, was doubtless a slap at Louis Malvy, minister of the interior. A young ambitious radical, Malvy did little or nothing to stop the growing anti-war furor; moreover, he convinced the cabinet to exempt from arrest the radicals behind the unrest. There were even those in or close to government circles who engaged in active pro-German activities, but remained suspiciously immune from prosecution. Rumors of government treason circulated, reviving memories of the notorious Dreyfus Affair of the 1890s in which a Jewish army captain was wrongly convicted of espionage as a scapegoat for an inept intelligence department and a self-serving general staff. Moreover, the army seemed helpless to stop the flow of rumor and anti-war propaganda. But Pétain stopped the propaganda literature and provocateurs by sealing the Zone of the Army and appealing to the soldiers to be careful with whom they associated.

Pétain, it is crucial to observe, despite all his perceptivity and sensitivity, did not formally note a common element that ran through all the mutinies. Undoubtedly he believed that low morale plagued his men. But the morale element was not profound enough to express the feeling that pervaded the front lines. As Richard Watt so keenly noted, the French Army was filled with despair. That despair was the taproot of the emerging disintegration, and it was fed by the conditions at the front. Sometimes narratives of Western Front conditions reach maudlin proportions, becoming latter-day Victorian melodrama, but the desperation was very real.

During the India Mutiny of 1857, fear of social change and denigration of native culture gave rise to the sepoys' desperation. In France an opposite current was operating. Stagnation, the fear that nothing would ever change, the fear that the war would go on forever, brought despair. Just as surely as in India, however, despair was the foundation for the alienation that emerged within the French Army.[16]

Meaninglessness, the confusion over what to believe, infected the French troops. They wanted to believe in patriotism and bravery, all the beliefs and values of French culture that had extolled militarism from the days of Napoleonic glory, but reality gave a different face to battle—grinding death, impersonal death, death on such a continuously massive scale that even the revered Napoleon might have blanched at the sight.

Powerlessness, the expectation by the individual that his actions will not influence outcomes of his behavior, emerged when the soldiers concluded that the army did not care about them and instead looked upon them as so much cannon fodder. The squalor of the rest camps, the bad food, the lack of leave, and the horrendous casualties confirmed their conclusions. The men grumbled and complained that no one in authority ever listened. The company officers often nodded in sympathy, providing a man was so bold as to address them with a complaint. But that was as far as it usually went. The officers did not dare take the issues to higher authority lest they be considered inadequate or, worse, cowards. During an offensive the soldiers struggled time and again to the German wire, fighting with all the *élan* they could muster. It seldom made a difference. When an offensive collapsed, strangled by the slaughter, the soldiers, not the generals, were blamed. What to do?

The answer was found in France, as it was in India, by normlessness, the expectation that socially unapproved behaviors were necessary to achieve given goals. In India, normlessness was a clearly drawn process as the British seemed bent on overwhelming Indian culture. The good guys could be differentiated from the bad guys. But that distinction was blurred on the Western Front. The Germans were not the source of alienation, despite the invasion. The French Army was the source, and that army was comprised of Frenchmen. Thus the mutineers' slogans were filled with references to the amorphous "they." *À bas l'armée!* Who? Nivelle? He was sacked by "the government." *À bas le gouvernement!* Who? The president, certain ministers, the cabinet? Or did the soldiers mean to reprise the 1789 revolution? Thus the reality of mutiny proved less noble than the slogans. The overt unapproved behaviors, those open acts of mutiny, were actually rather petty: shouting and waving fists: singing the *Internationale*; waving red flags; defying officers; marching to a copse and electing a revolutionary council; waiting to be arrested; or storming a railway station only to find all the tracks blocked and the trains rerouted. Spread across the vast front and between various units, these acts were small stuff indeed. Collectively, they defined an army heaving toward disintegration. The most defiant mutinous actions took place when entire divisions and corps, willing to defend the trenches, refused to attack the Germans.

Isolation was another expression of alienation. Soldiers assigned low value to goals and beliefs on which the army's upper echelons and, presumably, French society as a whole placed high value, thus superficially resolving their initial confusion over what to believe. The litany of values is long, but essential among them were devotion to duty, patriotism, loyalty, dogged determination, *élan*, and courage. The common soldiers displayed these values, these virtues, and fought and bled and died for them over the three years of the war. The soldiers found no reciprocity from the high offices of the army for their deeds. Medals were sprinkled about in the ranks, and some promotions were given; on the whole, the conformity to the revered values of the society meant little at the front. They were lies. No one died nobly or gallantly—they were unceremoniously blown to bits. The soldiers knew little beyond rumor what the majority of civilians at home thought about their plight; only that most must be in sympathy with the war and its ceaseless bloodshed.

The pervasive despair brought to a peak by the failed Nivelle offensive, the forms of alienation it engendered, and the mutinies that erupted from these processes must be understood against the background of the physical isolation of the troops within the Zone of the Army. The front was a self-contained world created by the generals, and communications with and travel to rear areas, even those only five miles away, were complicated and often dangerous. For weeks at a time the troops were exposed to the reality and capriciousness of imminent death.[17] Yet they thought of their trench sections as home, their companies as family. These were the stabilizing elements in their dangerous existence. But all of it was madness, a great aberration of the human soul.

As in India, the soldiers believed that the army was incapable of resolving their growing discontent. Again as in India, the mutineers directed their ire against what Richard La Piere termed a class of persons—generals, the government, the army itself—they believed were responsible for their intolerable circumstances. Unlike India, where overt verbal aggression moved quickly to overt physical violence against the British and then their own people, the French troops did not move beyond overt verbal aggression. However, the class of persons against whom that hostility was directed was unreachable, leaving the French mutineers without focus—without a tangible target—for their anger and despair. An irony interposes: Pétain's visits to the troops did not motivate violence. Here was a general. Real. Flesh and blood. But no one shouted, "Let's get him!" Quite the contrary. His sincere interest in their problems, his presence in forward areas, and his willingness to listen to them and order remedies for many of their grievances co-opted the soldiers to the army's interest in restoring order.

Mutiny leaders emerged but just as quickly disappeared into the mass from which they came. The most radical in the mutinous enclaves preached revolution and went through such revolutionary rituals as organizing councils and imposing puritanical discipline. The most impassioned soldier-orators, convincingly articulating grievances, failed to communicate means of ameliorating those grievances. Storming aboard a Paris-bound train was an exciting thought, but little consideration was given to what should be done if the train failed to appear or, if it did and they actually went to Paris, what actions they would take beyond marching along an avenue chanting slogans and glittering generalities. As La Piere stated in *Collective Behavior*, the assumption that inflammatory speechmakers rouse a mob to action "may be dismissed as a silly superstition."[18] Mob action usually must await the emergence of a fortuitous leader, the anonymous voice from within the mob, who cries out, "Burn the camp," "Kill the officers," "Attack headquarters and get the generals!" No such voices were heard. And yet another irony emerged for, as La Piere also noted, action spurred by the fortuitous leader may have no relation to the orator's goals. Certainly that was the situation in France. Getting drunk and collapsing in a muddy field was hardly the core of revolutionary action.

That lack of relationship contributed to the diffuse character of the mutinies. The orators who preached revolution, their understanding of the process little more than a shallow imitation of what they believed the Russians were doing, could do little to achieve their goals in the Zone of the Army's restrictive environment. What they engendered in the assemblies they addressed, besides much drinking, was a lot of shouting and fist waving, a few overtly defiant marches, and then a grudging return to the front. Most men would defend the terrible trenches with a near-incomprehensible sense of territoriality.

Uncoordinated, sporadic, spatially and temporally separated, lacking clearly stated goals, devoid of strong leadership, and with the soldiers responding positively to Pétain, the French Army mutinies of 1917 collapsed. The reforms instituted dragged the army from its despair and gave the men renewed hope. Thus, as Colonel John Etling concluded in his introduction to Richard Watt's *Dare Call It Treason*, the French mutinies were more like a soldiers' strike, much more orderly and certainly less violent than the earlier Indian Mutiny and the 1917–1918 mutinies in the Russian and German armies. The French mutinies, like a mid-range earthquake, rattled the Zone of the Army but did not fracture it.

5

The Siege of San Sebastian,
August 1813

The siege was one of many fought during the Peninsular War. After breaking through San Sebastian's defenses, the British troops ran amok, burning property, looting, raping, and allegedly murdering the survivors.

BACKGROUND TO A SIEGE

April 1810. A parliamentary inquiry exonerated Sir Arthur Wellesley, soon Viscount Wellington, following the generous surrender terms he granted the French Marshal Junot at Lisbon in 1808. Sent once again to Lisbon, he commanded a British Peninsular expeditionary force that numbered 26,000 troops. The hardy Portuguese Army needed more training to bring it to combat readiness, a task given General William Beresford. These troops were subsequently integrated into British divisions at a ratio of one Portuguese brigade to two British. Units of the King's German Legion still served the British in the Peninsula, just as they had under Sir John Moore, and there were Spanish troops available in varying numbers. Most welcome were the very effective Spanish guerrilla fighters who fought a savage, vengeful war of their own against the French.

Although the Allies faced an enormous French Army of 360,000, Wellesley believed they had two weaknesses: provisioning the army and their battle formation. Napoleon Bonaparte did not believe in commissariats but relied instead on the ability of his armies to live off the land. Had he learned from his 1798 Egyptian campaign, where he twice nearly lost his army to desert conditions, he might have changed his mind. Spain was economically worn out, the soil so poor that it barely sustained the native population. Thousands of French troops marching across Galicia or León must have seemed like a swarm of locusts. Wellesley concluded that such a limitation would bring the French to ruin if he could force them to besiege Lisbon where the surrounding area offered only scant gleanings. The French Army would starve.

Wellesley also believed he could shred the French Army in battle because Napoleon typically attacked in columns, massed battalions, that gave young and inexperienced soldiers a sense of security and which looked to an enemy like human juggernauts. The Achilles' heel of the column was restricted firepower. Only the men in the peripheral ranks could fire their muskets. The mass inside the column could not even see the enemy. Thus Bonaparte substituted weight of attack for infantry firepower. Wellesley arrayed the British line formation against the column. Regiments formed two or three parallel lines. Each line could fire in turn or they could fire all at once. A few regiments trained under Sir John Moore even learned to fire as they marched. The contrast with the French system was that the entire musketry of a British unit was brought to bear. Wellesley was convinced line would defeat column.

In April 1810, a French invasion force commanded by André Masséna, who lacked enthusiasm for the campaign and was heartily disliked by his subordinates, advanced through Salamanca province only to stall at the Portuguese border for six months. Then Wellesley began a slow retreat across Portugal, drawing Masséna after him to the Torres Vedras, the peninsula leading to Lisbon. But the city's defenses were so well prepared that Masséna dared not attack. Thus, from October 1810 to March 1811, the French Army withered away in a static siege, unable to resupply sufficiently, and lost 25,000 men.[1] Meanwhile the British were well supplied by ship convoys. Wellesley's assessment was right.

Wellesley went on the offensive in May 1813, leading a combined British-Portuguese force which, with the addition of 20,000 Spaniards, numbered 100,000 men (Map 7). One wing of the army marched from the region of Guarda toward the city of Salamanca. Six cavalry brigades and the British Light Division led the march, followed by the British 2nd Division, a Portuguese division, and two small Spanish divisions—a total of 30,000 men commanded by General Sir Rowland Hill. They captured the city on the twenty-sixth. Meantime, in Zamora, French General Augustin

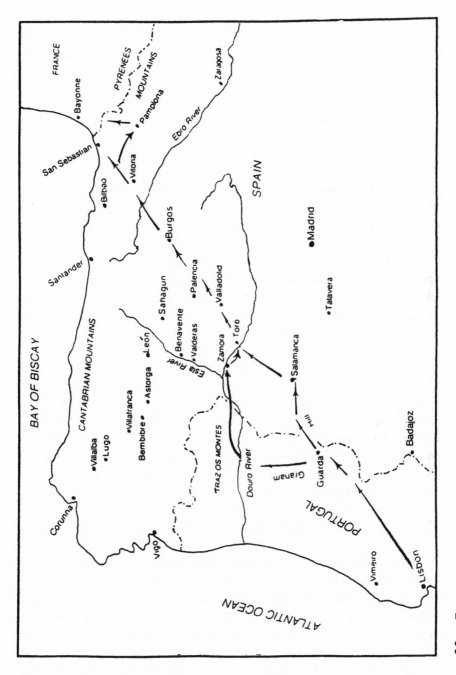

Map 7
Northern Spain: Wellesley's Campaign

Daricau carefully, even anxiously, mapped Hill's progress. He was shocked when he learned that another, larger British force was marching against his position from the north. This column of 65,000 commanded by Sir Thomas Graham was unleashed by Wellesley on the twenty-sixth, a day when Daricau was transfixed by Hill's operations to the south.

The march to Zamora was not easy for Graham's men. They crossed the mountainous Traz os Montes through gorges cut by the Douro River. For every valley there was a ridge; for every ridge another valley. The cannons were disassembled and the barrels, carriages, and wheels hauled up and down by ropes and pulleys. Panicked by Graham's surprising advance, Daricau struck camp and fled east. Graham occupied Zamora on 2 June and the next day joined Hill at Toro. Together they marched northeast toward Burgos.

King Joseph Bonaparte, plopped on the Spanish throne in 1808 by his brother, unaware of Wellesley's location, pulled his troops back to the city of Burgos on 3 June. Wellesley, by this time, was north of the French, forcing Joseph to evacuate Burgos on 13 June. He believed that Wellesley would not dare follow him because the northern route was through some very rugged and poor terrain. But the British did not have to live off the countryside as did the French. Wellesley, anticipating his needs, stockpiled supplies at Corunna, even refusing to let them be off-loaded from the cargo ships. He now ordered those ships to the north coast port of Santander. Never mind the distance between Spain and England. Wellesley's logistical fore-sight gave the British Army needed mobility. Pack trains connected the port to the army in a steady stream. The fine supply system increased morale. Malingering ceased to be a major problem, and the army was in overall excellent physical health. The attention to logistics gave Wellesley the basis for battlefield victory. He maneuvered toward the Ebro River, crossing on 16 June, his army now numbering 67,000 infantry, 8,000 cavalry, and 75 guns.[2]

Joseph, having marched to the Ebro River, and realizing on 19 June that Wellesley had made it through the northern route and was turning the French right flank, retreated further northeast to Vitoria. He determined to make a stand at the city with his force of 57,000 men and 104 guns, a decision undoubtedly made with great reluctance, for he was not a hero nor even much of a soldier.

The city of Vitoria was stuffed with refugees from western Spanish provinces, clamoring to get into France, a problem Joseph did not need. At the risk of diminishing his force, he sent many of these dispossessed people to Bayonne under escort. Left behind was treasure in abundance. Five million gold francs, the French Army's back pay, was stored in chests. Loot taken by the French from the Spanish—paintings, sculptures, crystal, silver, vases, carpets, jewels—was stockpiled, awaiting another convoy to France. Joseph could not begin to contemplate the extent of his brother's wrath if he abandoned his army, the gold, and all that loot.

Vitoria was strategically located. The Royal Road cut east-west across the Vitoria plain to the city, then arced northeast to Bayonne. A more northerly route went to Bilboa near the coast, and another went southeast to Pamplona. The Zadorra River, serpentining across the plain, was crossed by ten bridges.

Joseph deployed most of his army south of the Zadorra athwart the Bayonne Road and between the Royal Road and the river, with smaller contingents stationed north and east of Vitoria. Wellesley came at the French in four columns. One column of 30,000 men commanded by General Rowland Hill moved east between the Royal Road and the parallel Puebla Heights. A second column under Wellesley, 13,000 infantry and 4,500 cavalry, converged from the northwest, crossing the Zadorra at three points, and outflanking the French who faced Hill's column. A third column of two divisions commanded by George Ramsay, 9th Earl of Dalhousie, marched through the hills north of Vitoria to get behind the main French strength that was concentrating on Hill and Wellesley. The fourth column, 30,000 men led by Sir Thomas Graham, marched through the northern hills beyond Dalhousie's force, then turned south to cut the Bayonne Road near Gamarra Major and prevent Joseph's army from escaping. Mobility and surprise: these were Wellesley's ingredients for battle.

The British triumph at Vitoria was not predicated so much on a masterful plan as it was on a series of unanticipated developments. Dalhousie, leading the 7th Division, somehow was separated from Sir Thomas Picton's 3rd Division, the other half of the column, and promptly lost his way in the mountains. Picton, however, was in position on the banks of the Zadorra, ready to cross the Mendoza Bridge. He was smoldering in frustration, wondering what happened to Dalhousie. A staff officer from Wellesley arrived and told Picton to support Dalhousie's attack across the Mendoza Bridge. That was all that Picton needed. Damn, but he would have none of that nonsense. He turned on the staff officer, yelling at him that he could go back and tell Wellesley that he was going to take the bridge and that Dalhousie, if he ever bothered to show up, could support the 3rd's attack. With that, Picton turned to his men, shouting, "Come on, ye rascals! Come on, ye fighting villains."[3] The 3rd Division charged into the French grape and musket shot and across the bridge.

Wellesley, surprised by Picton's charge, nevertheless saw the advantage of battle swing his way. He launched his column at the French.

Now it was Graham's turn. His combined British-Portuguese column, supported by a division of Spanish irregulars, easily swept the French from positions above Gamarra Major. Graham then halted and dressed his lines. And waited. That delay allowed the French to occupy the village in strength. At 5 P.M., Graham sent forward an infantry brigade, supported by the 9th Regiment's light company, to take Gamarra Major. Colin Campbell, who was with the light company, observed the troops "did not take a musket from the shoulder until they carried the village."⁴ The French fell back to a bridge across the Zadorra. The bridge changed hands seven times that late afternoon; finally, after a vicious firefight between the British light infantry and the French *tirailleurs*, the French fled, abandoning their cannons. Graham's troops advanced to discover that the Zadorra was shallow enough to wade across. The fight at the bridge proved unnecessary.

With all his defenses collapsing, Joseph ordered his troops to escape along the Pamplona Road. This was an order easily given but difficult to obey. Hordes of civilians streamed from the city, choking the roads to the east. Artillery wagons collided with private carriages and carts. Soldiers lost their units and ran east. The more perceptive evacuees realized that the lighter the load, the faster the feet. They dumped boxes filled with household goods and clothing and flung aside expensive carpets and tapestries. Jewel boxes, fine silver, treasure chests heaped with coins and gold, paintings, sculptures, precious medallions and medals, the stuff of an aristocratic and privileged life, was jettisoned, easy pickings for British troops and Spanish peasants alike.

When the dust of battle settled and when the looters finally exhausted themselves, Wellesley calculated his casualties. British losses at Vitoria were 501 killed, 2,807 wounded, and 266 missing. Total Allied casualties were about 5,000. French casualties were estimated between 7,000 and 8,000, but no exact numbers were ever given. The London *Times* reported on 15 July that, even a month after Vitoria, there was no mention of the battle in Paris newspapers. The Duke of Fêltre, French war minister, interpreting the battle to suit his purposes as a Napoleonic apologist, concluded that French losses were mostly matériel but that British manpower losses were considerable. What he did not realize or did not care to know was that Wellesley's army was still intact.

THE SIEGE OF SAN SEBASTIAN

The First Attack, July 1813

Although intact, Wellesley's army was also exhausted. The long campaign across northern Spain was highly mobile for its day, and mobility came at a price: long, hard marches across mountainous terrain and intense fighting punctuated by costly sieges. The extent of the army's weariness was measured after the Battle of Vitoria by increased malingering, sickness, and even desertions. Any plans of a march northeast across the Pyrenees and into France meant a major commitment, one necessitating reinforcements and resupply. Moreover, two bastions of French resistance remained in Spain: one in Pamplona, some 50 miles east of Vitoria, and one in San Sebastian on the north coast. Wellesley sent a strong Spanish force to blockade Pamplona, while he placed in Sir Thomas Graham's hands the means to besiege San Sebastian.[5]

San Sebastian is located on a small peninsula about two-thirds of a mile long (Map 8). The eastern approach was then cut by the Urumea River which, at low tide, wound across a tidal flat about 1,000 yards wide. The west side of the peninsula is flanked by a small bay, with the little island of Santa Clara approximately 500 yards from the northwest corner of the peninsula. At its northern end, facing the Bay of Biscay, is Monte Urgull, 400 feet high, surmounted by La Mota Castle. Extending from the south base of the mount to the end of the peninsula was the town of San Sebastian. In 1813, a great hornwork—a fortification with horn-shaped or triangular projections—protected the town's southern flank. Behind the hornwork and encircling the town was a flat curtain wall 8 feet thick. Projecting from the south side of the wall was a cavalier or arrow-shaped strong point. On the wall's east side were two towers, Los Hornos and Las Miquetas. Two bastions, reinforced walls with gun emplacements, were at either end of the south curtain wall.

Beyond the hornwork on the landward end of the peninsula was the small suburb of San Martin with the convent of San Bartolomé located just beyond on the Heights of Ayete. The Chofres Sand Hills on the east side of the Urumea River gave an unobstructed view of the peninsula.

During the early phases of the Peninsular War, the French thought San Sebastian unimportant and depleted the garrison and its artillery defenses. After Vitoria, the fortress town was viewed as an essential link with France and a strategic pawn with which to distract Wellesley's attention. For Marshal Jean Soult, having reorganized the scattered and shattered divisions of King Joseph's army, had slipped back into Spain. Even though the British

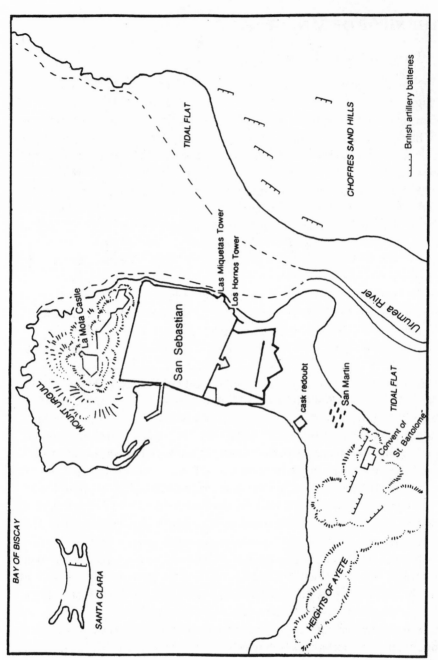

BAY OF BISCAY

SANTA CLARA

MOUNT URGUL

La Mota Castle

San Sebastian

Las Miquetas Tower

Los Hornos Tower

TIDAL FLAT

CHOFRES SAND HILLS

British artillery batteries

cask redoubt

San Martin

Urumea River

Convent of St. Bartolome

TIDAL FLAT

HEIGHTS OF AYETE

Map 8
Siege of San Sebastian

Royal Navy blockaded San Sebastian, the French managed to reinforce the garrison with comparative ease, increasing the numbers to 3,000 men. Command was given to General Emanuel Rey.

Rey harbored no illusions about San Sebastian's ability to withstand siege. The hornwork would be compromised if the British took the convent, giving their artillery a good view of the hornwork and the town. The Urumea River was easily forded, and the east wall was vulnerable to artillery fire from the sand hills.[6] Rey therefore fortified the convent and placed a supporting redoubt on the heights. San Martin was burned to the ground to create a killing ground in front of the hornwork, and a redoubt made of casks was constructed across the road leading into town. The French burned a bridge across the Urumea, and placed an artillery battery east of the castle, with two more along the east wall.

Wellesley developed a plan to take the fortress quickly. The Ayete Heights and the convent of San Bartolomé would be taken as artillery established on the sand hills across the Urumea River hammered the east wall. When a breach opened, infantry at the convent would move along the base of the wall at low tide, climb the breach, and fight their way into the town.

On 14 July, the convent was bombarded. Infantry attacking the next day could not take the position. After more shelling, two infantry columns of British and Portuguese units again attacked the convent. Men of the British 9th Regiment dashed forward; the Portuguese took their time. The 9th broke into the convent, moved beyond to San Martin, and advanced against the hornwork. French artillery fire forced the British back into San Martin, leaving behind 200 dead. But British sappers managed to place a mine under the southwest corner of the hornwork.

British artillery on the Chofres Sand Hills opened a ferocious bombardment against the town's east wall. By the twenty-fourth, two breaches were opened in the wall, and fires could be seen burning within the town. The next day, British sappers detonated the hornwork mine and an attack was launched, both a ruse to make the French believe a frontal attack against the hornwork was the principal British tactic. But the main attack was against the east wall breaches. The Royal Scots, supported by an assault party from the 9th, would storm the larger of the two breaches that was closer to San Martin. The 9th's unit, led by Lieutenant Colin Campbell, were placed in the center of the Royal Scots' light company. All huddled together through a long, cold, and very damp night in a narrow trench that was their departure point.

At the attack signal, the Royal Scots clambered from the trench and surged forward into the darkness. Then Campbell ordered his men forward.

The attack was confusion from the outset. The trench was too confined for orderly movement, the men were cramped from their all-night wait, and their scaling ladders were heavy and awkward. The assault party, stumbling over rocks and sloshing through deep tide pools that narrowed the tidal flat, dissolved into a jostling, knotted, serpentine line beneath the wall.

The regular companies of the Royal Scots, first to move along the wall and into the breach, were met by concentrated French fire that cut down those who tried to climb up the breach. The survivors spread themselves across the rubble created by the artillery bombardment. The attack stalled. Campbell and his party, coming up behind a mass of Royals waiting for directions, suggested to their light company commander that they try to skirt these men and assault the breach. There was no answer because the officer had fallen dead at Campbell's feet, a bullet through his head. Campbell formed his men into single file and moved to the top of the breach, but he was shot in the right hip and knocked back to the tidal flat. Finding he was not disabled, he joined two officers from the Royals and went up the breach again. He was shot in the left thigh. Captain Archimbeau, leading 90 Royal Scots, attempted to support Campbell's little force. But the Royals were so disorganized as they climbed through the rubble and the tangle of dead and wounded, and so intense was the French fire, that Campbell and Archimbeau ordered a retreat.

The withdrawal proved as difficult as the advance. They ran into detachments from the 38th and 92nd Regiments sent forward to assault the smaller and more distant of the two breaches. The entanglement, resembling a near mob scene, ended all hope of continuing the attack. The British lost 600 men. The French lost 60 soldiers.

William Gomm, an officer in the 9th, expressed the feelings of many fellow infantrymen when he wrote, "Our soldiers have on all occasions stood fire so well that our artillery have become as summary in the proceedings as our engineers. . . . [They] care not about destroying . . . defenses, or facilitating . . . what is the most desperate of all military enterprises."[7] Gomm went on to comment in the most bitter tones that engineers and artillery officers thought of infantrymen as so many mice in an air-pump experiment. The engineers and artillerymen complained that the infantry did not attack with sufficient vigor. Wellesley joined the argument, putting blame squarely on the men of the 5th Division from which the assault units were selected. They alone, Wellesley pronounced, were responsible for the failure. That judgment shocked the infantrymen. As Campbell later reflected, "One main cause of the failure was the narrow front and the consequent length and thinness of the column in which we advanced. This necessarily became loosened and disjoined by the difficult nature of the ground . . . so that it reached the breach in dribblets."[8] Thus the failure resided not so much in the execution of orders as in the plan itself.

For many soldiers like Gomm, the failure was yet another example of their general's willingness to let men die in poorly planned sieges. Despite the successful maneuvering by Wellesley of his army across Spain, and in the face of such victories as Salamanca and Vitoria, British siege operations were less than spectacular. For example, in January 1812, Ciudad Rodrigo was besieged at a loss of 1,300 British troops against only 300 casualties for the French. In April, at Badajoz, 5,000 British soldiers were lost. At Burgos, Wellesley mounted a half-hearted siege, allowing undermanned assault units to attack without adequate artillery preparations. The Burgos siege failed, a miserable six-week affair. San Sebastian promised to be a repetition. Feelings of desperation, reflected in all the finger pointing, seeped into the British forces.

The Second Attack, August 1813

25 July. Wellesley ordered that all bombardment was to cease, a situation reinforced when the big siege guns were shipped onto Royal Navy ships for safekeeping. The infantry remained in the trenches. Marshal Soult caused the hiatus by marching back into Spain and threatening the British front at Pamplona. Wellesley could not fight a two-front war. The siege would have to wait.

General Rey used the lull to rebuild his defenses. The hornwork was repaired, and all the rubble created by the bombardment was used to build a 15-foot secondary rampart behind the east wall. Clearing the rubble left a 20-foot drop from the top of the breaches into the city streets below. The breaches themselves were fortified and, within the town, the French erected mutually supportive street barricades. Rey slipped his wounded out by ship through the still ineffectual British naval blockade and brought in supplies, shot, powder, and reinforcements. By 15 August, his garrison again numbered 3,000 men, and 60 guns.

The British positions, especially those in the sand hills across the Urumea River, became a deadly hell for the troops. French soldiers manned sniper posts along the east and south walls, maintaining a steady fire into the British trenches. The allied troops remained passive, spatially separated from their enemy by the tidal flats. They had to take whatever punishment the French dealt them. Ignorant of the restrictions imposed by Wellesley, the London *Sun* blithely speculated on 29 July that San Sebastian would fall if only larger siege guns were used. That whisp of lounge chair wisdom did not help the common soldiers as they sat in their trenches wondering why, with the siege guns removed, they were there at all.

Wellesley fought Soult to a standstill by mid-August, forcing a French withdrawal from the Pamplona front into the Pyrenees passes. He then ordered a resumption of the San Sebastian siege. Graham had his siege guns put ashore, but the navy botched the operation. Arrival of the largest siege guns was delayed five days, and it was another five days before proper ammunition arrived.

26 August. A day-long bombardment reopened the siege. The east wall near the hornwork was hammered by 36 24-pounders on the Chofres Sand Hills, firing an average of twenty-three rounds per hour for fifteen hours. They opened a large new breach between Las Miquetas Tower and Los Hornos. A smaller breach was opened about 80 yards north. Guns near the convent disintegrated the hornwork itself, tore great chunks out of the curtain wall, rubble cascading down on the defenders, and turned the San Juan bastion into a cauldron of smoke and flame.

Once again the 5th Division was to attack the defenses, utilizing a plan nearly identical to that developed in July. Thus an assault party of two captains, four lieutenants, and a hundred men would storm the large breach. A brigade from the 5th was to follow as, simultaneously, a Portuguese contingent crossed the tidal flat—predicted to be a low tide during daylight hours—and attacked the smaller breach. Other units in boats would create a diversion by threatening to land on the peninsula's north shore.

Disgust with the strategy ran deeply through the 5th Division. Major General John Oswald, temporary commander, and all the brigade and regimental commanders viewed the attack as a design for slaughter. Lieutenant General Sir James Leith, permanent commander of the 5th, returned from sick leave only two days before the attack, furious that the plan was nothing more than a bleak repetition of the July failure.

Wellesley, hearing of the complaints, wrote Graham that he would have to disgrace the 5th by adding volunteers to the assault wave whose dash would demonstrate that the 5th were not being asked to do the impossible. Leith and Oswald were livid that Wellesley should continue blaming their division for the July failure, practically branding their men cowards in the bargain, especially since there were more than enough volunteers from the 5th willing to join the assault teams.

At 10:55 A.M., 31 August, the siege guns fell silent. A small British detachment was sent into the large breach to defuse a French mine. Most were killed when it detonated, and the French shot the few survivors when they reached the top of the breach. An assault team went forward, followed closely by a brigade from the 5th Division. French cannons and muskets opened fire. Dead and wounded British soldiers littered the ground. The survivors scrambled up the breach under heavy French fire only to discover the 20-foot scarp on the other side. Of 1,500 men from the 5th that charged the breach, 322 lay dead. Both Leith and Oswald were among the 530 wounded.

Andrew Hay's brigade from the 5th, supported by Wellesley's volunteers, attacked the breach. Their ranks were shredded. Survivors huddled against the wall as the defenders rained flaming pitch, grenades, and musket fire down on them. Graham was desperate as Wellesley's plan fell apart before his eyes. He was a stolid and loyal officer, imaginative a word not much used to describe his abilities. Yet, with the attack reaching crisis proportions, he made a daring decision, ordering all available guns to open fire once again, this time aiming at the top of the wall over the heads of his own men.

The British huddled at the wall were aghast that their own artillery would place them in jeopardy. But as defenders were swept from the wall, as more of the wall was completely pulverized, they understood the reason for the bombardment. The infantry sprang forward as the guns ceased firing, storming the southeast end of the wall, dominating the hornwork with their musket fire, and working their way behind the recently constructed rubble wall. Meanwhile, north of the hornwork, Wellesley's volunteers broke through some rubble into a ruined house which, by sheer luck, gave them direct street access. Then the sudden explosion of an ammunition cache tore out a corner of the south wall. The Royal Scots lunged through the opening and into the town. Now the Portuguese had their turn. They moved out of their sandy trenches onto the tidal flat, but, rather than splashing through shallow pools, they waded into waist-high water—someone again miscalculated the tide. The water turned red as intense French gunnery slowed but did not stop the Portuguese advance. The British and Portuguese attacks, relentless and brutal, broke unified resistance within the town.

Rey lost too many soldiers to the bombardment and could not plug the gaps in his perimeter defenses. The street barricades, so carefully planned for inner defense, collapsed under shell fire and burned. French resistance, reduced to small pockets, was wiped out. No prisoners. By 1:30 P.M., fires fanned by high winds consumed the town. The apocalyptic vision was completed later that afternoon by a thunderstorm and torrential rain. General Rey led his remaining men into the castle and shut the gate (they did not surrender until 9 September).

Aftermath: Mayhem

"Never surely," William Gomm, 9th Regiment, wrote of San Sebastian, "was there a more complete picture of devastation than this place presents."[9] Three thousand five hundred British and Portuguese soldiers were killed in five days but, of these, 2,376 fell during the 31 August assault. The piles of bodies—twisted, torn, blackened, often unrecognizable, killed by musket and cannon fire, exploding mines, and crushed under fallen masonry—testified to their bravery and tenacity, their silence a commentary on the ill-conceived plan.

San Sebastian paid an added price for resistance, the final chapter of the apocalypse. Wine and brandy casks found in ruined shops and houses quickly turned the British troops into a reeling, riotous mob. Men collapsed from drink, looking much like the corpses around them. And like the corpses, their pockets were picked clean of any loot by Portuguese soldiers who had sense to let the British troops do the grubbing about in the ruins. Close behind the soldiers were the British Army wives who swooped down like seagulls, and sat in circles dividing the scavenged loot.

The few surviving British officers tried to quell the mobs. There were tales of men turning violent and physically threatening officers, but, in most instances, the officers were simply defied or ignored, especially if they were from a different regiment. Other men, not so drunk and with greater professionalism than their comrades, looted more systematically. These men were thieves before they joined the army, and thieves they remained. They selectively plucked through the ruins, taking everything of value they could carry. Rape and murder were allegedly visited on the town's population, but no one knows the number of victims.

Rumors and some news reports of the wanton destruction spread to Britain. William Napier, who did not witness the siege, believing nonetheless that many atrocities occurred in San Sebastian, wrote about them much later with considerable zest, thus sustaining the horror stories.[10] In contrast, William Gomm, who was there, characterized the aftermath of the siege as a melancholy scene but did not find it especially horrifying. Of the two interpretations, the tales of devastation captured public attention in both Britain and Spain. The ruling Spanish *junta*, appalled by the destruction, accused Wellesley of demolishing the town by bombardment and willfully letting it burn in order to destroy an important Spanish port and thus serve British imperial interests. Despite the siege's notoriety, no one in Britain suggested an investigation.

ROOTS OF MAYHEM

Looking back to Sir John Moore's retreat to Corunna, we find a prelude to the rape, pillaging, and destruction that accompanied such Peninsular sieges as Ciudad Rodrigo and Badajoz. Thus San Sebastian's fate was hardly unique. Indeed, a mayhem-filled aftermath was a frequent companion to siege warfare throughout history. Honor required that cities be defended up to an unspecified yet well-understood point. A few cannons shot at the besiegers or repelling one attack would often do. But William Shakespeare's Henry V, angered by the stubborn defense of Harfleur, told the town's governor that, if he had to attack the city again, "I will not leave the half-achieved Harfleur till her ashes are buried" (Act 3, Scene 2, 7–9). Besiegers typically reached a point where they disregarded gentlemanly concern for those in the city or fortress, allowing the most bestial acts as full payment for prolonging the siege. Scipio Africanus' Romans slaughtered the inhabitants of New Carthage in 209 B.C. The Crusaders butchered the populations of Antioch and Jerusalem during the First Crusade. Constantinople met a similar fate in 1204. France's Charles VIII showed the defenders of San Giovanni no mercy in 1494. In 1573, Haarlem was looted, and its defenders, together with many women and children, were butchered. The British ran amok in Delhi in 1857 and in Lucknow the next year. The litany of savagery is long.

Nonetheless, the generalization that mayhem is a concomitant to siege warfare really serves no useful purpose beyond telling us what happened. There is little consolation in Correlli Barnett's conclusion that Peninsular sieges ended in "carnivals of drink, rape, robbery, and blind destruction."[11] What we need to understand is why, specifically, the British troops at San Sebastian fell from grace. Sir Charles Oman, in his study of the Peninsular War, concluded that "A certain amount of the horrors which took place at ... San Sebastian may be ascribed to mere frenzy, if the rest was due to more deliberate wickedness on the part of the baser spirits in the army."[12] Although this search for causes conforms to the usual narrations of the siege, it does not provide any greater insight than Barnett's statement; however, it does provoke the question of just what kind of men served in the Peninsula.

The officers were ostensibly "gentlemen" by virtue of purchasing their commissions. The amount paid depended on the rank and the regiment. A lieutenancy in a Guards regiment, for example, cost as much as a captaincy or even a major's rank in a line regiment. Yet, to think of the officers only as aristocrats or men from affluent and influential families would be a drastic error. Colin Campbell, for example, whose exploits we have had occasion to visit, came from a modest background. His father, John Macliver, was a Glasgow cabinetmaker. When Colin was 16 years old, his maternal uncle, Colonel John Campbell, introduced him to the Duke of York, the commander-in-chief. Colin was entered as a Campbell onto the army rolls without purchase as an ensign in the 9th Regiment. He was quickly promoted without purchase to lieutenant, an advance not unusual in the period of the Napoleonic Wars when subalterns fell in battle like dry straw. In 1813, he was promoted to captain without purchase in recognition of his gallantry during the first attack at San Sebastian. Lacking funds for further advancement, he remained a captain for 13 years. That, too, was very common. One captain in the 93rd Highlanders, for instance, remained at the rank for 35 years. The army gave such men a position but no promise of a future.

Officers in Wellesley's army learned on the job and by example. Campbell, the new 16-year-old lieutenant, was sent to Portugal, where he found himself in the Battle of Vimeiro. His first leadership lesson occurred when his company commander took his hand and walked him back and forth in front of their company in full view of the French artillery: learn how not to be afraid; set an example of courage to the men even if that meant dying; accept wounds and return to the battle. These were the moral lessons of a British field officer.

The enlisted men volunteered for 20 years service. What passed for training was up to six hours a day of close-order parade ground drill to instill instant obedience so that the battalion stood ready to attack or repel an enemy. Most musket practice was devoted to a complicated loading drill that ensured three shots a minute. The battalion, some 800 men, could unleash an impenetrable lead wall. Accurate firing was not a goal, except in the light companies, because muskets were not accurate beyond 200 yards and misfirings were common. Whether any given musket shot actually hit an enemy soldier was usually an unanswered question. At Vitoria, for example, only one musket ball of every 459 fired hit someone.[13] Mass firing made the difference. A volley from 800 muskets shredded an enemy column at 50 yards.

Life for the common soldier was hard. They lived in vermin-ridden barracks, lacking all privacy and without any recreation. Black bread, pork or beef, rice, oatmeal, raisins, butter, cheese, and boiled vegetables were standard barracks diet, according to Philip Haythornthwaite in *The Armies of Wellington*. Beer and wine were rationed, but stronger drink was purchased at pubs as a common release from tedium, pain, drill, the lash, and from living among other men that one might not like very much. Campaign food was a diet of coffee, hard tack, and bully-beef.

Wellesley, in an oft-quoted remark, thought his army was filled with the scum of the earth. The men, he believed, did not enlist for ideals like patriotism; instead they sought a steady source of drink, escape from crimes both petty and serious, and avoidance of the responsibilities of paternity. Undoubtedly there were men from what Sir Charles Oman, in his study *Wellington's Army*, called the criminal and semi-criminal classes. These included pickpockets, smugglers, local toughs who wore out their welcome in their towns and villages, petty thieves, robbers, and even a few murderers. More conniving men volunteered to obtain the enlistment bonus. They would desert and then reenlist someplace else, and receive another bonus, only to desert again. Every regiment had this range of criminals, but they never represented a majority. More numerous but less criminal were, as Oman put it, the raw stuff swept off the city streets. This class of recruits included dispossessed farmers, country boys escaping boredom, youths running away from tyrannical families, adventurers, debtors, and second sons of second sons. Thus, as Oman pointed out, and as Elizabeth Longford also concludes in her biographical study *Wellington: The Years of the Sword*, Wellesley's comment about scum was overstated, indeed overdramatized and, I might add, overquoted.

The British Army during the Peninsular War was expansive, needing more and more men, more even than the volunteer enlistment system could possibly provide. Lord Castlereagh, the war minister, juggled the bureaucracy and some rules, making it possible for the army to enlist local militia men, later known as territorial troops. Those taken into the regular army had at least one year of service in their local regiments, many of which possessed their own long and proud traditions, and were therefore familiar with discipline and the musket. The militia men became, in a very real way, the backbone of the Peninsular army.

Yet the behavior of the army at the San Sebastian siege plunged to its lowest behavioral denominator, according to such historians as Charles Oman, Elizabeth Longford, and Frederick Myatt. They concluded that the soldiers, following the lead of criminals and drunks, succumbed to a collective frenzied beastliness. These conclusions, containing one piece of the behavioral puzzle, remain obvious, simplistic, and too often repeated. In contrast, Richard La Piere stated in *Collective Behavior* that such frightful behavior "does not depend on the cultural status of those involved," but instead "is fortuitous, . . . the consequence of the coming together of a great many factors in entirely unpredictable ways."[14] How the troops that entered San Sebastian were transformed into a mob was not merely an instance of mass follow-the-leader but a more complicated process, initiated by a growing and shared discontent among the soldiers.

The first source of discontent was the conduct of the siege by Wellesley and his staff. The July assault against the east wall turned into a visible slaughter. The attacking units tried to advance along a narrow strip of uneven ground, a strip so inadequate that there was no room to maneuver, no place to hide. The French had an ideal killing ground. British soldiers, settling back into their trenches following that debacle, ignorant of Wellesley's need to counter Soult's moves, must have been dumbfounded when the siege guns were dismounted and taken away. They surely wondered what would be expected of them next. The answer came in the August plan, a tactical reflection of the first but to be executed in full daylight. The plan promised only more casualties, not a certain victory.

A second reason for discontent was that everyone knew, as indeed everyone was supposed to know, that Wellesley, following the first attack, maligned the 5th Division for not having enough guts to do the job, for being timid when they needed to be bold. Wellesley then added insult to injury by calling for volunteers in the second attack to show the 5th Division that the job was possible. The affair was a stroke of reverse, or perverse, psychology, stimulating men whom Wellesley knew to be good soldiers to greater deeds. Unfortunately such negative reinforcements often carry the seeds of their own destruction. The 5th Division, from generals to privates, was chagrined and angered by their chief's unbelievable accusations. Even if the 5th accepted Wellesley's broadside for what it was meant to be, there was no guarantee of its reception by the rest of the corps. The unfairness of the accusation was clear, and one can only speculate about how many men and officers wondered who would be Wellesley's next target.

Charles Oman, in his study *Wellington's Army*, explained a third source of discontent. There is no doubt that siege work was despised by the soldiers, not because it was dangerous—that was something they could accept as soldiers—but that it was irritable, painful, and demanding work. At the siege of Badajoz, the men wallowed in mud, and the trenches were 2 feet deep in water. At San Sebastian it was summer, and, although on the coast, the sun beat down, the trenches were narrow and cramped, and sand and flies were everywhere. Some men felt that keeping their heads down as they worked in the trenches was skulking from the enemy. Filled with bravado, they stood up in full view of the French, as if inviting the snipers to fire at them, challenging fate—a behavior common a hundred years later among the trenchbound Australians and British at Gallipoli.

Elizabeth Longford states that the troops waiting for the August attack reached a state of "unprecedented anxiety" signaled by a senseless, hysterical laughter.[15] Her source was a memoir by Ensign G. R. Gleig who, like William Napier, did not participate in the siege. Yet I have little hesitation in believing the description. Discontent and despair easily engender stress, and stress leads to anxiety. Death or terrible wounds awaited many. But with confidence in their officers, most men in similar situations will find a glimmer of hope. Such hope was dashed at San Sebastian when it was obvious that the second attack would be a repetition of the first.

The palpable anxiety of the troops moved them from mere discontent to desperation. Similar to the desperation felt by the Indian sepoys and the French soldiers along the Chemin des Dames, the British assault troops from the 5th Division lost hope that the precarious situation in which Wellesley placed them would change. Certainly men willingly stepped forward as part of what promised to be another Forlorn Hope. But they were less driven by noble thoughts of gallantry and patriotism than by their anger at Wellesley. That was probably the reaction Wellesley wanted: better to be mad at him and get the job done. Nonetheless, his posturing contributed directly to the riotous behavior that followed and must be counted as a failure of generalship. In that context, the only reasonable conclusion is that Wellesley did not care what happened within the town as long as it was destroyed as a French fortress. If that is correct, the Spanish junta's accusations against Wellesley were uncomfortably close to reality, but for the wrong reasons.

The desperation of the British troops generated feelings of alienation: meaninglessness, powerlessness, normlessness, and isolation.[16] Despite his overt concern that his men lacked patriotic motives for enlisting, Wellesley never asked his men to die for king and country. He did not give grand speeches or publish perorations in daily orders. Yet the men followed him unhesitatingly across Spain, risking their lives in sometimes questionable battles but usually winning. Now the great general reheated a plan stinking of death and, in the process, denigrated an entire division. Despair among the troops allowed the processes of alienation to work their way through Wellesley's troops at San Sebastian. Meaninglessness, their initial confusion and uncertainty about what they should believe, their consternation at their general's accusations, fed isolation. Thus isolation was the form of alienation through which the men shifted their values from duty to survival to revenge. That meaninglessness and isolation could develop at all was a reflection of powerlessness, the feeling that their actions could not influence future outcomes. They could not do anything about their situation because there was no legitimate recourse for their concerns. That void pushed the

men to normlessness, finding escape, however temporary, from their intolerable situation in the unapproved, violent behavior they heaped on the town
and its inhabitants.

Tracing the emergence of the violence is not too difficult at San Sebastian. The second attack began well enough, the soldiers moving against
the French defenses, obeying orders, fighting with determination, doing
what was expected of them. The expense of meeting expectations was, as
the men anticipated, very high. The lead units were held in the large breach
by French fire for two hours. Dead and wounded were everywhere. Then
Graham ordered his artillery to rake the wall, wiping out the defenders, and
opening the way for his men to get into the two streets.

That shift of battle from external wall and breach to internal streets
redefined the physical context of battle, indeed redefined the siege itself.
The town was afire and there was fighting in the streets. And more: the men
fought in confused and mixed small groups as all battalion order was lost.
This was the moment when formal leadership and discipline failed. The
casualties during the attack and the confusion that followed deprived the
men of their officers. Of 200 officers serving in the 5th Division, half were
dead or wounded by mid-afternoon. In the 47th Regiment alone, only five
officers escaped death or wounds, and in the 59th Regiment only four
officers survived the attack unscathed.

As in the Indian and French mutinies, the real leaders among the soldiers
in the streets of San Sebastian emerged by chance out of the situations that
equally by chance came their way. A soldier running—it could be to
anywhere—stimulated others to follow simply by his action. This is the part
of the behavioral puzzle held by historians. A booming voice from a cellar
calling out "Wine!" was an attraction many found irresistible. As La Piere
points out in *Collective Behavior*, the person setting the example of action,
or somehow calling attention to himself or to an object, such as loot, often
engages in an activity that is advantageous to him alone. However, when his
action is replicated by others and intensified through interaction, then what
began as a jostling, yelling, collection of men, each bent on serving his own
individual desire, can become and, in the case of San Sebastian, did become
violent mob behavior.

That mob behavior erupted in San Sebastian is, with the usual wisdom
of hindsight, not surprising. Historical precedents notwithstanding, the
behavior of the British troops was inseparable from the conditions of the
siege. The anxiety preceding the attack suggests the men were panicked—
that they perceived the situation as threatening their survival. But any battle
threatens survival. What made San Sebastian different from, say, Vitoria, is

that the soldiers lost confidence in their leaders because the plan they were ordered to execute had been tested in July and failed miserably. The usual response to panic is escape, fleeing from the source of danger. The dilemma facing the British soldiers, much like the French in 1917, was that their own leaders were the real source of danger. Yet they could not and would not attack Wellesley. Graham was readily available, but they did not attack him. Instead they turned their enmity on San Sebastian, the town and its inhabitants becoming the tangible focus of all their pent-up anxiety, fear, and rage.

The flash point of aberrant collective action ignited, and then its energy faded. Exhausted, fear vented by their rampaging, rage spent in what Longford called a degraded catharsis of terror and drink,[17] the mob became an army once again. They marched off to do battle with the French at the Bidassoa River, cross it, and invade France, astonishing the southern French peasantry with their professionalism and discipline. Not long after, many of the same infantry coldly faced Napoleon and his French columns at Waterloo. Their discipline never wavered.

6

Surrender: The Disintegration of a Division, December 1944

In December 1944, the Germans made an unexpected attack against American forces in the Ardennes region. Two regiments of the 106th Infantry Division, operating in a leadership vacuum, were cut off and surrendered.

SETTING UP FOR A DISASTER

Normandy, France, 6 June 1944. The Allied armies—American, British, Canadian—the largest invasion force ever assembled in human history, pushed ashore against savage German resistance. Slowly the Germans fell back from the coast, unable to endure the devastating Allied naval gunfire and the incessant aerial bombardment from the Allied-dominated skies. As British and U.S. aircraft, really aerial artillery, continued to scream down on their positions, the Germans came under heavier and heavier artillery fire after the Allies moved their big field guns ashore.

The Allies fought costly battles to break out of Normandy as they moved east toward Caen and south to St. Lo, Caumont, Vire, Tinchebray, and Falaise. By early August, the German 7th Army's south flank was hemmed in by General George Patton's U.S. 3rd Army. Canadian and British troops near Caen attacked south toward Falaise. The German 7th Army and the 5th Panzer Army were soon trapped in the so-called Falaise Pocket. Elements of the U.S. 3rd Army surged north toward Argentan as Canadians and Poles moved further south to join them and close the gap at the pocket's east end. But a substantial German force escaped entrapment before the pocket was zipped on 21 August, leaving behind scenes of great carnage.

The Germans retreated to the Seine River, attempting to establish a defensive line, but the Allied drive swept on to free Paris. Patton's 3rd Army knifed east toward Lorraine. The British attacked north, taking Brussels on 3 September and Antwerp the next day. Adolf Hitler meanwhile ordered that various channel ports, such as Le Havre, Calais, Dunkirk, and Boulogne, hold out at all costs. Taking Antwerp should have caused Allied celebration; its shipping facilities would have eased their growing supply problem. However, the Germans mined the Scheldt estuary leading to Antwerp, and their artillery made even the approaches hazardous. Barely enough supplies were transported laboriously from Normandy, either from the beaches or through Cherbourg, the one major port the Allies controlled.

By 15 September, the Allied armies held a front from the English Channel near Bruges, east to Antwerp, then curving south to Maastricht, the Ardennes, the eastern front of Luxembourg, and further south into the Moselle region. Two months later, the front was extended north when the Canadians assaulted the Scheldt, opening the shipping lanes to Antwerp. A salient was also created around Aachen, the ancient Carolingian capital, and the Hürtgen Forest. East of the Ardennes, more a moral victory than a strategic maneuver, U.S. forces penetrated the German West Wall or Siegfried Line (Map 9). This line of fortifications—pill-boxes, bunkers, artillery positions, and tank traps—suffered from neglect after the 1940 invasion of France and was empty of German armaments. The Allied armies were tired, undersupplied, and undermanned. U.S. forces alone experienced 3,000 casualties a day during the November fighting around Aachen and in the Hürtgen Forest. With the coming of winter, the troops happily settled down to what they believed was going to be a long winter's nap in the West Wall positions.

Many Allied leaders, both military and political, and many of the soldiers who survived the fighting, assumed the German Army was finished. The battles in Normandy and across France cost them 50,000 dead and 200,000 prisoners. Fifteen of fifty-six German divisions were obliterated. A total of 1,300 tanks were destroyed—none of the panzer divisions escaped with more than 15 tanks in fighting condition.[1] The British and American tactical air attacks also destroyed countless trucks and personnel carriers, gun tractors, armored cars, and utility vehicles. The German Army, famed for blitzkrieg, was rendered nearly immobile. It was only a matter of time before they collapsed. The Allies had earned a rest. And certainly, as the November

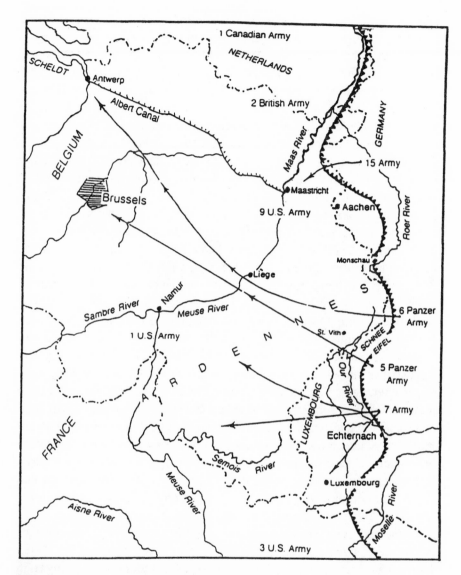

Map 9
German Attack Plan, November 1944

fighting demonstrated, there was no sense getting involved in attritional battles for so little gain.

A few Allied officers voiced dissent. British Major General Kenneth Strong, intelligence chief to supreme Allied commander Dwight Eisenhower, at first joined the optimistic chorus when he commented in August that the end of the war was near. Yet, after an intelligence review of the November battles and of continuing German activity along the West Wall, he concluded that the German Army was stronger than assumed by Allied commanders, and that Allied inactivity signaled Hitler that their armies had run out of gas, both figuratively and literally. Strong also believed Hitler would work his will on his generals, using the time given him by the Allies to regroup and mount a winter offensive during a spell of bad weather. The offensive would aim at the Ardennes. Similarly, Colonel Oscar Koch, U.S. 3rd Army intelligence section, did not view the German retreat from Normandy as a rout. He believed the Germans were buying time for an offensive to be launched when conditions turned most favorable to them. Both officers argued their cases in the strongest terms. Neither was believed.

Indeed, Strong and Koch were fighting the proverbial uphill battle to get their opinions heard. For a consensus had emerged among Allied leaders, from supreme Allied command down to the intelligence sections of the various field armies, that the Germans were incapable of mounting an offensive, and certainly not one in the Ardennes. Eisenhower, his chief of staff Bidell Smith, Omar Bradley, commanding the 12th Army Group, and Bradley's intelligence chief, Brigadier General Edwin Sibert, all believed the Germans lacked the capacity to mount an offensive. Besides, Gerd von Rundstedt, an old-line Prussian, commanded the German Army in the west, and he knew better than most to avoid an offensive in the narrow and wooded Ardennes defiles during winter when the twisting roads, covered with mud and snow, were at their very worst. Furthermore, the Germans held a very thin line, having little armor and artillery for an offensive. Their troops were either battered veterans, and not too many of them, old men, or mere boys. The observed German movement along the West Wall only proved that Rundstedt was plugging holes left by the troop drain of the November battles.

Hitler had other ideas. As early as 16 September 1944, senior staff officers were summoned to his command bunker, the *Wolfschanze* or Wolf's Lair, in East Prussia. With Alfred Jodl, chief of operations of the Army High Command, standing beside him, Hitler abruptly announced, "I have made a momentous decision. I shall go over to the offensive . . . out of the Ardennes, with the objective Antwerp."[2] No one in their right mind would have dared suggest such a campaign. But then the man had been nearly blown up in an assassination attempt, his body was wracked with pain, and he consumed a host of drugs that were a collective death sentence. Hitler held another briefing on 27 October. Rundstedt and his chief of staff Siegfried Westphall were there, as were Walther Model, the operational commander of the offensive, Hasso von Manteuffel, commander of the 5th Panzer Army, and "Sepp" Dietrich, an old beerhall fighter that Hitler had known since the 1920s, who commanded the 6th Panzer Army. They all thought the plan overextended, and that the limit of the attack ought to be the Meuse River. Antwerp was 100 miles away. Fuel requirements would be staggering. Any columns along the roads were fair game for the Allied tactical fighters. Besides, the generals did not believe there was sufficient manpower to sustain such an attack.

Hitler, with Jodl acting as his yes-man, airily waved aside all objections. There were too many positive results to be obtained. A drive to Antwerp would create a gap between the British and American forces, and the recapture of Antwerp would deny the Allies their strategic port. The British Army to the north and the American forces at Aachen could then be surrounded and destroyed. The terrible losses inflicted on the Allied armies would cause the war-weary civilians at home to demand a negotiated peace. If the Allies refused to negotiate, then Hitler was prepared to unleash the power of his secret weapons. He suggested that the V1 and V2 rockets sent to terrify England were only the beginning. The Allies would be forced to submit.

Hitler believed the Ardennes was a feasible front along which to launch an offensive. The area east of the Ardennes was sufficiently wooded to disguise German troop and equipment concentrations, giving the Germans the advantage of surprise. Moreover, Allied generals obviously did not think the Germans would attack in that sector because the thin, poorly conceived American positions around the West Wall were manned by burned-out veterans or young, inexperienced soldiers who did not know how to survive in winter conditions. Any difficulties the German Army faced by launching an attack across the rugged terrain were equally shared by the Americans facing them. Thus, surprise in their favor, the Germans required fewer divisions to achieve significant results. Hitler code-named the offensive *Wacht am Rhein* (Watch on the Rhine). The opening salvos would smash into the Allies on 25 November.

The Germans would attack along a 50-mile front extending from Monschau in the north to Echternach in the south. The area around Monschau, the Hautes Fagnes, is a line of ridges, marshland, and forest. The Hürtgen Forest spreads southeast. Another ridge line, cut by ravines and forests and called the Schnee Eifel, curves farther south, its population dispersed in small villages. Sections of the West Wall surmounted the east side of the Schnee Eifel. On the west side, the gorge created by the Our River formed a major barrier. Many roads in the Eifel, built by the Germans in World War

I, were narrow routes with sharp and blind turns. About 3 miles west of the Our River is the town of St. Vith, a regional road center.

The only viable east-west corridor across the Eifel was the Losheim Gap in the north. The Gap has been described as a clutter of abrupt hills, some bare, others covered with forest and thick undergrowth, in which most of the villages are in draws and potholes.[3] Hitler, ever mindful of German military history, remembered its use in 1914 as the German invasion route into Belgium and, in 1940, as Erwin Rommel's corridor to the Meuse River.

Model's Army Group B would carry the main attack in three thrusts. Dietrich's 6th Panzer Army was to attack in a line from Monshau to the Losheim Gap, take Liège and Brussels, and carve a path to Antwerp. At the 6th's left flank, Manteuffel's 5th Panzer Army would penetrate the Gap and the Schnee Eifel, take St. Vith, cross the Meuse, then swing northeast to protect Dietrich's flank. The 7th Army commanded by Erich Brandenberger would envelop Echternach in the south, advance toward the city of Luxembourg, and maneuver toward the Semois River, thus blocking Patton's U.S. 3rd Army. Two days after the main attack, the German 15th Army was to attack toward Aachen and Maastricht, and continue toward Liège.

But Hitler's generals delayed implementing the plan. The November battles required Rundstedt to shift units to the Hürtgen Forest and around Aachen. He sustained 12,000 casualties and further losses in armor and transport. No matter to Hitler. With visions of glory playing across his mind, he ordered his panzer divisions reequipped and the infantry divisions brought to full strength. He had to do a lot of scraping to accomplish that goal. For example, the 26th *Volksgrenadier* Division, mauled in Normandy, became a patchwork of small units that had never before fought together. The 18th and 167th *Volksgrenadier* Divisions were comprised of drafts from the navy and airforce. Only a few divisions in the assault force, such as the 2nd and 116th Panzers, were held together by cadres of battle-seasoned veterans.[4] Even with Hitler's juggling of resources, Model knew the army could not sustain an attack for very long and managed to delay activation until mid-December.

Hitler's assessment of American forces certainly applied to the units defending the Allied center. In December 1944, U.S. Major General Troy Middleton's VIII Corps took position along the Ardennes's east face. The corps's main tasks were resting, reequipping, and training. The 4th Infantry Division, at about half strength following the Hürtgen Forest battle, deployed along a 20-mile line from Echternach to Luxembourg, was the link with American forces farther south. The 28th Infantry Division, which lost 5,000 men in the Hürtgen Forest battle, took more than a 25-mile front along the Our River. They were supported by elements of the 9th Armored Division. The 106th Infantry Division, just off the boat from the United States, without combat experience, took position along an 18-mile front, including the Schnee Eifel, most of which was on the German side of the Our River.

Major General Alan W. Jones, commanding the 106th, realized that he held a difficult sector. His 422nd Infantry Regiment commanded by Colonel George Descheneaux occupied old West Wall fortifications atop the Schnee Eifel, a sector 8,000 to 9,000 yards long. They were supported by combat engineers and a field artillery battalion. There were also 155mm howitzer batteries located at Auw. Jones' 423rd Regiment commanded by Colonel Charles Cavender covered an 8,000-yard sector at the division's center. One battalion occupied part of the West Wall, another battalion held a line curing west around the Schnee Eifel, and a third battalion, a scratch force from various units, anchored the right flank. The regiment's 2nd Battalion was held at St. Vith as a reserve force. The 424th Regiment, commanded by Colonel Alexander Reid, occupied a 6-mile sector that curved to the southwest. There was a 4,000-yard gap between the 423rd and 424th.

Two squadrons—a mere 800 men—of the 14th Cavalry Group, commanded by Colonel Mark Devine, were attached to the 106th. They defended the Losheim Gap and maintained communications with the 99th Infantry Division to the north. The 14th, a mechanized cavalry group, was deployed into eight static strong points. But they had the support of a dozen 75mm towed anti-tank guns, two reconnaissance platoons from a tank destroyer battalion, and some self-propelled 105mm howitzers.

The key senior officers of the 106th lacked battle experience. Jones, a stateside officer in World War I, Descheneaux of the 422nd Regiment, and Cavender of the 423rd, although an enlisted man in World War I, never commanded in combat. Even though there was a cadre of professional enlisted men, the personnel of the division, as a whole, were as green as grass. When still in the United States and after basic and advanced infantry training, 60 percent of the 106th Division were appropriated as replacements for units serving in France. They were replaced by 1,200 men from the Army Specialized Training Program (men who, in effect, continued their college careers after being inducted into the army), 1,100 more from air cadet schools, another 1,500 drawn from divisions not yet scheduled for overseas duty, and 2,500 service troops (such as cooks, clerks, drivers). They went into the line with fewer machine guns than the division they replaced, without an integral tank battalion, and anti-tank artillery that was mostly towed rather than self-propelled.[5] Major General Jones was a justifiably worried man.

THE BATTLE FOR LOSHEIM GAP AND THE SCHNEE EIFEL

16 December 1944. A battalion of the 18th *Volksgrenadier* Division slipped quietly through the black, predawn forest toward the village of Auw at the north end of the Schnee Eifel. Taking the village would secure access south to the important crossing at Schönberg, and also open the way to the so-called Skyline Boulevard, the major north-south road behind the Schnee Eifel. No artillery barrage covered the battalion's advance. A mile-wide gap leading directly to Auw had been discovered in the American defenses, and Manteuffel wanted to exploit it quickly. Surprise was the key; artillery would only alert the Americans.

At 5:30 A.M., well after the assault battalion was on its way to Auw, German mortars, artillery, and *Nebelwerfer*, 6-barreled electronically fired rocket launchers, sent their projectiles tearing across the front lines of the 14th Cavalry Group and the 106th Division. Shells crashed into positions along the Skyline Boulevard and St. Vith, hit artillery emplacements, and cut communications. Manteuffel's barrage was short but powerful, each field gun firing 40 rounds in 20 minutes, followed by a rolling barrage of 60 rounds per gun. Suddenly the black, cloudy sky came alive with flickering light. Manteuffel knew his assault troops needed some kind of illumination in the dense winter forests, so he used searchlight beams bounced off the cloud cover. Even though the false light sometimes helped the defenders as much as the attackers, the atmosphere was near-spectral, adding to the surprise.

Two regiments of the 18th *Volksgrenadiers* advanced into the Losheim Gap headed for Weckerath, Roth, and Kobscheid, the zone defended by Devine's 14th Cavalry Group. The *Volksgrenadiers* were supported by most of the divisional artillery, plus 40 75mm assault guns, and 40 self-propelled tank destroyers that mounted 75mm guns. Their goal was to swing around the shoulder of the Schnee Eifel, turn south, and form a link with the division's other regiment advancing to Bleialf (Map 10).

Roth was an immediate target for the 18th *Volksgrenadiers*. The defense was thin: a platoon of the 14th Cavalry Group, two towed 75mm anti-tank guns, and a few headquarters' company clerks. Captain Stanley Porche, in charge of the little force, called his commander for help. Colonel Devine sent a platoon of M3 Stuart light tanks. They could travel at 35 miles an hour

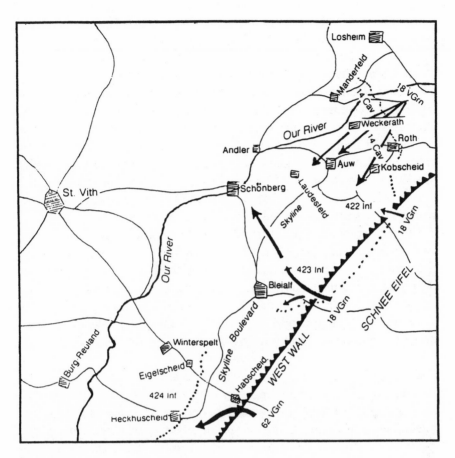

Map 10
German Attack Along Schnee Eifel

under optimum conditions (the British made great use of them in the Western Desert in 1941), but winter voided any speed advantage. Certainly their light armor could not withstand the German artillery. Indeed, most of the Stuarts were destroyed by German 88mm and 75mm self-propelled guns as they crossed a meadow, leaving Porche's men to battle the Germans as best they could. A German tank fired projectiles directly at the command post. All hope of resistance gone, Porche surrendered his command—only 90 men—after they destroyed their vehicles and weapons.

Kobscheid was defended by only two platoons of the 14th using .50-calibre machine guns dismounted from their armored vehicles. About 11 A.M., they received a radio transmission from Porche at Roth, before he surrendered, that he was going to withdraw and that the men at Kobscheid should also move back.[6] The Kobscheid group held out until 6:30 P.M., then walked through the forests and snow fields to St. Vith, a three-day trek.

There was little or no defensive perimeter established at Weckerath. Only a few Stuart light tanks and 75mm gunfire from atop a nearby ridge assailed the Germans. Other units of the 14th Cavalry Group in the path of Sepp Dietrich's 6th Panzer Army were just as defensively shallow. Some units fought the onslaught with determination, hanging onto their little positions. In the end, they were outgunned, outarmored, and outnumbered. As Charles MacDonald comments in *A Time for Trumpets*, Manteuffel's flanking maneuver around the north end of the Schnee Eifel was moving as planned, and Devine's small force could do nothing to stop them.

Devine's command post was at Manderfeld, on the seam between the German 5th and 6th Panzer Armies. He called General Jones, requesting a counterattack to restore the positions lost in the Losheim Gap. Jones, his own infantry regiments imperiled, offered no assistance; however, a little later, with the Germans outflanking Manderfeld, he gave permission to withdraw the 14th to a ridgeline behind the Our River. Devine ordered everyone to evacuate. The headquarters unit first set fire to their secret papers—maps, code books, orders—and in the process set the village ablaze. Trucks, jeeps, personnel carriers, and armored cars drove from the village only to find the road clogged by vehicles and foot soldiers from other units escaping the front. Abandoned equipment filled the landscape. Artillerymen simply walked away from their battery of 155mm howitzers. Items such as backpacks and gas masks, and heavy equipment, such as trailers, kitchen trucks, and jeeps were all abandoned. Vehicles were parked on the road shoulder. Others stalled in the middle of the road, fuel spent. Others skidded on the slippery surface and careened into snowbanks and trees. In the middle of the chaos, Colonel Devine left his command and went to St. Vith to talk with Jones. But the general had bigger problems, it seemed, and told Devine he had no time to talk with him at the moment; best he sit down and wait.

One of Jones' biggest problems was that he did not have the means to communicate with his regiments and support units, and with General Middleton at corps headquarters in Bastogne. The German bombardment cut many telephone wires; they also jammed radio transmissions. Jones was worried that his 422nd and 423rd Regiments, some 6,000 men together with supporting artillery, might be subjected to a German pincer movement in the Schnee Eifel. Finally getting through to Middleton, he suggested withdrawing the units to positions where they could better maneuver. Middleton replied, "You know how things are up there better than I do. . . . " At that point, the telephone transmission was disconnected by the operator, who told an incoming caller from the 99th Division that the line was engaged and that he would get back to him when it was free. The military historian Charles MacDonald, an infantry officer in the Battle of the Bulge, suggests it may have been during that disconnect that Middleton also said, "but I agree it would be wise to withdraw them."[7] Jones, of course, did not hear that last remark and told his staff that Middleton wanted the regiments left in their current positions. The telephone operator's ill-timed act and Jones' incorrect assumption sealed the fate of two regiments.

The 423rd Regiment, deployed around Bleialf, was attacked on 16 December by the 293rd Regiment of the 18th *Volksgrenadier* Division. Cavender immediately called Jones for reinforcements, but Jones refused the request as premature. The Germans penetrated Bleialf but at considerable cost because the Americans stood their ground, forcing close-quarter, hand-to-hand combat. That determination doubtlessly surprised the Germans, who had assumed that U.S. infantrymen avoided close combat. More than 200 Americans and Germans killed each other in one firefight for the village square. The German attack succeeded, and the Americans were forced back. But a counterattack was quickly organized by infantry, combat engineers, and the headquarters company that forced the *Volksgrenadiers* from Bleialf. By mid-afternoon the 423rd had blunted the German attack in their sector. The offensive would not be the walk-over Hitler and Jodl envisioned.

The German assault battalion that had slipped through the gap in the American lines toward Auw in the early morning did not know what to expect. They discovered the village was occupied by a company of the 81st Engineer Combat Battalion. On seeing the Germans, the engineers responded quickly with rifle and machine gun fire. Unfortunately for them, the Germans reinforced their advanced battalion with self-propelled assault guns. The engineers, unable to withstand the shelling, withdrew south to link with the 422nd. Supporting guns of the 589th Field Artillery, 105mm and 155mm howitzers, finally brought the Germans in Auw to a standstill. The *Volksgrenadiers* sent out squads, using submachine guns, grenades, and mortars, to destroy the American artillery batteries. Somehow many of the American artillerymen fought off their attackers and stuck by their guns. When the German squads reported uneven results, assault guns were sent forward. At least three of these self-propelled machines were destroyed by artillery fire, forcing the Germans to bombard from afar. With their own casualties mounting, the 589th pulled back to Schönberg. Some gunners made it, some never did, and others kept going past Schönberg.

Jones realized that the north flank of the 422nd was in a precarious position and that supporting artillery was in even more imminent danger. He sent his reserve battalion, the 423rd's 2nd Battalion, Lieutenant Colonel Joseph Puett commanding, to extricate the gunners. Puett was supposed to attack north, but he somehow lost direction and took his battalion south. Thus the Germans enveloped the north flank and rear of the 422nd, enabling them to bring their fire down on the regimental command post at Schlausenbach.

The Germans also attacked Colonel Reid's 424th Regiment at Heckhuscheid. The objective of the 183rd Regiment of the 62nd *Volksgrenadier* Division was to take high ground held by the 424th's 3rd Battalion. At the same time, the German 190th Regiment was to attack to their right along a ridge near Eigelscheid, giving them access to the Winterspelt road and beyond to St. Vith. The 183rd penetrated the 3rd Battalion's positions but could not dislodge them. The fighting continued. The Germans took Heckhuscheid, then gave it up to an American counterattack. By midnight, the Germans controlled the village and the high ground, but so resolute was the 424th's defense, and so severe were German casualties, that the Germans abandoned plans to penetrate the 424th's lines.[8] What the Germans probably did not know was that the 424th and its support units were barely operational. The 591st Field Artillery Battalion fired all its ammunition in one day, the soldiers were emotionally and physically spent, and the 424th's communications with the 28th Division just to the south no longer existed.

The American forces in the Ardennes needed reinforcements. General Omar Bradley, 12th Army Group commander, approved moving the 7th Armored Division from Holland to a staging area at Vielsalm, 14 miles west of St. Vith. However, one of the division's three combat commands—Combat Command B or CCB—led by Brigadier General Bruce Clarke, was designated to assist Jones' 106th Division immediately. Jones was told CCB would arrive in St. Vith at 7 A.M., 17 December. Middleton and Jones planned to have the armored unit attack the Germans. Jones' elation when Clarke arrived at his command post turned to despair when Clarke reported that he was only an advance man and did not really know when CCB would arrive. In fact, CCB arrived in Vielsalm at 11 A.M. on the seventeenth, hours behind schedule because of road traffic south. The road between Vielsalm and St. Vith was even more clogged, and it was early evening before a few tanks reached St. Vith. Maybe, just maybe, the main body of CCB would arrive the next day.

1:30 P.M., 17 December. Colonel Devine of the 14th Cavalry Group burst into Jones' command post: "General, we've got to run. I was practically chased into this building by a Tiger tank, and we all have to get out of here."[9] Clarke, who was talking to Jones, realized that Devine had reached the end of his emotional reserves. As Lord Moran put it in his *Anatomy of Courage*, the will to fight is like a bank account against which combat makes deductions. Sooner or later, everyone's balance hits zero. Clarke diplomatically suggested that Devine be sent to corps headquarters at Bastogne so he could explain the situation to Middleton. Devine left but did not go to Bastogne; instead he and his intelligence officer, escorted by an armored car, headed back to the 14th's command post. They ran into Germans on the road, and, in attempting to maneuver, the armored car pushed Devine's vehicle off the road. Devine's driver made it to safety on the back of the armored car. Devine and his intelligence officer escaped on foot, dodging German patrols, walking and crawling back to their command post. Once there, Devine excused himself, went to bed, and never again asserted command. He was finally evacuated as a nonbattle casualty.

Colonel Devine's reaction, however psycho-medical, was nonetheless symptomatic of the growing confusion permeating the 106th. Telephone communications were sporadic, and the Germans jammed radio frequencies. Messages were repeated again and again until, hours after being initiated, they were completed—maybe. By that time, the situations they addressed changed, rendering their intent obsolete. Jones, for example, sent a message to Cavender and, through him, to Descheneaux, at 10 A.M., 17 December, telling them to withdraw if their positions became impossible, and that the area to the west would be cleared of Germans by the afternoon. Cavender did not receive the message until mid-afternoon and did not contact Descheneaux until midnight. The colonels decided to stay where they were. Their perimeters were stabilized, but there appeared to be no appreciable clearing of the area to the west. Furthermore, the 7th Armored Division was coming, and Jones promised air transport supply drops. What the two colonels did not really understand at the time was that they were completely surrounded, the 18th *Volksgrenadiers* having achieved the pincer movement that Jones feared might develop. The German 293rd Regiment had taken Bleialf and maneuvered north to Schönberg where they met units of the 18th moving south.

2:15 A.M., 18 December. Jones ordered Cavender and Descheneaux to abandon their positions and dig in south of the Schönberg-St. Vith road where it paralleled the Our River. They were to destroy a German panzer regimental combat team that controlled the road. Jones again promised an air supply drop. The message reached Cavender at 7:30 A.M. He and Descheneaux decided to advance at 10 A.M., forming a front of all six battalions. No sooner did the regiments leave the relative security of their positions than Jones sent Cavender another message. Clarke's armored combat command was unable to attack and help the regiments break out because CCB was fighting a major action around St. Vith in which half its armored strength was destroyed. Thus the first mission given the 422nd and 423rd was scrapped. Instead they were ordered to attack Schönberg itself. From that point, very much on their own, they would have to cross the Our River and fight their way down the road to St. Vith.

The two regiments spent much of 18 December maneuvering in the forests to attack Schönberg the next morning. Puett's battalion unexpectedly met Germans on the Bleialf-Schönberg road. He called for help. Cavender sent forward his 1st Battalion, but it was late in the day, the fading light casting strange shadows on the snow. One direction looked very much like another, objects fusing into each other, disorienting the troops. Cavender ordered the battalion back to its original line.

By nightfall, Cavender brought some order out of the growing confusion, forming his three battalions into line for a morning attack on Schönberg. Cavender's immediate problem was that, having lost contact with Descheneaux, he did not know where the 422nd was located. He assumed his regiment would be attacking Schönberg by itself. Descheneaux, for his part, receiving the order to move against Schönberg, assumed he would be attacking in line to the right of the 423rd. He also assumed that the 7th Armored Division was coming to the rescue and that the promised air drop was still on schedule.

ATTACKING INTO SURRENDER

The attacks by the 422nd and 423rd Regiments against Schönberg—and here it is difficult to be overdramatic—were doomed. With minimal communications, and without one regiment knowing where the other was located, the first steps toward Schönberg were necessarily confused. And more: the Germans had surrounded the two regiments, outnumbering and outgunning the Americans. Those first steps were bloody.

At 10 A.M., 19 December, the 423rd Regiment moved forward, Lieutenant Colonel Earl Klink's 3rd Battalion on the left flank. One of its companies on the Schönberg road ran into German self-propelled assault guns and half-track mounted anti-aircraft guns, and was raked from the rear by infantry fire. The company was shredded. The survivors moved to the slopes of a nearby hill. But the Germans charged, overrunning the group. Thirty-two men lived to surrender.[10] Another company of the 3rd Battalion moved across Hill 504 but were cut to pieces by artillery fire as they approached the Schönberg road. Klink, joining his remaining company, scaled the hill and also came under German artillery fire. They dug in and established a perimeter defense.

Joseph Puett's 2nd Battalion, on the right flank, moved along another slope of Hill 504. Reaching a crest, they looked down into Schönberg. Unable to contact Cavender, Puett led his men into a little valley that cloaked his approach to the village. The downhill trek was not easy. The forested slope swallowed the battalion. One tree looked like another. Narrow trails crossed and recrossed, creating a tangle of confused directions. The battalion might have survived all that, but, as they approached the valley, a stream of infantry fire enfiladed one flank, causing some casualties. This turned out to be so-called friendly fire. Puett's men had found the 422nd Regiment's 3rd Battalion, who mistakenly thought they were Germans.

The 422nd Regiment was also experiencing problems. A company of the 1st Battalion was destroyed by tank and machine gun fire as they tried to cross Skyline Boulevard. Another two companies moving toward the Boulevard came under German assault gun, machine gun, and rifle fire. Most of the men were killed or surrendered. The 2nd Battalion, accompanied by Descheneaux, crossed Skyline Boulevard and moved uphill. Once at the crest they saw vehicles stretched along the Schönberg road leading north to Andler. Someone called out that the column was American—the 7th Armored finally come to the rescue! No sooner did the Americans start walking down the slope than they were raked by gunfire on one flank from tanks and self-propelled guns and on the other by infantry fire. The 2nd Battalion made a ghastly mistake. The column was the *Führer Begleit* Brigade (the Hitler Bodyguard), stalled by traffic. Their gunfire cut into the battalion's ranks. They managed some retaliatory 81mm mortar fire, destroying three assault guns, but most of the surviving men fled into the woods. Their hopes for a breakout by a relief column and of continuing the attack on Schönberg lay bleeding on the exposed hillside.

Colonel Descheneaux huddled with his staff in a trench, helpless as wounded men struggled past him to a nearby aid station. He reached a decision: surrender. Earlier, when he received orders to attack Schönberg, he had sobbed, "Oh, my poor men—they'll be cut to pieces!"[11] He was tragically right. Each time his battalions moved in any direction, the Germans were waiting for them. His men were pounded by rocket and artillery fire; German armor made it impossible to move along the roads.

Descheneaux's anti-tank gunners and bazooka teams did their best, but their jobs, always dangerous, became suicidal as the Germans responded at point-blank ranges. His infantrymen were exhausted, his support artillery overrun. Ammunition was nearly gone. There was little food left and no safe water. Medical supplies were dwindling. Descheneaux sent runners to contact Cavender but none returned. He looked into the faces of his men and saw hunger and exhaustion. Were there also flickers of hopelessness? The promised air drops never came. The armored breakthrough never materialized. He and Cavender could not even coordinate an attack to fight their way out of the encirclement. Descheneaux could not find any alternatives to surrender, for he saw no valor in dying under those conditions. Most of his officers, reluctantly agreed. The one dissenter was Lieutenant Colonel Thomas Kelly of the battered 589th Field Artillery. He wanted to wait until dark and try slipping through the German lines in small groups. But Descheneaux was adamant. He was going to save the remnants of his regiment even if he was eventually court-martialed. He gave the order for everyone to break their weapons. Then he slumped down in the trench and cried.

Colonel Cavender reached the same conclusion as Descheneaux at about the same time. He called his officers together and reviewed their situation. Casualties were heavy. No one knew the whereabouts of Puett's battalion. The men were hungry and thirsty, and they were almost out of ammunition. The Germans were all around them. He announced that the regiment would surrender at 4 P.M.

THE ANATOMY OF SURRENDER

The word went out: surrender! From the regimental command posts, to the battalions and companies, platoons, squads, and finally from foxhole to foxhole—surrender! Many men were apprehensive, and with justification. Surrendering, as John Keegan points out in *The Face of Battle*, is a chancy if not dangerous act. *Waffen SS* troops had shot Canadian prisoners in Normandy. Would these Germans do the same? Would the Germans even understand them? Would they understand the Germans? Of course, officers of the two armies made arrangements and came to terms, but would the Germans keep their word? A terrible quiet blanketed the young American troops as they clambered from their positions, destroyed their weapons, and waited for the enemy to appear. What would the Germans be like? The answer arrived in a short time as joyous *Volksgrenadiers* came through the woods. Laughing and joking among themselves, they saw the Americans, hands raised, holding up their helmets in a sign of final surrender. Some of the *Volksgrenadiers* were openly contemptuous of their vanquished enemy, going among the men, rudely pushing them, and taking watches, rings, and other personal property. When American officers complained to German officers of this behavior, the belongings were returned. The Americans were formed into columns and marched to the rear, into Germany, and finally into the barbed wire enclosures of prisoner-of-war camps.

The men had mixed feelings. Many of their comrades earlier fled west to the alleged safety of St. Vith in a torrent of what Colonel R. E. Dupuy called in his history of the 106th, *St. Vith: Lion in the Way*, sheer, unreasoning panic. Soldiers who stayed on the line thought these men had "bugged out," run away and, not to put a fine point on the assessment, were cowards. Now that certainty of judgment faded in the reality of being a prisoner of war. Other men felt guilty. Maybe, they thought, they did not fight hard enough. The same thought crossed the minds of officers, who mentally tortured themselves about what they did and did not do, what they might have done, what they should have done. Other men felt ashamed and tore their divisional patches—the golden lion—from their uniforms.[12] Still other men did not know why they had to surrender. These included the men who never saw a German, never fired a shot, and never knew they were surrounded. And then there were those who thought they were fighting rather well, who believed that they could have held out until help arrived, who wanted to continue fighting because it was what they were there to do. Finally, and inclusive of all those already mentioned, were the soldiers who resented the whole miserable situation. They had not been in the army very long and had received only perfunctory training. They landed in Europe and were pushed into the front line without adequate preparation. And now, after only a few days of fighting, their war was over. A few lousy days! That was no war at all. If only the army had given them a chance.

Not every man in the two regiments and their support units received the surrender orders, and there were those who, getting the orders, defied them. By midnight, 19 December, about 500 men gathered on a hill near Laudesfeld. Major Albert Ouellette from the 422nd's 2nd Battalion led the aggregation. The Germans quickly surrounded the hill, bringing down artillery fire on the Americans. The next day the Germans arranged a truce and suggested Ouellette surrender. More death was unnecessary. Ouellette surrendered his men on the twenty-first. Another group of 68 men from the 423rd did slip through the German lines and made it to St. Vith. Perhaps a total of 250 from both regiments escaped.

Charles Whiting states that between 8,000 and 9,000 men were captured during all of the fighting. In contrast, Charles MacDonald reasoned that because the six infantry battalions, together with their supporting artillery-men and cavalry, were much reduced by battle casualties—half-strength would not be overstated—a figure close to 3,000 would be a more realistic number of those who surrendered. I think MacDonald is probably right. Hugh Cole, reviewing the situation in his official history *The Ardennes*, concluded that, even though precise casualty and surrender numbers will never be known, the battle on the Schnee Eifel represented "the most serious reverse suffered by American arms during the operations of 1944–45 in the European theater."[13]

Important among the military elements contributing to the 106th's disintegration were tactical failures. As Gay M. Hammerman points out in a study of some of the 106th's survivors,[14] the division was moved into a topographically difficult defensive position. They were spread thinly along the line, occupying sections of the West Wall, but most deployed were on the German side of the Our River. Their position was rationalized by intelligence estimates from Eisenhower's headquarters, through the 12th Army Group command, to VIII Corps command that the Germans were incapable of mounting an offensive and that the Ardennes was the last place they would choose. Conventional thinking dulled imagination and silenced argument. From the viewpoint of the men on the battlefield, the 106th was left vulnerable. The situation was exacerbated by a lack of armor to contest the German advance, too few anti-tank weapons, not enough ammunition, poor maps, and, within a short time period, low rations and dwindling medical supplies. All that was supposed to be ameliorated by the arrival of the 7th Armored Division's CCB under Brigadier General Clarke. However, seeing the confusion in Jones' headquarters, and recognizing that it was too late to counterattack the Germans and relieve the two stranded regiments, Clarke unilaterally altered his mission to make a stand at St. Vith for as long as he could hold out. The airlifts were botched from the start. Bad weather in England grounded most flights. Twenty-three C-47s arrived over Belgium but were diverted from one field to another without any fighter escort. The crews lacked preflight briefings, had no maps, and were not given any coordinates. The planes finally landed in France where they waited, and waited, and then were diverted to Bastogne. This was confusion at the highest command levels. Certainly none of this incompetency was the 106th's fault, but the consequences fell upon them like a rock.

Leadership within the 106th also failed. Undoubtedly Major General Jones wanted to make the right decisions, but he was incapable of doing so.

His communications fell apart with the first German bombardment. Rather than visiting his regiments or sending out officers to discover what was happening, he paced back and forth in his command post, surrounded by a lackluster staff, ignorant of the actual situation, believing that the German attack was not serious, and that his men could handle it. General Matthew Ridgway, commanding the Airborne Corps and sector commander, arrived at Jones' headquarters on 22 December to discover for himself what was happening. Officers such as Clarke of CCB and Reid of the 424th told Ridgway the unvarnished truth: their units were less than 50 percent effective. Yet Jones answered questions with a naive optimism that angered Ridgway. Jones was relieved of his command.

Cavender and Descheneaux responded to the crisis by doing little or nothing. The Germans infiltrated their lines and endangered their flanks; yet the colonels, their communications with Jones garbled, held their positions. Individual units within the 422nd and 423rd Regiments fought with great determination, causing grievous casualties among the Germans. Small units of the outnumbered and outgunned 14th Cavalry Group fought brave delaying actions. Nonetheless, it was clear from the first German shelling that these American units would be on their own. Instead of maneuvering westward, keeping the Germans always to the east, the two infantry regiments remained static and were surrounded. Jones, ignorant of the frontline situations, often issued impossible orders, such as attacking directly into the German strength at Schönberg. Thus the divisional commander compounded his regiments' isolation and fed their growing hopelessness.

Largely absent from all this commentary are the actions of Reid's 424th Regiment. They initially stopped the *Volksgrenadier*'s advance, thereby delaying the planned German envelopment of the Schnee Eifel and the capture of St. Vith. Supported by Brigadier General William Hoge's Combat Command B from the 9th Armored Division (not to be confused with Clarke's CCB from the 7th Armored), the 424th refused to be encircled, retreating across the Our River from Winterspelt to Burg Reuland. The regiment's orderly withdrawal was costly. The effective fighting force was cut in half; they lacked ammunition, rations, and medical supplies; and they lost contact with the other two regiments. Like the 422nd and 423rd, their communications with Jones' command post were sporadic. Thus all the factors usually cited as contributory to the other two regiments' disintegration were also present in the 424th. But Reid's men continued to function as a potent fighting unit, helped to establish and sustain a salient around St. Vith until the position became completely untenable, and, in doing so, once again threw off the German timetable. Thus, with armored assistance that the other two regiments lacked, Reid's willingness to maneuver, rather than remain static, was the principal element in the survival of his regiment as a unit.

The 424th provides an example of what is fast becoming a truism in military history: the physical condition of a fighting unit is not necessarily an indication of its fighting spirit; conversely, diminishing that fighting spirit, that will to combat, leads to collapse and disintegration. This generalization shifts our search for the sources of the 106th's disintegration from military factors to those more sociological.

The imaginative commander, Robert Leonhard points out in *The Art of Maneuver*, aims his attack at the enemy's point of greatest vulnerability.[15] The purpose is not to annihilate the enemy, in contravention of textbook military wisdom, but to disrupt its combat effectiveness. That was exactly Manteuffel's goal. The surprise and ferocious character of the German attack left the Americans on the Schnee Eifel confused. Tactical control, especially within the 422nd and 423rd Regiments, broke down. Platoons fought without company support, and companies were cut off from their battalions. Battalions, such as Puett's, lost contact with regimental headquarters, and the regiments lost contact with each other and with the divisional command post. Without communication, there can be no command. Thus the two regiments became disorganized and ineffective.

Gay Hammerman's study of the defeat, using an admittedly tiny sample of the 106th's survivors, identified key elements in the division's short history that, when combined with the conditions on the Schnee Eifel, promised disintegration. Poor leadership, poor staffwork, poor training and fitness, little or no combat experience, high personnel turnover, and inexperienced officers leading inexperienced troops were among those mentioned by the men Hammerman interviewed.[16] In short, the division never really had the opportunity to become a cohesive unit. Sixty percent of the men who originally formed the division were taken away as replacements for other units. Those replacing them did not expect to be in the infantry. They did not know their officers, and many of the officers were themselves new. There was no real *esprit de corps*.

By the time the survivors reached the prison camps, the lack of *esprit de corps* simmered into widespread resentment. Younger officers openly defied Cavender who was camp senior officer, and the German camp commander had to restore order. The men, both officers and enlisted personnel, were sullen and showed no inclination to organize themselves into committees within the camp and showed no inclination to escape.[17] The impact of failure, earned and imposed, destroyed them.

I think that the factor of alienation, so contributory to disintegration in other examples used in this study, emerged in the 106th, but in a different way. All the glory words learned about their role as soldiers and the part they played in the war came to nothing. The war was over for most in the space of two or three days. Their commanders failed them; the army itself failed them. The orders to surrender surprised many men. As Hammerman points out, soldiers of all ranks did not know they were being defeated by the *Volksgrenadiers* until it happened. Thus I think that three forms of alienation were predominantly at work within the 106th.[18]

The first is isolation. The men in the camps found they had little regard for the values, meanings, and beliefs the army thought they ought to have as good soldiers. They did not know if they were good soldiers. Many did not feel like soldiers at all. Their sullenness and disrespect for higher ranks were indicative of a growing breach between normative military expectations and those emerging within the situation caused by defeat, surrender, and imprisonment.

The second form of alienation is meaninglessness, the feeling that the soldiers were not certain what to believe. This is well illustrated by a participant in Hammerman's study who was convinced that the 106th was purposely put in the line to entice the German attack. He could accept at an objective level the demonstrated fact that the Germans planned their offensive long before the 106th made its appearance on the Schnee Eifel. But, at a gut level, he could never accept that explanation. He was faced with choosing between alternative explanations of the disaster and could not decide where the truth was to be found.

The third form of alienation is powerlessness, the feeling that individual behavior cannot determine future outcomes. The men did not have the chance to fight their way out of the encirclement, nor did they really have the opportunity to fight where they stood. Their commanders surrendered before most knew about the decision. Soldiers, of course, do not make command decisions. No vote is taken. But many veterans of the 422nd and 423rd felt cheated of the opportunity to demonstrate that they were good soldiers.

What makes these forms of alienation different from those in the other examples studied is that they emerged mostly after the organizational disintegration rather than directly contributing to it. Certainly the elements that allowed the forms of alienation to be expressed were inherent in the division's *esprit*—or lack of it. Some men did panic and run away in spurts of normlessness, feeling that such nonconforming behavior was the only solution to the crisis befalling them. Most held their ground and fought as well as circumstances allowed. Suddenly everything was taken from them. Once in prison, the value and belief structure that even marginally sustained them in battle collapsed.

The fate of the 106th was ironic. The division was reconstituted but never again saw combat. Instead they guarded German prisoners of war. The division's history was buried beneath the brash defense of Bastogne by the 101st Airborne Division and Patton's sweeping maneuver northward to help rescue them. Soon the West Wall was broken, the Rhine was crossed, and Germany surrendered in May 1945.

The Sand Creek Massacre, Colorado, 1864

Having helped spawn hate and fear of the Indians in the Colorado Territory, Colonel John Chivington led units of Colorado Volunteers in an attack against a Cheyenne camp, killing and mutilating mostly women and children.

THE GENESIS OF FEAR AND HATE

Colorado Territory, 1858. Gold in Colorado! The words shot east. Pikes Peak was a mountain of gold. Nuggets, 4 and 5 pounds each, were just waiting to be picked up from the ground. Cherry Creek was awash in gold. The Arkansas River and the South Platte overflowed with gold. Fact, rumor, wishful thinking, greed, and hope—the constant ingredients of American frontier life—pulled thousands of people west. Some even came east from California where, ten years earlier, hope often grounded in barren stream beds. Now there was a second chance. Prospectors panned the rivers and streams, shoveled sand by the ton, and chopped into barren hillsides. Most found nothing. Even though many of the disappointed and destitute seekers returned east, rumor continued to draw still newer waves of emigrants west, their hopes buttressed by such newsmen as Horace Greeley, an editor of the New York *Tribune*, and William Byers, who hauled a press across the prairie and founded the *Rocky Mountain News* in the boomtown called Denver. Eventually enough gold was found to entice large-scale mining to the territory, disgorging gold and silver in greater quantities by more efficient methods than panning and pick and shovel. The larger corporate approach necessitated an army of hard-rock miners—tough, independent, hard-drinking, and sometimes violent men.

The inevitable symbiotics chased after the gold-seekers: tradesmen, teamsters, tailors, blacksmiths and barbers, carpenters and bricklayers, lawyers, adventurers, get-rich-quick schemers, gamblers, land speculators, ranchers and farmers, and those seeking power in the open civic life of the territory—the best and the worst that American society offered a new land. To secure the persons and property of these Americans, the United States Army extended the promise of protection.

Protection was needed because the Colorado Territory and neighboring western Kansas and Nebraska were the traditional ground of such tribes as the Cheyennes, Arapahoes, Kiowas, the Southern Sioux, Pawnees, Comanches, Crows, Utes, and the Delawares. They did not view the westward movement as a benign in-migration of American settlers but as an invasion of their homelands. Rudely shoved aside in the name of progress, misunderstood, stripped of their traditional hunting grounds, the Indians were quickly reduced to desperation.

Long-time white settlers in the territory also resented the new settlers. William Bent, for example, was a trader who came to Colorado in the 1820s with his three brothers, married a Cheyenne woman, and built a fort that was sanctuary to all. As early as 1850, when he was a government Indian agent, Bent warned that white incursions into Colorado were disrupting tribal life and the Indians faced extinction if it continued. In 1851, the Cheyenne and Arapahoes signed a treaty promising not to attack the whites if the government ceded to the Indians western Kansas and Colorado. In effect, the United States government gave to the Indians lands that were already theirs.

The emigration launched by the 1858 goldrush was a wholesale violation of the treaty. The burgeoning population settled wherever they pleased, irrespective of the 1851 agreement. Thus, without any attempt by the government to stop them, the Indian lands along Cherry Creek, Colorado, were overrun by prospectors. Small settlements, mostly rude collections of tents and wooden shacks, soon dotted the creekside, followed by the formation of Denver City.

Bent viewed the emigration with renewed alarm. A delegation of Arapaho and Cheyenne chiefs visited him, telling him that the government had to enforce the treaty and stop the emigrants.[1] There was nothing Bent could do. The two tribes, frustrated, bewildered, distrustful of the white man's word, angrily ceded their Cherry Creek lands to the settlers under a new treaty. The Cheyennes even volunteered to give up their traditional nomadic prairie life for farming if the government would send them the proper tools and farm experts to teach them how to work the soil. Thus, on 5 December 1861, President Abraham Lincoln signed the Fort Wise treaty, guaranteeing the Indians expert help, cash subsidies, mills and shops, and land grants for farming. They were to live on a reservation bounded on the south by the Arkansas River from Booneville to a point just beyond Bent's so-called New Fort. The northeast boundary, giving the reservation the look of a right triangle, followed the line of Sand Creek. The Cheyennes were to occupy the western half of the reservation and the Arapahoes the eastern half (Map 11). As the historian Stan Hoig concludes, "The whites in Colorado now legally owned the land they had invaded."[2]

The settlement of Colorado, uncoordinated and motivated by greed, was seen as another expression of America's God-given right, their Manifest Destiny, to expand from sea to shining sea. The Indians were an impediment to the Great Idea. Never mind that treaties were broken or that whites decimated the buffalo herds for a thrill or for the profits from hides. The Indians were considered no better than blacks. In fact, they were worse because they often fought back and because they lacked economic value. Not being white, Christian, and useful, the Indians were despised as lazy, dirty, treacherous, bloodthirsty savages. And the Indians were everywhere. They lounged about stagecoach stations, roamed across ranch and farm lands, lived around army posts, and were an everyday sight on Denver streets. Who knew when these strange people would rise up against the whites and kill everyone in their beds?

The American Civil War exacerbated fears of Indian intentions. Many able-bodied men had gone east to join the Union Army or headed for Texas to join the Confederate cause. Western army garrisons were stripped, leaving only a few hundred regulars patrolling thousands of square miles. If the Indians started a war or, as was commonly feared, if the Confederates brought the Indians to their side, the settlers would be in great danger.

In 1861, William Gilpin, Colorado territorial governor, received permission to raise the 1st Colorado Volunteer Regiment. Men from all walks of life were attracted—a veritable cross section of territory life—but the regiment's core consisted of miners. Unfortunately the federal government lacked funds to supply and arm the regiment. Gilpin solved the problem by issuing bank drafts on the U.S. Treasury, a cavalier move because he did not get federal permission to issue the drafts. Thus, when Denver businessmen submitted the drafts for payment, the treasury understandably refused to

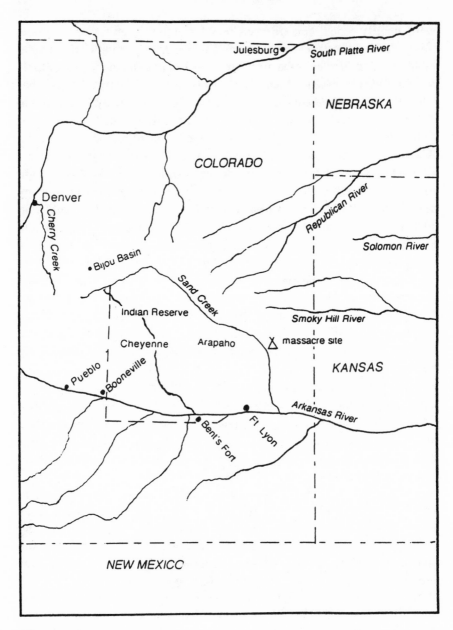

Map 11
Colorado Territory, 1864

honor them. Many businesses floundered, and some went bankrupt. Gilpin resigned, engulfed by the ensuing scandal and accused of empire building, fraud, and incompetence. He was replaced by John Evans, whose approach to the Indian problem was completely naive: he denied a problem existed. If the natives did become restless, the 1st Colorado Volunteers would handle them.

John Slough, an attorney, was appointed colonel of the 1st Colorado, and John Tappin, a newspaperman, was his executive officer. John Chivington, a minister, became regimental major. The regiment they commanded was an unruly and sometimes violent band. The men resisted drill and often defied their officers. When in Denver, with or without leave, they got drunk, started fights, broke into stores and houses, and if arrested were freed by their comrades who broke down the jailhouse doors. Slough and Chivington made matters worse because they did not like each other and frequently quarreled in front of the men.

In the fall of 1861, fear spread through the territory as a confederate brigade of 3,000 men commanded by Henry Sibley left Texas and marched into New Mexico, capturing Santa Fe and Albuquerque. Their objective was to invade Colorado and take the gold fields. In March 1862, the 1st Colorado was sent to rescue the situation. They made a remarkable forced march of 64 miles in 24 hours to Fort Union. To celebrate, the men looted the sutler's store and got drunk.

25 March. Slough led the 1st Colorado, together with elements of the New Mexico command, a force numbering 1,342 men, from Fort Union to find the Confederates. The next day, Slough sent Chivington ahead of the main column with two companies of the 1st Colorado and a cavalry detachment to Apache Canyon. They came upon 700 Confederates marching into the canyon. Chivington ordered his men to fire, catching the enemy in the open and unable to maneuver. The survivors were sent back to Slough.

On 27 March, a thousand Confederates cautiously approached Apache Canyon. Slough deployed to meet them but, in the interim, sent Chivington and 430 men into the mountains to surprise Sibley's troops from the rear. The march was arduous. When they reached Glorieta Pass, they saw the Confederate supply train below. Chivington ordered his men down the hillside. Slipping and sliding, many using ropes, they recklessly charged into the Confederates. Surprise worked its magic. With little fighting, Chivington captured 80 wagons filled with munitions, food, and animal forage. The wagons were burned and between 500 and 600 mules and horses were bayoneted to death.

The Confederates withdrew to Texas. Slough was not allowed to pursue them and resigned his commission in a huff. Chivington, hero of the day, savior of the Colorado Territory, was promoted to colonel and given command of the newly created Colorado Military District.

Chivington catapulted into prominence when his exploits were vividly portrayed in Byers' *Rocky Mountain News*. He fit the role of hero. He was a large man, standing more than 6 feet tall and weighing more than 250 pounds. His resounding speeches, trumpeting Gospel authority and the fire of a true believer, gave needed reassurance to Denver's civic groups. But Chivington realized with the terrible insight often possessed by the demagogue that he could not rest on his narrow military accomplishment. He needed a new enemy, one to which the entire population could have a common response—fear.

That enemy was the Indians. Chivington did not trust Indians. He considered them to be rude, crude, bloody-minded, treacherous savages who plotted to drive all white men from the territory. He blatantly called for the killing of all Indians—and he meant all of them.

There were just enough Indian depredations during 1862 and through the winter of 1863 to maintain the edge of fear among Colorado's whites. Curiously, one incident that captivated Denver citizens took place in faraway Minnesota. The Sioux attacked Fort Ridgely and the town of New Ulm. Nearly 800 whites were killed. The militia defeated the Indians in late September 1862 and hanged 38 Sioux. Denver citizens, following the incident in the *Rocky Mountain News*, were terrified because the Minnesota Sioux had been peaceful, then unexpectedly rose against the whites with great ferocity. The Cheyennes and Arapahoes might do the same.[3]

Closer to home, the Indians raided ranches, rustling cattle and horses. That these were considered honorable activities among the Indian tribes, tests of guile and manhood, gave cold comfort to the whites. Far less harmful was the Indian game of chasing stagecoaches down the prairie roads, shouting and gesturing with their weapons, and then turning aside, while those inside the coaches dissolved in fear. The tribes also warred against each other in time-honored fashion. Thus a common sight was the passage through Denver's streets of Cheyenne war parties, Kiowa scalps dangling from poles. The Denver citizenry, imagining their own scalps fluttering in the freeze, did not know that the trail the Indians followed beside Cherry Creek was a long-used route. Yet, for all the imaginings of the whites, and despite the raids and the occasional murders, the Indian tribes generally remained peaceful.

The spring of 1863 brought change as drought hit the region. The Indians were impoverished because the agricultural transformation promised in the Fort Wise Treaty never materialized. No farm experts or tools were sent, there were no mills and shops, and no crops to feed the hungry. The Indian agent at Fort Lyon (the new name given Fort Wise) reported that the nearest buffalo herds were 200 miles away from the reservation and that there was little or no local game. Major Scott Anthony, 1st Colorado Volunteers, concluded that the government would have to assume full support of the Indians or let them starve to death, the latter being the easiest way to eradicate them.[4]

Governor Evans, although initially convinced the Cheyenne and Arapaho were peaceful, underwent a change of attitude in May 1863, a change influenced by Colonel Chivington's beliefs as well as by Indian depredations. For Evans was now convinced that the Cheyennes and Arapahoes were plotting to join with the Sioux to drive all whites from the territory. He warned the tribal chiefs that the whites would fight back in a war of extermination. The Indians, conceding that some warriors went raiding, were nevertheless taken aback by Evans' level of hostility, unable to understand that to Evans and the white settlers, some Indians meant all Indians.

As a response to the settlers' concerns that the army was not doing much about the Indian problem, Chivington put into motion a scenario to punish the Indians and, at the same time, advance his own agenda of an Indian war. On 9 April 1864, he sent a report to Major General Samuel Curtis, his commanding officer, stating that Indians rustled 175 head of stock from a government cattle contractor. He believed the information reliable because it was told to him by cowboys supervising the herds. These men were never named. The anthropologist George Grinnell concluded that the herdsmen probably invented the rustling story to cover their own negligence.[5] The Indians, a group of Cheyennes, admitted they found the stock but said that the animals were wandering about the prairie, a common occurrence. As a matter of course, finders-keepers as it were, the Indians drove the stock into their camp. Chivington knowingly exaggerated the whole affair in his report. Curtis took the statement at face value, and dispatched a unit of the Independent Battery of Colorado Volunteer Artillery, Lieutenant George Eayre commanding, from their post near Denver. The orders were to retrieve the cattle and punish the rustlers. Even though some cattle were found, probably strays rounded up from the prairie, Eayre searched on into May, indiscriminately attacking Indian camps, looting, and burning lodges (tepees). In one attack he reported killing 28 Indians, including three chiefs.

Returning to Denver, he commandeered some wagons, loaded them with supplies, and headed back to the prairie with 85 men and two howitzers.

On 16 May, not far from Fort Larned on the Arkansas River, Eayre's column encountered a large Cheyenne band, probably on a buffalo hunt. A sergeant was sent to talk to the Indians, returning with Chief Lean Bear. He had been among the Arapaho and Cheyenne chiefs invited to Washington, D.C. in 1862, and he wanted to show Eayre the medal he received from President Lincoln and documents testifying to his friendship with the whites. No one cared. The soldiers killed him, and they attacked the band. As the battle was about to erupt beyond some preliminary artillery shelling and skirmishing, the peace chief Black Kettle rode from the nearby Indian camp, calling upon the band not to fight the whites. They broke off any further action.

Eayre led his column to Fort Larned. A band of Kiowas arrived soon after. Distracting the soldiers with a ceremonial women's dance, they rustled the fort stock together with 240 cattle that Eayre found. The next day an Arapaho chief named Left Hand approached the fort, carrying a white flag and wanting to help the soldiers retrieve the stolen animals. But Captain Parmeter, the post commander who may have been drunk at the time, ordered his cannons to open fire. Doubtless, the firing on Left Hand and the earlier murder of Lean Bear were the consequence of a message Chivington sent to all his subordinates, warning that they should be alert to cattle-thieving Indians and that the only recourse left was to kill them.[6]

The Indians were confused. Their intentions were peaceful, they carried medals and papers to prove those intentions, and their actions, especially those by Lean Bear and Left Hand, did nothing to earn the white man's violence. The Indians, however, did not take into account Chivington's enmity toward them, nor did they understand that many whites lumped all Indians together into the convenient stereotype of bloodthirsty savages. The Cheyennes and Arapahoes, two tribes essential to peace in the Colorado Territory, were stirred to anger and revenge for the insults and death dealt them. Within a week of the cannonade against Left Hand, Cheyennes raided ranches, farms, and stagecoach stations along the Fort Larned road, reducing them to burned-out shells, drove away the stock, and murdered the occupants. The Indian violence that the whites feared had become a self-fulfilled prophecy.

Chivington's wish and Evans' fear that several tribes would unite were realized in May 1864 as the Cheyenne and Arapaho warriors joined Sioux war bands at the Solomon River. Small raiding parties rode out from this central camp, killing an estimated 200 ranchers, farmers, traders, and travelers between May and September.[7] They burned scores of ranches, attacked stagecoaches and way stations, and rustled the stock. Wagon trains bringing supplies to Denver became a favorite target. These attacks created direct and severe consequences. The stage line to Denver was shut down, and, with supplies drastically reduced, the city experienced a food shortage. Denver, fear spreading like a plague, was under siege.

In June, Denver experienced its worst nightmare. Ward Hungate, a ranch manager, and a hired man named Miller went looking for some stray cattle. They were a few miles from the ranch when smoke from the ranch buildings caught their attention. Hungate's wife and two children were in the ranch house. He knew it was an Indian raid. Sending Miller galloping to Denver for help, Hungate—despite Miller's pleas that there was nothing left to do—wheeled his horse around and raced back to the ranch. When Miller reached Denver, he sought out the ranch owner Van Wirmer to tell him what happened. Wirmer tried to enlist help, but none of Denver's stalwarts volunteered. He hitched a wagon and went to the ranch, accompanied by Miller. What they found varies with the narrator. Hungate certainly never reached the ranch. His body was later discovered at a nearby creek, shot full of holes, mutilated, and scalped. One narrative placed the bodies of Ellen Hungate and her two daughters Florence and Laura about a hundred yards from the house. Another account claims that the three were bound together and stuffed down a well. There is no disagreement regarding the circumstances of their murders. Mrs. Hungate was raped, stabbed several times, and scalped. The throats of the two girls were so severely slashed that they were nearly decapitated. The four Arapahoes who committed these murders also burned down the ranch and took about thirty head of cattle. The Hungates' bodies were transported to Denver and placed in a wooden box, the daughters between the parents. The macabre scene was put on public display. Denver was shaken.[8]

July, August, September: more murders and burnings. Public outrage at the continuing Indian depredations bombarded Governor Evans: Do something! The governor, despite public impatience, was not idle. He certainly realized that Denver was vulnerable. The 1st Colorado Volunteers were back in New Mexico to block a suspected Confederate attack, and the recently organized 2nd Colorado was in Kansas fighting Indians. Evans received permission from General Curtis to establish the 3rd Colorado Volunteers. Unlike the first two units that were infantry, the 3rd was cavalry and the men would serve only one hundred days. To spur enlistment, Evans and Chivington spread a rumor that anyone not serving in a volunteer force would be drafted and sent to the big war in the east. Within a few weeks, 650 men enlisted in the 3rd.[9]

The regiment was commanded by 28-year-old Colonel George Shoup, originally of the 1st Colorado. The men he commanded were issued Union blue uniforms and armed with antique muskets of dubious quality. Even though many Denver residents were pleased if not blatantly proud of their new soldiers, old problems soon erupted. The men were just as rowdy, if not more so, than the old 1st. They awakened when they felt like it, wandered away from their duties, including standing guard, refused to drill, ignored orders from their officers—some of whom were drunkards—and crowded into Denver looking for drink, loot, and a good punch-up. A more obnoxious and undisciplined body of troops is difficult to imagine. Because of their term of enlistment, the name "hundred dazers" was attached to the regiment. They were also known as the "bloodless Third" because they saw no action.

In addition to obtaining another regiment, Governor Evans also developed a plan to further diminish the Indian threat. On 27 June, he issued a proclamation to the Indians that distinguished friendly from unfriendly, pointing out that the latter were rustlers and murderers. The Great Father—the U.S. president—was angry and was going to punish the guilty. In contrast, he wanted to care for friendly Indians and make certain no mistakes were made by inadvertently punishing the innocent with the guilty. Therefore, Indians of all tribes were to congregate at various forts and military camps where they would receive provisions and find safety. The Cheyennes and Arapahoes, for example, were to gather at Fort Lyon. The conclusion derived from the proclamation was simple enough: any Indian found on the prairie must be unfriendly and was subject to being killed.

4 September 1864. Three soldiers of the 1st Colorado were on their way to Denver to be discharged when they encountered two Cheyenne men and a woman. The soldiers almost opened fire, but one of the Indians made peace signs and waved a paper. The soldiers took the Indians prisoner and rode to Fort Lyon. John Smith, an old trapper who knew three Indian dialects, was asked to interpret. One of the captured Indians was One-Eye, a Cheyenne subchief. The other man was a warrior, and the woman was One-Eye's wife. One-Eye was to deliver two identical letters from Black Kettle and other Cheyenne chiefs to William Bent and to Sam Colley, the Cheyenne Indian agent. Dated 29 August, they were written in English by Edmund Guerrier, a half-French, half-Cheyenne trapper. The letters stated that the Cheyennes held a council and were willing to make peace with the whites providing the whites made peace with other tribes such as the Kiowas, Arapahoes, and Sioux. A prisoner exchange was also promised. One-Eye told Major Edward

(Ned) Wynkoop, commandant at Fort Lyon, that Black Kettle knew of Governor Evans' proclamation but was reluctant to enter the fort because there had been so much betrayed trust and so much killing. One-Eye also said that 2,000 Cheyennes and Arapahoes together with 46 Sioux lodges were camped at the headwater of the Smoky Hill River, waiting for a white man to meet them and discuss a peace settlement. Would Wynkoop be that man?

Wynkoop, suspicious that the Indians were setting a trap for him and his men, told One-Eye that he would meet the Cheyennes and Arapahoes but would keep him and his two companions hostage. One-Eye did not flinch. Instead he told the major that he would rather die if the Indians betrayed their word. Wynkoop, a disciple of Chivington, firmly believing that all Indians were treacherous, bloodthirsty, and devoid of personal feelings, had a completely unexpected reaction. Suddenly he felt that he was "in the presence of Superior beings."[10] That moment was an epiphany for Major Wynkoop.

Two days later he led a detachment of 130 men, with two howitzers, out of Fort Lyon, riding north and then east into Kansas. After five days, the column was met by several hundred warriors who appeared to be spoiling for a fight. Wynkoop deployed his men for battle. Then, wisely, he hesitated, swallowing his fear and rising distrust. He sent One-Eye to the Indian lines to tell them that the soldiers did not want a fight. One-Eye soon returned and told Wynkoop that Black Kettle indeed wanted to meet him but, seeing the cannons, did not trust the soldiers' aggressive intentions. Wynkoop withdrew his column several miles and made camp.

The next morning Black Kettle and several chiefs rode into the army camp accompanied by George Bent, one of William's sons, who acted as interpreter. Wynkoop asked if the letter asking for peace and a prisoner exchange was genuine. Most of the chiefs said yes. But some chiefs at the meeting, such as Bull Bear, brother of the murdered Lean Bear, doubted peace was possible because the whites were too treacherous. The Indians, he said, must go to war. One-Eye, although a subchief, rose to denounce Bull Bear's position, making an impassioned speech favoring peace. Thus the peace chiefs, led by Black Kettle, prevailed. Further avenues to peace would be explored.

Wynkoop told the chiefs he was not empowered to make peace. In a bold move, he brought the Cheyenne and Arapaho chiefs, including Black Kettle, to Denver to meet with Governor Evans. The governor was furious, telling Wynkoop that he wanted nothing to do with the Indians, and that such a meeting would only make him look foolish to federal authorities for having pressed so hard to raise the new volunteer regiment. Moreover, the Indians had not been punished for their depredations. Because the Colorado 3rd was organized to punish Indians, they would have to do some punishing.

Miraculously, despite formidable opposition, Wynkoop had his meeting. Evans, some of Denver's leading citizens, and several army officers, including Chivington and Shoup, met the chiefs at Fort Weld just outside Denver. Evans made it clear that a general Indian uprising would provoke severe military retaliation, driving from the territory those few who survived. Their only hope was to submit to military authority and, by giving information on hostile tribes and by scouting for the army, demonstrate their friendship. Evans went on to ask about hostile tribes, about the culprits of several raids, and where certain chiefs were to be found. The assembled chiefs answered as best they could.

Neither Evans nor Chivington explicitly offered peace at that meeting. Evans said he did not have the authority to do so (doubtlessly leaving the chiefs wondering who did), and that the Indians must place themselves under military protection at the various camps and forts designated in this proclamation. The chiefs left the meeting believing they had successfully communicated to Evans their desire for peace, and believed they were already under army protection.

What the Indians did not understand, could not understand, was the web of ambiguity that lay beneath all the words just spoken. As far as Evans was concerned, the Indians gathered at Fort Lyon had surrendered to military authority. Major Wynkoop also assumed they surrendered. Riding a fine point, Chivington considered the Indians at Fort Lyon still hostile because he did not personally accept their surrender.[11]

Wynkoop returned to Fort Lyon, believing the meeting had made progress toward peace. Several days later, 700 Arapahoes arrived at the fort in destitute condition. Wynkoop distributed government supplies and allowed them to trade freely within the fort. That was his downfall. On 5 November, Major Scott Anthony arrived from Fort Riley, Kansas, with orders from General Curtis to relieve Wynkoop as post commander. Curtis had received reports, some would say rumors, that the Indians moved freely within Fort Lyon, a clear violation of Curtis' order to keep them at arm's length. No one knows the exact origins of these reports/rumors, but the accusing finger is often pointed at Colonel Chivington. Curtis reiterated to Anthony his order to keep Indians away from the fort. That order contradicted Evans' proclamation, placing the Indians in an impossible situation: they could not gather at the forts under army protection if the commanding general ordered the army to keep them away. Wynkoop's departure removed from Colorado the one man of any stature in the territorial hierarchy who possessed a knowledgeable empathy for the Indians and who understood that the Indians' problem was really the white man.

THE SAND CREEK MASSACRE

Major Anthony, according to Duane Schultz in his *Month of the Freezing Moon*, was a master of duplicity. The day after taking command at Fort Lyon, he persuaded the Indians that they would be safe if they camped at the big bend of Sand Creek, about 40 miles northeast. He then wrote General Curtis that the Indians only pretended to want peace. Anthony was also impatient, unable to wait until guilty Indians were separated from the innocent. Begging for a fight, he again wrote Curtis that when reinforcements arrived, he intended to attack the Indians. The Sand Creek camp was a classic set-up created by Anthony. The Indians had to leave the fort by orders of General Curtis. Then, because the Indians were no longer at Fort Lyon, they had to be considered hostile, according to the governor's proclamation. No matter what happened next, Anthony was on the side of right because he operated within the bounds of official policy. That Wynkoop and Evans thought the Indians surrendered was irrelevant. George Grinnell concluded that Anthony selected the Sand Creek site because it placed the Indians within easy reach when he decided to attack.[12]

Sand Creek was dry in November except for some scattered pools. The creek was about 200 yards wide with banks varying in height to 10 feet. Seven hundred Indians occupied the camp—200 men and 500 women and children. Most were Cheyennes, but about 10 percent were Arapahoes. Black Kettle was in camp, and so too were Lone Bear and One-Eye. Prominent among the Arapaho leaders in camp were White Antelope and Left Hand.

On 13 November, Chivington ordered the 3rd Colorado to camp at Booneville on the Arkansas River. He joined them ten days later. Major Hal Sayr, who led seven companies from Bijou Basin to Booneville, observed that Chivington's assumption of command was not greeted enthusiastically. Three interconnected causes withered the hero's laurels. First, Chivington had not been in a battle since Glorieta Pass. That void, together with the 3rd Colorado's reputation as the "bloodless Third," hastened his fading popularity. Second, in 1862, five members of a robber band, the so-called Reynolds gang, were caught and sent by Chivington from Denver to Fort Lyon under an army escort of 100 men. The five robbers were shot, allegedly trying to escape. Their unburied remains were later found still bound by chains and with a bullet hole in each skull. Chivington bragged that he had ordered the guards to shoot them. Third, Colorado was seeking statehood, a hotly debated issue in the territory, and Chivington, still the hero to his intimates, was nominated for Congress. The bid for statehood failed, and Chivington, the Reynolds affair haunting him, went down to a resounding defeat. Thus the Cheyenne gathering at Sand Creek was not only an opportunity for action, a means to bloody the "bloodless Third," but the means by which to resurrect his reputation.

Chivington led the 3rd Colorado and a few companies of the 1st out of Booneville east along the Arkansas River. The first day they marched 12 miles, despite the terrible cold. The next day was warmer and they covered 28 miles, reaching Bent's Fort. Chivington ordered that no one leave the fort lest word of his march reach the Indians. In fact, the route along the Arkansas was so secure that when the column reached Fort Lyon on 28 November, the garrison was surprised.

Captain Silas Soule, who attended Wynkoop's Denver meeting with the chiefs, and who was now at Fort Lyon, was shocked that Chivington planned to attack the Indians at Sand Creek. Soule believed that the Indians surrendered, that they were sincerely interested in peace; he also knew firsthand that their actions even saved soldiers' lives when they had warned of a Sioux trap. Soule talked to Lieutenants Baldwin and Joseph Cramer, who agreed with Soule that Chivington needed to be stopped. Soule went to Major Anthony whom he believed wanted to protect the Indians because, on taking command of Fort Lyon, he promised to continue Wynkoop's practices. But Soule did not know that Anthony's statements and his actions were often different. Anthony now blatantly admitted to Soule that he wanted to attack the Indians, having written Curtis of his intentions, and was merely waiting for the right moment. Furthermore, he thought all hostile Indians ought to be killed. Lieutenant Cramer had the forthrightness to confront Chivington directly, telling him that as an officer under Wynkoop he was pledged to fulfill Wynkoop's agreements with the Indians; therefore, the proposed attack violated his personal honor. Chivington replied that it was right and honorable to kill Indians who massacred whites, and anybody who sympathized with the Indians, such as Soule, Wynkoop, and Cramer, should leave the army.[13]

Dismissing all further attempts to alter or cancel his plan, Chivington ordered his force to fall in on the evening of 28 November. He commanded 450 men of the 3rd Colorado under Colonel George Shoup, some 125 men of the 1st Colorado led by Lieutenant Luther Wilson, and 125 men under Major Anthony from the Fort Lyon garrison. They were supported by a battery of 12-pound howitzers. Robert Bent, one of William's sons, was conscripted as guide and interpreter.

The column marched through the night, the 1st Colorado showing much better route discipline than the 3rd. Mile after mile they rode across the plain without pause, fighting off sleep and numbed by the cold wind. Chivington wanted complete surprise. Speed was his ally. At dawn, 29 November, Chivington and Shoup galloped ahead, topping a rise from which they could see the Cheyenne camp, a circle of a hundred lodges on the north side of Sand Creek. To the west were several Arapaho lodges. Six hundred ponies grazed on the creek's south side. A smaller herd was behind a bluff a little farther south. Chivington dispatched a company of the 3rd Colorado to round up the latter herd, while Lieutenant Wilson and three companies of the 1st Colorado scattered the larger pony herd. Once the ponies were dispersed, Wilson dismounted his men and ordered them to fire into the village. Anthony's men followed behind and opened fire. Chivington then brought the 3rd Colorado to the creek bed, telling them to take off their coats so that they could fight better. "Take no prisoners," he shouted. "Remember the slaughtered white women and children. Remember the Hungates!"[14] The men opened fire.

As Robert Bent rode in with the army, his brother George, who was living with the Cheyenne, found himself under fire in the Indian village. Years later, he gave George Grinnell his account of what happened when the attack developed.[15] When the troops opened fire and as the first howitzer shells exploded in the village, Black Kettle rushed out of his lodge and attached an American flag to a pole as a display of friendship. To no avail, he called out to his people that there was no reason to be frightened because the camp was under army protection. The Indians were bewildered; it was the army firing at them. Some warriors ran after the pony herd, George Bent among them. Intense fire drove him back into the village where he joined the main body of Indians running along the curve of the creek bed. Bodies were everywhere, some wounded, most dead. The Indians stopped running at a point on the west side of the curve. Desperately they dug pits in which to hide or fight, according to Bent. Chivington later rationalized his attack by testifying that the Indians had dug the pits in expectation of battle.

Silas Soule, following his conscience rather than Chivington, did not allow his men to open fire but kept them riding along the creek's south bank from which they observed men of the 3rd Colorado attacking the sand pits. The Indians tried to fight back with guns and knives, but their efforts were overwhelmed by the eager troops who first killed the warriors, then the women and children. Many were scalped and their bodies mutilated. Fingers and ears were commonly lopped off to get at silver jewelry.

Soldiers in the village battled their way through the maze of tepees. They shot One-Eye, Bear Man, and a half dozen other Cheyenne chiefs. White Antelope, wearing the medal given him by President Lincoln, ran toward the soldiers shouting at them to stop. He was met by a fusillade of musketry, bullets kicking up dust at his feet and whistling about his head. He suddenly stopped in the middle of the creek bed and folded his arms. Bullets smashed into him. Soldiers raced to his body, scalped him, cut off his nose, and ears and, it was alleged, cut off his testicles to use the scrotum as a tobacco pouch. Some officers were as bestial as their men. Sergeant Lucien Palmer, 1st Colorado, later testified that he saw Major Sayr scalp an Indian for a silver hair ornament. Lieutenant Harry Richmond, 3rd Colorado, shot three women and five children, then calmly scalped them.

Even though the fighting slackened by mid-afternoon, the killing did not stop. Some live infants found beside their dead mothers were killed by slitting their throats or smashing their skulls. And Jack Smith, half-Indian son of the trapper John Smith, was taken as a prisoner, placed in a tent, and then shot. Although various officers approached Chivington, asking to release Smith, he considered him an Indian. His order stood: no prisoners.

That night Chivington penned a report to Major General Curtis, describing the attack, stating that there were 130 tepees and 900 to 1,000 warriors in the camp. He claimed between 400 and 500 were killed. His men actually killed around 125 Indians, two-thirds of whom were women and children. Chivington also wrote to his friend William Byers of the *Rocky Mountain News*. Predictably, on 17 December, the paper editorialized that "Among the brilliant feats of arms in Indian warfare, the recent campaign of our Colorado volunteers will stand in history with few rivals. . . . Colorado soldiers have again covered themselves with glory."

On 10 January 1865, the U.S. House of Representatives approved a resolution to investigate the massacre. Chivington, back in Denver after the fight, said that a white man's scalp, no more than three days old, was found in the village, proving that the Indians were hostile. Yet, in a sworn deposition taken later in Denver for the congressional committee, Chivington said he found 19 scalps. He also stated there were 700 warriors in the camp. The committee condemned Chivington in the strongest terms. They found "he deliberately planned and executed a foul and dastardly massacre which would have disgraced the veriest savage among those who were the victims of his cruelty."[16] The committee found that Evans gave shuffling testimony filled with misleading statements to obscure his complicity, and also found that Major Anthony's conduct demonstrated the attack was both unprovoked and unwarranted. Yet Chivington was not held accountable. His commission officially expired 23 September 1864, fully two months prior to the massacre, even though he continued in command into early January 1865 by some bureaucratic fluke. The congressional committees considered him beyond the reach of military law. Furthermore, the committees took no notice of the army's chain-of-command failures and ignored the government's complicity related to its failed Indian policies.

Even though saved from complete disgrace, or worse, Chivington was nevertheless on a steep slide into obscurity. Yet many citizens felt that any criticism of him or of the 3rd Colorado was treachery. With the moral certainty that often mantles the violent among us, self-appointed avengers "took care" of those whom they believed betrayed Chivington and the "bloody Third." Captain Soule, for example, whose testimony fixed responsibility for the massacre on Chivington, was murdered. Then the army officer who arrested the murderer was in turn killed.

Sioux and Cheyennes, enraged by the Sand Creek massacre, together raided Julesberg in northeast Colorado, and turned the banks of the South Platte River into a wasteland. Black Kettle, however, never gave up his quest for peace. He was involved in the vacuous treaties of the Little Arkansas in 1865 and of Medicine Lodge in 1867. He was killed during the battle at Washita Creek, 27 November 1868, by the 7th U.S. Cavalry, George Armstrong Custer commanding.

THE ARMY AS LYNCH MOB

The events at Sand Creek, once isolated from the emotional tangle imposed by wanton butchery, reveal a significant sequence. First, Major Anthony brought his men of the 1st Colorado to the creek bank. They opened fire on the village. Second, Chivington led the 3rd Colorado to a position just behind Anthony's formation, ordered them to shed their overcoats, and open fire. But they had to shoot through Anthony's line. To avoid the danger coming from behind Anthony's men fled into the creek bed. Third, the 3rd Colorado moved forward, some men going along the creek bed and others crossing into the village. Fourth, all order was lost among the troops as they fired wildly at the Indians and even at each other. Nowhere is there clear indication that Chivington tried to direct, much less control, his force beyond the initial deployment. With only a few exceptions, company officers, most certainly in the 3rd Colorado, did not control their men. Silas Soule testified that, from his vantage point back across the creek, he could not observe any order to the fighting. Fifth, many of the men and some of the officers fell to scalping and otherwise mutilating the Indian dead. As Schultz noted in his book *Month of the Freezing Moon*, Chivington's men turned into an unrestrained barbarous mob.[17]

Unfortunately Schultz does nothing to elaborate his important insight that the 3rd became a mob. His picture invites the interpretation that the soldiers were temporarily deranged by events, as it were an infectious madness, that reduced them to the lowest forms of behavior. Such phrases as "the madness of the mob" or "mob frenzy" are familiar descriptions of such behavior. Never accurate, they are distractions that lead away from the realities of the situation and, for those interested in doing so, provide thinly veiled excuses for inexcusable conduct. The answers to why the 3rd Colorado in particular became a mob are found within the unit and in social conditions and existed prior to the massacre.

The men who enlisted in the 3rd Colorado Volunteers avoided military service for most of the Civil War. Only the threat of conscription and service on the main battlefronts drove many to enlist. That their service would last only a hundred days was a bonus. The men and many of the officers were already hard, rude, crude, and violence-prone when they entered the service. Their military training was nil—not only was there little time to train them, but the men openly resisted or ignored the training that was attempted. The troops were literally given uniforms, guns, and horses and told to be soldiers. Born an undisciplined unit, the 3rd Colorado remained undisciplined.

The men carried into their military service their civilian hopes and fears. The Colorado Territory was a breeding ground for discontent among the white settlers. They moved in with the gold rush which, for most, was either a fantasy or led to brutally hard work in the mines at low wages and at high risk. Ranchers and farmers were marginally better situated. But they all shared, regardless of economic status, the common experience of invading the land of native Americans about whom they knew nothing. For most whites, the Indians were an impediment to progress and to the fulfillment of their personal dreams. How much easier to blame the Indians than themselves if anything went wrong on the road to wish-fulfillment. The situation was exacerbated when some Indians resisted the invasion, engendering fear among the whites.

The discontent that arose from the fear, much like the examples of military mutiny and riotous behavior already discussed, produced desperation—a widespread collective attitude that not much was being done to resolve the Indian problem and, with the Civil War raging, that not much could be done to ensure public safety. The threat of a general Indian uprising seemed very real when, in May 1864, depredations escalated and Denver seemed besieged. The incendiary public display of the slaughtered Hungate family fueled the desperation.

The vitriolic messages of Chivington, Byers, and Evans, sowing more hate and suspicion, further shaped the settlers' attitudes and beliefs. Never mind that some Indians were more guilty than others. Never mind that the Indian culture was shredded by the white emigration. Never mind that whole villages were living near extinction, reduced to dependency on the white man's government. It was easier to agree with Chivington: kill the Indians; kill them all.

Any hope that the settlers could solve the Indian problem by legitimate means lay buried under the widespread inability or unwillingness to recognize that their emigration, their own invasion, initiated the Indian problem. They sought escape from their rising feelings of desperation by attacking the Indians, who were equal captives of the intolerable situation.[18]

The inability to solve the problem by legitimate means, resorting instead of violence that reached barbarous proportions, was an expression of normlessness. Unlike the previous examples of alienation, the normlessness felt by the soldiers doubtlessly existed prior to their enlistment and was legitimized by their role in the army. The men felt empowered, rather than powerless. Thus, rather than feeling morally isolated, sharing beliefs that the rest of the society did not, the men of the volunteer regiments found in Chivington, the principal representation of military authority and Christian certitude, confirmation of their own invented and errant morality.

The capacity of the 3rd Colorado's men to use the army spuriously to reshape their alienation into what they believed were normative behaviors was a failure of their leadership. However culpable his masters, Chivington was directly responsible for the massacre at Sand Creek. Hardly the charismatic leader, he bullied any opposition into submission. He led his men to the creekside, ordering them to kill the Indians. Then he stepped back. Not unlike the leader of a lynch mob who cynically directs events leading to the hanging, Chivington would not be the executioner. He summoned participants to the self-declared righteousness of the action, demonized the alleged transgressors, brushed aside legalities in favor of expediency, and held those with higher military authority in contempt for their alleged indifference to those offended. Standing aloof from the slaughter, imperious, and without blemish, he gave orders but did not swing his sword.

Consequently the functional leadership during the attack was fortuitous and even anonymous. As in other situations of disintegration, seemingly disconnected voices in the crowd pulled the men in various directions, with the actions of one group building on those of another, creating the conditions for an amplified, intensified behavior that burst forth in the barbarisms committed against the Indians.

8

The My Lai Massacre, Vietnam, 1968

On 16 March 1968, C Company, 1/20 Infantry Regiment, 11th Infantry Brigade, Americal Division, entered the hamlet of My Lai 4 on a search-and-destroy mission against Viet Cong guerrillas. They massacred more than 400 noncombatant men, women, and children.

THE VIETNAM WAR: THE ENVIRONMENT OF AMBIGUITY AND FEAR

The French returned to Indochina after World War II, expecting to pick up the pieces of their humpty-dumpty southeast Asian empire. Many Vietnamese objected because the French treated them brutally before the war, and their country was handed to the Japanese by the collaborative French Vichy government during the war. Many Vietnamese, wanting freedom from colonial rule, followed the path to independence offered by Ho Chi Minh. In May 1945, Ho organized a separate government and in September declared Vietnam a sovereign state. The French seemed willing to bargain. However, they soon declared South Vietnam a French Republic and, in December 1946, attacked Haiphong, killing 6,000 Vietnamese, starting a war that lasted eight years.

The French believed they could annihilate Ho's peasant army by using massive firepower, much of it financed and directly supplied by the United States. The Americans and Ho Chi Minh experienced good relations during

World War II, but, fearful of upsetting the easily bruised French, President Harry Truman's government determined that France should return to Indochina. By 1953, with Ho's Viet Minh Army much harder to defeat than anticipated, and with public opinion turning against the war, many in the French government and military thought Vietnam a lost cause. The troops fighting in the jungles felt deserted, even betrayed, believing that if the Viet Minh were brought to a major battle, French arms might yet succeed. The opportunity seemed to present itself at Dien Bien Phu. The French fortified the area, hoping to draw out the Viet Minh. The Viet Minh did respond, besieging the position and handing the French a humiliating defeat that forced a peace treaty. As a result, Vietnam was divided north and south. The south declared a republic and the north, under Ho, went communist.

By 1957, South Vietnamese communist guerrillas, the Viet Cong, started a revolution that escalated into a civil war. Terrorism, torture, outright murder, and assassinations were methods used by both sides. The United States took the position that if South Vietnam fell to Ho's forces, then the gates of southeast Asia and the western Pacific would be opened to communist expansion.

President Dwight Eisenhower sent military advisers to South Vietnam to train their army. In 1961 President John Kennedy increased the number of advisers, and soon American-supplied planes were being flown on combat missions by American pilots. But neither the Viet Cong nor the North Vietnamese Army would stand and fight. They used the same guerrilla tactics that so confounded the French, rendering the South's increasing firepower irrelevant. Thus, by 1964, reeling from a guerrilla war they could not win, wallowing in their own ineptitude and corruption, the South Vietnamese government neared collapse.

In May 1965, President Lyndon Johnson sent the first American combat troops to Vietnam. Given the lack of a definite front line, the American military concluded that winning ground meant nothing. The alternative was a war of annihilation. The U.S. Army and Marine Corps embarked on search-and-destroy missions to kill Viet Cong guerrillas and North Vietnamese soldiers, disrupt their supply sources and village havens, and root out their infamous tunnel systems that held everything from arsenals and supplies to aid stations and barracks. Officially, burning villages and killing livestock were the purview of the South Vietnamese Army.

The effectiveness of the missions was measured by body counts. The soldiers doing the fighting determined and reported how many they killed. The totals were tabulated each week and reverentially delivered to the news services for distribution to the American public. As the war dragged on, the body counts became a contentious issue. Lieutenant General William Peers wrote in his official army report of the My Lai massacre—the so-called Peers Report—that "the news media blew up the daily 'body count' out of all proportion and made it sound as though killing VC and members of the North Vietnamese Army was a bad thing."[1] This comment had merit only within the Army's ideological cocoon. The U.S. Army's Rules of Engagement defined who was and who was not to be considered an enemy combatant. Troops received instruction about the Geneva Convention, and the army issued more than 14 directives within Vietnam regarding the treatment of noncombatants and prisoners. Even though avoiding civilian casualties was officially emphasized, the war's realities obviated attempts to implement limitations on those casualties.

Among the most decisive factor working against attempts to limit civilian casualties was the impact of firepower. When an area was declared a Viet Cong sanctuary, be it a stretch of jungle or a village, it was declared a free fire zone upon which unlimited firepower could be unleashed. And that could be massive. If near the coast, U.S. Navy destroyers came inshore and bombarded the area with their 5-inch guns. Army artillery blasted the area with high explosive, shrapnel, and phosphorus shells. Helicopter gunships fired rockets and strafed the ground with 7.62mm machine guns and 30mm cannons. Fighter bombers swooped in to drop their bombs, loose their rockets, and burn the area with napalm. All of that lethality was both concentrated in relation to the actual target size and indiscriminate. A 155mm howitzer shell, a 500-pound bomb, or napalm did not distinguish between aggressors and noncombatants. Everyone died under the onslaught. Thus, as lethality increased proportionally to American combat involvement, so too did the annual number of civilian casualties. In 1965, an estimated 100,000 South Vietnamese were killed and wounded by American military action. By 1968, the number grew to 300,000.[2]

Another factor that increased the number of noncombatant casualties was faulty U.S. intelligence. The distinction between so-called friendlies and the Viet Cong (VC) was not easily made and in many instances, not even attempted within free fire zones. Of course, the VC took full advantage of their ability to fade into the general population. Consequently the slightest suggestion that a village was a VC base or sanctuary could bring down the full power of American forces. Vietnamese informants were frequently inaccurate, and they sometimes paid back old enmities by making false accusations. The U.S. Central Intelligence Agency (CIA) unwittingly fostered such personal agendas when it formed and supported the Phoenix Program to identify Viet Cong, make lists of suspects, and carry out assassinations and torture. Although military intelligence took a jaundiced view of the program, the CIA continued to promote its value.

Distinguishing good guys from bad guys continued to plague American soldiers. The incessant drain of killed and wounded men left the U.S. troops with the conclusion that any Vietnamese—an old man, a mother, a child—was capable of throwing a grenade, laying a mine on a trail, boobytrapping a house, or taking a shot at a soldier. The soldiers took the next step toward dehumanization of the enemy; it was not difficult.[3] If "they" were responsible for killing a friend, or shredding his arms and legs, if the next casualty might be you, then how easy to hate this undefinable enemy. Combat veterans, during training, told recruits about the Vietnamese: they all looked alike; none were to be trusted; they were not people like us; they were gooks, slants, slope heads, dinks, easy epithets for 18- and 19-year-old American soldiers to learn.

These generalizations need significant qualification. Not all American combat troops equally shared a suspicion and hatred of the Vietnamese. The evidence offered by Philip Caputo in *A Rumor of War* illustrates the two sides of the issue. His Marine company engaged the Viet Cong around the village of Giao-Tri 3, but the enemy, after a short firefight, disappeared into the jungle. The Marine company's 3rd platoon charged down a hill into the village, firing wildly, throwing grenades, killing livestock, and setting huts afire. The panic-stricken villagers ran from the inferno. The company and platoon commanders tried to stop the destruction, but it was too late. Nothing was left. Yet the Marines did not kill or wound any of the villagers. That incident took place in the spring of 1965. By October, attitudes within Caputo's company changed. Four Marines were found in a common grave, their hands and feet tied, and each had been shot through the head. Another Marine was captured by the VC, bound, beaten with clubs, and then shot. A patrol was ambushed, and the wounded were systematically shot by the VC. Caputo says the Marines exacted their revenge in full. Reminiscent of the comment by the Marine sergeant on Guadalcanal, some companies did not take any prisoners or, if they did, routinely shot them when they allegedly tried to escape. "Take no prisoners," the World War II Marine sergeant had said; "kill them, kill them all." The atmosphere of hate and fear was not much different in Vietnam. The growing disinterest in differentiating combatants from noncombatants was reflected in the oft-heard statement, "If he's dead and Vietnamese, he's VC."[4] That was the rule for body counts.

The rule was created by the men in the field, a certain response to common pressures to be aggressive and have meaningful body counts, the only real measure of success given them. Thus, dissembling or not, the

American high command in Vietnam provided their men the necessary avenue by which to violate the overtly displayed Rules of Engagement.

That this ambiguous environment could exist at all was a direct result of leaving to the common soldier the task of distinguishing between VC and friendlies.[5] True, the army informed General Peers during his My Lai investigation that combat soldiers were issued little pocket-sized cards describing how to treat noncombatants, and that men going into combat attended meetings before each operation to remind them about the Rules of Engagement. The cards, according to the research of Bilson and Sim in *Four Hours in My Lai*, were usually pocketed and forgotten and the meetings canceled amid combat preparations. There were more important things to do.

Cold stares and the appearance of hostility toward their presence often greeted the young American troops when they entered a Vietnamese village. Whether the particular unit earned it or not, a stereotype often preceded them of Americans routinely burning villages, raping women, and shooting whom they pleased. Seeing the hostility of the Vietnamese civilians, the soldiers wondered how they could know for certain who was friendly and who was not.

There was little experience upon which the soldiers could rely. The tour of duty in Vietnam was 12 months. Those who survived the first six months usually finished the tour in one piece, and were sent home for discharge. New men were cycled into the units to replace the veterans. This constant turnover affected not only enlisted personnel but also officers and noncommissioned officers. No wonder then that the common soldiers whose judgment would decide friendly and unfriendly could not find consistent guideposts to right conduct. Given enough provocation, they slipped from behind civilization's veneer. The result was the massacre at My Lai 4.

Robert McNamara, President Johnson's defense secretary, confirmed the indiscriminate character of much of the killing when, in late 1966, he wrote Johnson that the Viet Cong and North Vietnamese Army, based on the number of weapons counted after an engagement compared to the body counts, lost only one-sixth as many weapons as men. That suggested to McNamara that the remaining dead were porters used by the combat troops or were innocent bystanders. Major David Gavin, a U.S. military adviser in Vietnam, explained to General Peers during his inquiry that the discrepancy between the weapons count and the body count resulted from the efficient battlefield weapons retrieval system developed by the Viet Cong. But U.S. troops, based on Caputo's combat experiences as a Marine officer, often had great difficulty finding dead Viet Cong to add to their body counts. Surely the Viet Cong, even granting their combat prowess, when seeking to disengage after a firefight and slip back into the jungle, would find the task of locating their dead equally difficult. That leaves McNamara's bystanders not, as it were, gatherings of curious people standing about watching the battles, but the populations of villages who were defined as the enemy and consequently cut down by powerful weapons in the hands of young and inexperienced soldiers.

In 1968, an infantry unit designated Charley Company was thrust into the maelstrom of the Vietnam War. Superficially they were much like a dozen other Charley Companies in a dozen other battalions in a dozen other regiments. But what happened to this Charley Company and what they did, although not entirely uncommon in an uncommon war, nevertheless mortified a nation, at least for a while.

THE BAD BOYS OF CHARLEY COMPANY

Charley Company was part of the 23rd or Americal Division activated in October 1967,[6] a paperwork unit of widely scattered brigades. Of the division's three brigades, the 196th was already in Vietnam, the 198th was training in Texas, and the 11th was training in Hawaii. The 11th, reactivated in 1966, was reorganized the next year as light infantry to conform with the other two brigades. The number of infantry was increased, and the number of allotted vehicles and the amount of heavy equipment was decreased. The functional alterations complicated the brigade's training program as different missions were imposed. Further complications arose because of a large personnel turnover. Under then existing deployment regulations, fully 1,300 men were ineligible for Vietnam service. Replacements arrived, but at different times and in inadequate numbers. The brigade's training cycle was shortened from eight weeks to four, but some compensatory training was conducted once in Vietnam. They were moved to Duc Pho in southern Quang Ngai Province where a South Vietnamese division taught the newcomers scouting techniques and methods of securing and clearing a village. That lesson lasted one day.

One of the subunits run through 11th Brigade training was Charley Company (C Company), 1st Battalion, 20th Infantry Regiment. Before March 1968, the unit's authorized strength was six officers and 175 men. Actual fighting strength in Vietnam was 120 officers and men organized into a headquarters platoon, a heavy weapons platoon, and three rifle platoons.

Michael Bilson and Kevin Sim, in *Four Days in My Lai*, concluded that Charley Company was an average infantry unit, displaying both plus and minus elements. More than three-quarters of the noncommissioned officers were high school graduates, and several had additional college credits, a statistically higher ratio than usually found in the army. Seventy percent of the enlisted men were high school graduates. Most were between ages 18 and 22. Half were African Americans. Forty percent of the men had enlisted; the remainder were drafted. Even though, as the Peers Report notes, the men registered high aptitudes for infantry training, those drafted were less educated and considered less trainable than the army norm. None of the company's personnel, including officers, had any significant combat experience.

Captain Edward Medina—at age 30 the company's old man—commanded Charley Company, an assignment given him in December 1966. The son of a Mexican-American farm worker, he was reared by his grandparents in Colorado. He enlisted in the army and quickly became a noncommissioned officer. Selected for Officer Candidate School, he graduated fourth in a class of 200. He had been in the army 10 years when he met the recruits who comprised his company at Schofield Barracks, Hawaii. They were, like many raw rifle companies, a diverse lot fresh from basic training. That promised little because, as one Vietnam veteran told me, much of the equipment used in basic training was left over from World War II and Korea, and many of the same pointless tasks, what Paul Fussell called "chicken-shit," still shaped the routine.

Medina's job was to make his company into a fighting unit, and, by all indications, he did an excellent job. The Peers Report comments that both his men and his superiors considered him an outstanding officer. Even though he could be abusive and was considered tough and authoritarian, he was also thought to be fair and interested in his men's welfare. Charley Company, on completing training in Hawaii, was rated the best in the battalion. Indeed, Medina welded the men into a unit that was efficient and proud of its achievement.

Doubtless, Medina's impoverished childhood and his tenure as an enlisted man and noncommissioned officer allowed him to build bridges between himself and his men that other company commanders might envy. But what was considered a strength in the balmy clime of Hawaii became a failing in combat. Medina alone controlled the company, the Peers Report concluding that he "exerted an extraordinary degree of influence over [his men]."[7]

Medina's platoon leaders, as the Peers Report notes, were not considered outstanding leaders. The company may have had bad luck in getting weak lieutenants. More likely, their lack of leadership was a reflection of Medina's influence and his unwillingness, if not inability, to let his subalterns develop as leaders, an essential function of a company commander. He preferred to place himself in a completely dominant position. That the platoon leaders did not have combat experience was hardly their fault. They were, but for one of their number, thought to be "nice guys" by the enlisted men. Unfortunately the officers crossed the invisible barrier between the ranks and tried to be buddies to their men. The Peers Report, based on the testimony of the platoon leaders themselves, points out that the situation within Charley Company deteriorated when they entered combat and discovered how little control they actually exercised over their men. Authority was centered on Medina. The lieutenants were actually fearful of their men and were hesitant to exert any leadership lest they become disliked and targets of Medina's wrath. The Peers Report comments that Medina was often condescending, probably because he was older than the lieutenants, had been in the army 10 years, and worked his way up through the ranks. I think there was a well-earned self-satisfaction in the man; unfortunately he turned smug, as if brandishing a preening proletarian moral superiority over his subordinates.

Certainly Captain Medina harbored no affection for 2nd Lieutenant William Calley, Jr., leader of the 1st Platoon. According to Bilton and Sim, Medina regularly belittled Calley in front of his men, constantly referring to him as "shithead." Although Calley tried to appease Medina, he was rebuffed. Medina's attitude toward Calley rubbed off on the enlisted men, many of whom thought Calley incompetent. He did not know as much as he pretended, and when he made a mistake he would not admit it. Others thought he was a glory seeker who would willingly sacrifice his men to advance his own interests. Still others saw Calley as a small man, both physically and psychologically, who did not understand his leadership role and shouted a lot as compensation for his shortcomings. Bilton and Sim concluded that the men had no respect for him and that their opinions regarding him were "universally hostile."[8]

Whatever problems lurked in Charley Company stayed just beneath the surface when, during the second week of December 1967, they were flown to Vietnam via Continental Airlines and, with the rest of the brigade, deployed to Quang Ngai province.

QUANG NGAI PROVINCE: THE VIET CONG
AND U.S. FORCES

A travel book could be written about Quang Ngai province (Map 12). Its northern border is 50 miles south of Da Nang and the southern border is a crow's 300 miles north of Saigon. The province is bordered on the east by the warm waters of the South China Sea that lap white sand beaches lined with palm trees. Rivers flow to the sea, establishing broad, rich deltas. The elevation gradually increases inland, forming a kind of piedmont region. Fifty to 60 miles farther inland are the jagged peaks of the Annamite Cordillera, a long mountain chain that separates much of Vietnam from Cambodia. The city of Quang Ngai is the provincial capital. In the 1960s it was a dusty gathering of shacks, lean-tos, and shops straddling the major north-south highway. In fact, the so-called city was a small town of about 14,000 inhabitants, overflowing with "the flotsam of the international war effort."[9] Duc Pho far to the south was the only other town of consequence in the province. Most of the province's population lived along the coastal belt in villages and hamlets organized around rice farming.

The province was notable as a center of rebellious activity. During the 1870s and 1880s, the people strongly opposed French occupation and, in the early 1900s, participated in anti-French, anti-tax movements, and sheltered various Vietnamese nationalist leaders. During World War II the communist Viet Minh—the League for the Independence of Vietnam—was established, recognizing guerrilla warfare as an integral strategy for revolutionary independence. After the war, the Indochina Communist Party energetically organized the Vietnamese people. For example, they sponsored national welfare associations which, in Quang Ngai province, recruited more than 100,000 people. When the French returned to Vietnam, they failed to dominate Quang Ngai. Duc Pho was even a major rest area for the Viet Minh Army during the ensuing war. At the end of the war, and with partition, many Viet Minh soldiers sought sanctuary in the north. By 1959, however, an estimated 90,000 Viet Minh filtered south again, rekindling old communist ties, organizing villages, and laying the foundations of the Viet Cong. Quang Ngai province emerged as a VC stronghold, controlling about fifty villages and creating an area independent of Saigon control. In that area, the VC recruited and trained troops, built defenses, and established medical and educational programs in the villages.

According to the Peers Report, total Viet Cong and North Vietnamese Army strength in Quang Ngai varied between 10,000 and 20,000 for the years 1964 to 1968. In early 1968, strength was estimated to be between

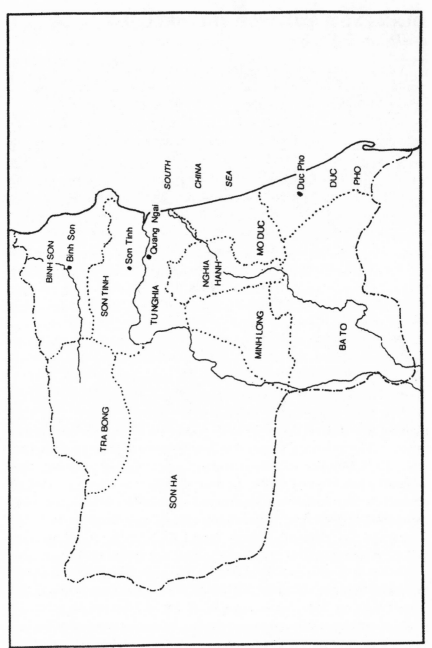

Map 12
Quang Ngai Province

10,000 and 14,000, two-thirds of whom were combatants. VC units were usually small, numbering from five to ten to thirty. They were called local-force units because they lived in the hamlets and villages around which they fought. The VC also mustered units up to battalion strength, between 500 and 1,000 soldiers. In 1968, four battalions and 11 companies were responsible for guerrilla activity against areas controlled by the Army of the Republic of Vietnam (ARVN) and the Americans.

Quang Ngai province was politically divided into 11 districts. Immediately north of Quang Ngai city is the district of Son Tinh. This was homeground to the VC's 48th Local Force Battalion. Formed in 1965, the unit's strength varied from 500 men at its activation down to 200 to 250 by March 1968. In 1965, the 48th was repeatedly attacked by U.S. Marines, yet managed to keep fighting. The infamous Tet Offensive of 31 January 1968 began when the 48th was joined with another battalion to form the 328th VC Regiment, and let loose a barrage of rocket and mortar fire against Quang Ngai city. Even though the VC attack was repulsed, American and ARVN troops failed to overtake the elusive 48th and destroy their operational base. One reason for the failure suggested in the Peers Report was that the 48th's soldiers were thought to live in Son Tinh villages and hamlets, working as farmers by day and engaging in guerrilla activities at night. Who, then, among the civilian population were VC and who were not?

In 1965, the military situation in Quang Ngai province grew critical as the Viet Cong continuously mobilized strength and support. The U.S. Marines who arrived that year were positioned in the province's south region. A Korean marine brigade was already stationed in the north, and the 2nd ARVN Division held the central province. Quang Ngai was also declared a free fire zone. Over the next two years, as Jonathan Schell, a reporter for *New Yorker* magazine learned from South Vietnamese civilian authorities, 70 percent of the province's villages were destroyed by South Vietnamese and American military actions. For example, during one surveillance flight from Duc Pho to Quang Ngai city, Schell's helicopter flew over a belt of rice fields near the coast and a stretch of villages some 13 miles long between the fields and the sea. "The houses along this strip," Schell observed, "have been destroyed almost without exception,"[10] the result of artillery bombardment, air strikes, and incessant search-and-destroy missions by ground forces. Between 20,000 and 30,000 Vietnamese civilians were displaced. No one knows how many were actually killed or wounded.

The Rules of Engagement of the 3rd Marine Amphibious Force participating in these missions required that a psychological warfare unit warn targeted villages that they were about to be bombarded. Leaflets were widely used until it became apparent that they had little effect because most of the villagers were illiterate. Next loudspeakers attached to planes and helicopters were used. The Marines told the villages forthrightly that they would not hesitate destroying any village that was a VC stronghold, harbored VC, or from which a hostile shot was fired. Often, in the last instance, no warning was given at all. Contrary to American expectations, the villagers proved resilient and stubborn, returning to their burned-out homes and rice fields. The next Marine warning read in the past tense: the village has been bombed as punishment, so do not show further sympathy of any kind to the VC. The final warning was future tense: the village will be bombed again. The Marines and, later, army enlisted men, were allowed to believe that any civilians still in such ravaged villages must be VC.

The first U.S. Army units entering Quang Ngai province in 1967 operated from the 4th Infantry Division as Task Force Oregon. With more and larger artillery pieces, with helicopter gunships, the task force could deliver much greater firepower than the Marines. In Operation Benton, Task Force Oregon destroyed the houses of 17,000 Vietnamese. The body count was 400 VC. The operation was considered a success.

In 1967, the 11th Brigade arrived in Quang Ngai province, establishing an initial position along Quang Ngai's south coast, replacing the Marine units that were deployed elsewhere. The 2nd ARVN Division remained responsible for the central coast. When the Korean brigade, responsible for the north coast, was redeployed, the job of filling the vacuum was given the 11th Brigade.

Brigadier General Andrew Lipscomb, the 11th's commander, formed a task force to replace the Koreans and to hunt the VC. Task Force Barker, named after its leader, Lieutenant Colonel Frank Barker, numbered 500 men. The unit included a battery of four 105mm howitzers, a platoon from the 1st Cavalry Division, an engineer platoon, a military police squad, and three rifle companies. Charley Company was attached to the task force on 26 January 1968. The force was positioned in two fire bases named Landing Zone Dottie and Landing Zone Uptight that provided facilities for helicopter troop transports and artillery fire in support of infantry operations.

During the Tet offensive, Charley Company moved from Dottie to a position a few miles south, their mission to block the expected Viet Cong retreat. Even though the VC 48th Local Force Battalion made significant gains in Quang Ngai city, enveloping a South Vietnamese training center near town, an armored counterattack forced their withdrawal north toward the coast. Charley Company, from a hillside position, watched the battalion disappear northward, unable to do anything because they were in an ARVN zone and needed South Vietnamese permission to open fire. Communications stalled. As Bilton and Sim concluded in *Four Hours in My Lai*, Charley Company would never again have the VC 48th so conveniently in their sights.

THE MY LAI MASSACRE

Charley Company was ordered to chase down VC in northern Quang Ngai province. For two weeks they mucked through rice paddies and rooted through villages whose inhabitants gave them mixed greetings: sometimes ignoring them—often from shyness; greeting them with smiles as their curious children clustered around the men; sometimes staring at the Americans with hostile eyes. The patrols, boring and arduous, sucked strength and determination from the men. The heat and humidity were crushing. Morale dropped. Michael Bernhardt was an enlisted man in Charley Company. A graduate of a Long Island Catholic military school, he first trained as a paratrooper, and he understood the meaning of discipline. He harbored many doubts about Charley Company's combat fitness, but these were subordinated to the feelings he shared with his comrades that the fruitless patrols were wearing them out. The men believed that no one cared about them and that they were physically isolated. "We were abused," Bernhardt said. "[The army] wore us down to nothing."[11] March, march, march. One stinking, pointless patrol after another through an alien world that to many in Charley Company seemed primitive, a world a million miles from home. As one veteran who fought in the Mekong Delta told me, a single question beat in his head, as if keeping time to his throbbing, heat-induced headaches: "How do I get out of this chickenshit country?"

The Viet Cong, much like a tiger turning to hunt its hunters, found Charley Company's 1st Platoon on 12 February. Lieutenant Calley made his first mistake of the day by leading his men to an area along the Diem Diem River exposed to VC fire. He anxiously called for help. Quickly the guns at Landing Zone Uptight responded, giving the platoon the opportunity to withdraw. Then Calley made his second mistake. Instead of leading his men away from the river, he became disoriented and led them back into another exposed position, enabling VC snipers to open fire. The platoon's doubts about his leadership abilities were confirmed.

13 February. Task Force Barker was ordered to clear Viet Cong from Son My, a collection of hamlets in eastern Quang Ngai. A half dozen of these hamlets were named My Lai and numbered 1 to 6 by the Viet Minh. The

complex, part of the Son Tinh district, was bordered by the South China Sea to the east, mountains to the west, the Diem Diem River on the north, and the Tra Khue River on the south.

The attack by Task Force Barker did not go well. As Charley Company moved into a blocking position, Bravo Company advanced toward My Lai 1. Viet Cong fire from My Lai 4 forced them back. The next day, Alpha Company attacked but could not penetrate the VC defenses. On the fifteenth, attacking together, the companies entered the village, wary of mines and boobytraps. The VC were gone.

25 February. Charley Company walked into a minefield. They were moving into a blocking position, this time south of Loc Son. The march was not easy. Bamboo stands, thick undergrowth, and a steady drizzle fatigued the men. About 7:30 A.M., an explosion and a piercing scream rent the thick air. Captain Medina yelled, "Freeze!" Fear stripped reason. Men broke down, screaming and crying. Others continued to move about, trying to escape the certainty of death only to embrace it. Six men lay dead, one ripped from the crotch to the sternum. A dozen more were wounded. Medina ordered the area swept for mines, marked them, and delineated an exit path. He personally helped rescue some of the wounded, nearly getting killed in the process. But Medina pulled his company through the crisis, his exemplary conduct earning him the Silver Star. Charley Company concluded that the VC laid the minefield, the sneaky bastards. They kept to the jungle, hidden from view, and refused a stand-up fight. Michael Bernhardt remembered that the mines were in an area previously occupied by Korean marines who were notoriously lax in mapping and reporting mine locations.[12] No one in the company wanted to hear that explanation. They invented their own truth. The next step was to invent their own amorality.

The endless search for the Viet Cong continued into the second week of March as mines, boobytraps, and snipers took their toll. The VC remained a shadow. What did change was the company. As the odds against getting home in one piece diminished, as the men felt more and more isolated, as fear and mistrust of the Vietnamese gripped them, their violence toward the civilian population increased. Captain Medina set the tone. He bullied, beat, and terrorized civilians brought in for questioning, and often laughed at the tortured antics of his victims. Calley followed his leader, leaving the impression among his men that if they did something wrong, something beyond the Rules of Engagement, it was fine with him. For example, an old man, obviously a farmer, was brought in for interrogation. Calley was convinced he was Viet Cong, even though the company interpreter disagreed. Calley was about to shoot the man when Private Herbert Carter picked up the old man and threw him into a swell, then pushed him further and further down. Calley looked over the edge and blew out the man's brains; Carter fired several shots into him. At the slightest suggestion of an enemy presence, civilians were regularly shot, women were routinely raped, and the soldiers stole what they wanted from the villagers. The officers did not care as long as the men were not caught. There was one rule: survive.

As Charley Company honed its brutality during the vain search for the Viet Cong, U.S. intelligence officers gathered new information about the VC 48th Local Force Battalion. They issued an intelligence assessment in February, stating that the VC 48th possessed heavy weapons such as 12.7mm machine guns, mortars, and rockets, and that their manpower was supplemented by two Local Force companies. When fully supplied, they would launch a new offensive against Quang Ngai city.

Enough was enough for Lieutenant Colonel Frank Barker. He conceived a plan whereby his task force would strike the Son My village complex, destroying the VC 48th and its support base. Of particular interest within Son My was the hamlet My Lai 4, the purported headquarters of the VC 48th and its two supplemental companies. That hamlet was to be Charley Company's principal target. Alpha Company would attack three hamlets north of My Lai 4 across the Diem Diem River. Bravo Company, landing near the coast between My Lai 6 and My Lai 1, would maneuver north toward the river.

As Barker pieced together his plan, Andrew Lipscomb was replaced by Colonel Oran Henderson as commander of the 11th Brigade. Lacking combat experience in Vietnam, Henderson nevertheless came to his new post with a definite idea about why the war was not progressing more satisfactorily. The troops did not close on the enemy. He let his staff and Barker know that new operations would be pursued aggressively.

Barker did not receive written approval for the operation from either division or brigade headquarters. Nor did he himself issue any written orders or retain, if they did exist, any operational papers. What he knew died with him in a helicopter crash some months later. What is clear is that the operation against Son My was to last three days. Howitzer fire from Landing Zone Uptight would secure a helicopter landing area near My Lai 4 and, together with fire from helicopter gunships, clear a tree line on the hamlet's west side of any hidden defenders. No warning of the attack was to be given the inhabitants, an operational procedure based on two assumptions: first, Son My complex was a known Viet Cong stronghold and all the inhabitants were therefore VC guerrillas or sympathizers; second, noncombatants in the hamlet would be away at market by the time the attack began.

Barker briefed his company commanders, and they relayed to their men what they thought Barker said. Captain Medina later testified that he believed Barker told him to burn the hamlet, kill the livestock, and destroy wells and crops. He said that his men did not have permission to kill unarmed civilians, and that the men must use common sense. In contrast, as reported in *Time*, 5 December 1969, Sergeants Kenneth Hodges and Martin Fagan, and Private Lenny Lagunoy, among others, believed Medina told them to kill everyone. Bilton and Sim concluded that "there can be no doubt about the impression [Medina] left on most of the men. . . . [He] let slip the dogs of war."13

At 7:30 A.M., 16 March 1968, gunners manning the 105mm howitzers at Landing Zone Uptight fired the first rounds into My Lai 4 (Map 13). In three minutes, 120 shells landed in the helicopter landing zone and within the hamlet. The inhabitants, who were not at market as anticipated, dove for shelter. Then helicopter gunships chattered overhead, unleashing a torrent of machine gun fire and rockets. American war in all its fury and lethality fell upon My Lai 4.

As Lieutenant Colonel Barker flew overhead in a command helicopter, Charley Company's 1st Platoon landed west of the hamlet. The pilots were surprised to find the landing zone "cold"—there was no hostile fire. Yet the bombardment from artillery and gunships continued. Lieutenant Calley and his men tumbled from the helicopters. A farmer came out of a rice paddy, waving his upraised hands, but was cut down by machine gun fire. The 2nd and 3rd Platoons arrived during the next half hour. The men quickly deployed, positioning machine guns and mortars, and advanced in line toward the hamlet. A woman and infant, spotted in the undergrowth near the trees, were killed by a burst from an M-16 rifle. More Vietnamese were sighted, all greeted by gunfire. But no VC fired back.

The 1st and 2nd Platoons moved into My Lai 4, the 3rd and Medina's command squad staying behind in a defensive position. The two assault platoons lost all cohesion, breaking into small groups, loosing long streams of fire from M-16s and discharging rifle grenades. They ordered people from their houses. Silence was met with a hand grenade pitched through the door. As Herbert Carter described the action, reported in *Newsweek*, 22 December 1969, "We didn't see any VC. People began coming out of their hootches [huts] and the guys shot them and burned the hootches—or burned the hootches and then shot the people when they came out." A villager pulled from his house was bayoneted, another was thrown down a well, a grenade pitched in after him. A clutch of old women and children were herded together and shot. Another 80 villagers were brought to an open area where

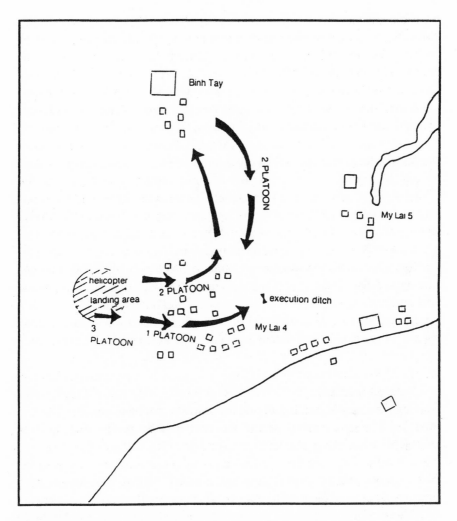

Map 13
Charley Company at My Lai 4

Lieutenant Calley told the soldiers, "You know what I want you to do with them," and walked away. Returning several minutes later, he found the villagers still standing about. He shouted to the men guarding them, "I want them dead. . . . Waste them." Calley, Private Paul Meadlo, and radioman Charles Sledge opened fire.[14]

The 2nd Platoon shot their way into the village, firing at anyone who moved, shooting blindly through walls, and tossing hand grenades through open doors. They cut down a group of children ages six and seven, and machine gunned a group of inhabitants who gathered together, undoubtedly thinking there would be safety in numbers.

The platoons pushed through the hamlet. Carter later told Seymour Hersh that many soldiers joked and laughed about what they were doing, evidently enjoying the massacre. Other men, horrified by what they or those around them had already done, refused to be sucked in any further. James Dursi, who killed the mother and child when first landing, refused to kill anyone else, even under direct order from Calley. Robert Maples refused to obey Calley's order to machine gun a group of people.

But the killing went on, Vernado Simpson admitting to Hersh that he killed about 25 people. The killings, taking place in a tiny world isolated from the parameters of military control and bereft of familiar moral guideposts, spawned barbaric acts completely unrelated to the search for the Viet Cong. Women were gang raped, sodomized, and then murdered. According to Bilton and Sim, one woman was killed when a gun was thrust into her vagina and then fired. Vietnamese were beaten with fists and rifle butts, tortured, and bayoneted. Some were scalped. Still others had "C Company" or the figure of the ace-of-spades cut onto their chests. Lieutenant Calley did nothing to stop the depredations. Lieutenant Stephen Brooks, commanding the 2nd Platoon, did nothing to stop the massacre—indeed, like Calley, he often joined his men.

Captain Medina looked grim when he entered My Lai 4 with the 3rd Platoon. But he did nothing to stop the slaughter. When asked by Barker what was going on, he gave his commander body counts that were in themselves lies. When the brigade executive officer, Major Charles Calhoun, asked him if civilians were being killed, Medina replied that the helicopter gunships killed between 20 and 28 civilians. Having walked over and around piles of dead bodies, he knew that the real number was greater, much greater.[15]

How much greater was discovered by Warrant Officer Hugh Thompson, a helicopter scout pilot. He overflew My Lai 4 at 9 A.M., sighting what he thought was an armed Viet Cong soldier. One of Thompson's two-man crew fired at the man and missed. What they unquestionably did see were dead and wounded civilians scattered all about the hamlet. Wanting to help the wounded, Thompson dropped smoke markers near them so that medical corpsmen could give assistance. He saw a group of soldiers approach one girl that he marked. An officer in the group, whom he later identified as Captain Medina, shot her. Flying to the hamlet's east end, Thompson and his crew sighted a ditch containing dozens of Vietnamese. Many were dead, but many were still alive. On landing, Thompson confronted Calley who, in effect, told him that ground operations were none of his business. The two men argued, Thompson gesticulating wildly. Frustration boiling, he took off and flew over the ditch again. Calley and his men were executing the villagers.

Lieutenant Stephen Brook's 2nd Platoon moved on to Binh Tay, another hamlet in the Son My complex. The 2nd had the dubious reputation of being the rapists of Charley Company, according to Sergeant Leonard Gonzalez who saw them "in action" several times. Their behavior in the hamlet lived up to that reputation. For two hours the men raped their way through the hamlet. Gonzalez found seven women, all naked, all dead, killed by the buckshot from several M-79 grenades fired into the group.

Thompson spotted the 2nd Platoon returning to My Lai 4, chasing a group of villagers. He put down his helicopter between the villagers and the platoon, ordering his crewmen to fire on the American soldiers if they starting shooting the civilians. Eventually, to the displeasure of the 2nd, Thompson coaxed the villagers from a bunker where they had run for safety. He called down two helicopter gunships to evacuate them to a secure area. Thompson and his crew took off again but quickly landed when someone was seen moving among the bodies in the 1st Platoon's execution ditch. They rescued a small boy from among the pile of bodies and flew him to a hospital in Quang Ngai city. Thompson reported what he had seen, and, upon confirmation from other helicopter crews, the information was given to Barker. He in turn told Major Calhoun, his executive officer, to find out if civilians were being killed and to stop it. Charley Company was ordered to cease fire.

After final mop-up operations in My Lai 4—burning remaining houses, killing livestock, and burning crops—Charley Company moved to a designated link with Bravo Company between My Lai 5 and My Lai 6. They left behind in My Lai 4 between 450 and 500 dead.[16] The only casualty in Charley Company was one man who shot himself accidentally.

General Westmoreland commended Charley Company for an outstanding action that dealt the Viet Cong a severe blow. The commanding general did not then know the extent to which a conspiracy of silence overshadowed the massacre. Barker suggested to Medina that he tell his men not to say anything, and few did. Colonel Oran Henderson, the new brigade commander, made a cursory inquiry and then kept changing his narrative of events. Barker soon died in a helicopter crash, and Calhoun kept quiet. Then, gradually, whispers circulated about a second massacre perpetrated by Bravo Company at Co Luy, a village at the south end of the long, thin peninsula flanking the Son My coast. Ninety civilians were killed. Like My Lai 4, that event was wrapped in silence.

The massacre was not known to the public until the fall of 1969, urged by soldiers' letters to the Pentagon and to U.S. senators. The Army was ordered to make an official inquiry, resulting in the Peers Report. The Report's conclusions now seem tepid in places because General Peers found it difficult to believe the events described to him by common soldiers. The incidents were outside the parameters of Army regulations; therefore, they could not have happened as described. Peers was much more stern with the Army bureaucracy when he found that reports about My Lai were never written down or somehow disappeared, that existing records were incomplete, that memories conveniently failed, and testimony changed time and again. Officers up and down the chain of command were subsequently indicted on various charges ranging from murder to dereliction of duty, making false statements, participating in a coverup, to altering records. None was court-martialed. Of all the participants in the massacre, only four were brought to trial and only one, Lieutenant Calley, was convicted of murder. He was sentenced to life imprisonment but was released pending his appeal. After three years, President Richard Nixon gave him a full pardon. My Lai, as Bilton and Sim point out, faded from public memory, any moral outrage either long spent or twisted into a clever public relations travesty in which Calley was transformed from a monster into a victim of political persecution and a convenient scapegoat for the Army, leaving the generals free of any blame. To many Americans, Calley was a hero.

A SOCIOLOGICAL PERSPECTIVE OF THE MASSACRE

The Peers Report briefly discusses some factors that led to the massacre. Notable among these was the failure of leadership. Colonel Oran Henderson, the new brigade commander, was hampered by a lack of adequate brigade headquarters staff, resulting in poor communications, coordination, and supervision. Faulty staff work compounded the difficulty that Henderson faced because he did not fully grasp the Son My operation and did not know Barker. Even though Barker was considered an outstanding officer, the Peers Report concluded that his assumptions, plans, and orders revealed an operational incompetence. This was demonstrated when he failed to obtain brigade and divisional approval for the Son My attack, and by his lack of control over the operation as it unfolded beneath his command helicopter. Officers within Task Force Barker did not impress subordinates with the need to distinguish between combatants and noncombatants—partially the fault of an intelligence report that said noncombatants would not be in the village. The veracity of the report was not challenged, nor was a contingency plan developed if the report proved incorrect. Orders to kill everyone, burn the hamlets, kill livestock, and burn crops were illegal.

Captain Medina, considered an outstanding officer, dominated his company. Ironically, at the moment when his leadership was most needed, he failed to exercise control over his two assault platoons, and he should have communicated to Barker that there was no VC return fire. He was much like Colonel Chivington at Sand Creek, bringing his men to the edge of disintegration, standing back, and letting them fall. An argument along formal lines of military authority could be made that he depended on his platoon leaders to control the men. That would be a reasonable assumption in most companies but not Medina's. He did not think much of his lieutenants, especially Calley whom he humiliated before his men. Lacking much authority, the young officers compensated by trying to be buddies with their men, an effort that significantly contributed to the permissive attitude within the company.

The platoon leaders failed to control the men as they entered My Lai. Having long before dehumanized their enemy, and running off Medina's leash, these dogs of war became a violent mob. Lieutenants Calley and Brooks did give orders but they were more those of mob leaders than army officers. Rather than restricting or terminating the violence, the two lieutenants encouraged its expansion. As Bilton and Sim comment, no one along the chain of command supervised the troops. No one in authority, with mendacity poisoning the atmosphere, said stop until it was far too late.

Overlooked in the descriptions and explanations of the massacre is the desperation felt by Charley Company, the end of the process by which discontent gave way to hopelessness. The men were convinced the Army forgot them. They went on endless patrols that netted only more company casualties. They were worn out. Morale dropped. At the same time, an intense group identity developed that transcended military norms as the company became a kind of family, one facing the stark reality of possible extinction, a crisis from which the men sought escape. There was a problem: the source of the crisis was the U.S. Army. The Army put them in Vietnam. The Army sent them on patrols. The Army wore them down to nothing. The Army forgot them. But Charley Company could not strike back at or run away from the Army. Instead, typical of crowd behavior, and as we have seen at San Sebastian and Sand Creek, the soldiers directed their frustrations, anger, hate, and ultimately their violence toward the people who became convenient scapegoats for their crisis—the My Lai villagers.

The causes are still more complex. Bilton and Sim concluded that Charley Company was alienated. Unfortunately, except for describing the appalling physical and emotional isolation of Charley Company, little is made of the concept. However, alienation is central to understanding what happened at My Lai.[17]

Desperation left Charley Company with the feeling that they were caught in a machine that fed men into one end and spewed death from the other. The soldiers knew there was nothing they could do to alter the system that put them in that situation, so they concluded that the Army was unconcerned about their fate. The men believed they were alone, a distorted and subjective judgment but one that nonetheless conditioned their perceptions of reality. That was powerlessness, the kind of alienation that leaves one with the feeling that his actions will have little effect on what happens in the future.

The Military Assistance Command issued many directives regarding proper behavior toward noncombatants. Lieutenant Calley once gave a three-minute canned lecture during their training period on how to treat Vietnamese women properly. Field commanders were advised to control their weapons to minimize civilian casualties.[18] But the same army preached aggressiveness, exemplified by Colonel Henderson's directive to have his infantrymen close on the enemy. Body counts were the measure of combat effectiveness. When engaging the enemy, with howitzer shells screaming overhead from 3 or 4 miles to the rear, with helicopter gunships spraying machine gun and rocket fire into enemy positions, and napalm bombs burning the edge of a village, there was no time for the niceties of distinguishing enemy combatants from noncombatants. Thus there was an enormous discrepancy between what the Army officially sanctioned and the reality of battle. The U.S. soldiers in Vietnam were in an intolerable situation, confused about what to believe, a form of alienation termed meaninglessness.

As a result of their perceived powerlessness and meaninglessness Charley Company, moving toward disintegration, assigned low reward value to goals and beliefs that the Army officially valued—that form of alienation designated as isolation. The company, during the weeks it chased the VC through northern Quang Ngai, gradually increased its level of violence toward the Vietnamese. Greg Olsen, an enlisted man in the company, said, "We believed this [violent] behavior was commonplace. . . . You really do lose your sense . . . not of right or wrong, but your degree of wrong changes. . . . [It's] a different set of rules and I don't think any of us knew what those rules were."[19] The company ceased to be a military unit in all but its outward appearance. They even ceased to be a family. They became a mob. Believing their brutal behavior was the combat norm, confirmed by the absence of punishment for what they did, they invented new values and beliefs out of the crisis of survival. Thus, as Fred Widmer, another enlisted man, told Bilton and Sim, the company believed they lived in a culture of violence. The values and beliefs replacing those formally proffered by the Army were outside the parameters of accepted military conduct because, through the form of alienation called normlessness, the soldiers developed the expectation that only socially unapproved behavior would relieve their crisis; certainly the formal system did not ensure survival—it threatened survival. That is why Charley Company ignored directives about the treatment of noncombatants, left the information cards on right conduct unread, and why Calley later commented that his canned lecture on the treatment of women was a joke.

The foundations of Charley Company's emergence as a violent crowd or mob were inherent in its composition and short history. When the formal value system of the Army failed them, when desperation and alienation overcame them, with Medina setting an example of brutality, when placed under the stress of what they believed would be close combat in the My Lai operation, and when their leadership failed, most men in Charley Company easily walked the path to massacre.

9

Toward a Sociology of Military Disintegration

Mutiny, mayhem, surrender, massacre: these, among the worst failures of regimental behavior, are often disguised behind the heroic posture of military history. When they are discussed, we are told what happened, and, as if rendering courts-martial judgments, who was responsible. What such narratives overlook is the considerable complexity that lurks behind the historical facade.

I have offered six in-depth examples of disintegration as a way of exploring that complexity. My interpretations evolved from two ideas. First, the events were not discreet. Instead, granting their separation by time, place, army, and type of disintegration, the examples all touch one another because they share common processes. Second, what happened to the military units experiencing disintegration occurred because they were human groups. These two ideas required me to link history with sociology. What follows is a recapitulation and elaboration of the four sociological processes that I believe are the foundations of military disintegration, and a systematic analysis of the crowds that developed within each example. All this will necessitate some repetition of facts already presented in order to give the discussion proper context. Personal reflections are added at the end.

FOUNDATIONS OF MILITARY DISINTEGRATION

Failure of Leadership

Many officers discussed in this study had fine, even distinguished, careers. Yet those same leaders, together with officers of lesser ability in their commands, either failed to act or acted inappropriately when faced with crises. Those failures abetted the crises and hastened the disintegration of their commands.

At Meerut in 1857, Lieutenant Colonel George Carmichael-Smyth, 3rd Bengal Light Cavalry, was warned that any attempt to foist the infamous greased cartridges on his sepoys would cause trouble. His men even filed a petition to stop the firing-parade. Carmichael-Smyth ignored their pleas. Most troopers refused the cartridges, were arrested, court-martialed, and imprisoned. Mutiny, wild and violent, followed. Old General Hewitt, the Meerut garrison commander, mutiny seething around him, did not believe the sepoys would ever raise a hand against their officers. The opacity of such officers is more easily understood than forgiven. Paternalistic and supercilious attitudes dulled their thinking, lulling them into insensitivity to the sepoys' discontent and eventual despair over the British invasion of their culture. When violence fell upon Meerut, Delhi, Cawnpore, Lucknow, and a dozen other garrison towns and cities, the British were surprised and unprepared to meet the consequences of their failure.

There was little disparity between the conditions of the French field-grade officers and enlisted men along the Western Front in 1917. Unlike India, where enormous social gaps existed between officers and native troops, those occupying the trenches in 1917 were all caught in the same hell. Not surprisingly, some officers had great sympathy for the expressed discontent of the enlisted men—presuming the particular officer was trusted enough or courageous enough to hear it. The general staff, in contrast, was reviled. They remained far behind the lines, aloof and untouchable, blaming the men in the trenches for their bankrupt strategies. Having created a fiefdom called the Zone of the Army, impervious to governmental scrutiny, Joffre and his minions conducted a war beyond their understanding. When Nivelle took command, hope rose within the ranks that a breakthrough of the German lines was possible. But Nivelle was a pompous blowhard, truculent, and unable to accept sound advice. When his offensive failed, half the frontline divisions mutinied. Some soldiers merely talked, some demonstrated, many got drunk. Eventually, most returned to duty without much trouble. Only Pétain's reforms, none particularly earth-shattering but all important to the troops, restored hope in men who, for so long, knew only despair.

British leadership failed at San Sebastian for two reasons. First, Wellesley, a first-rate leader in so many, many ways, blundered when he blamed his 5th Division rather than a poor plan for the failure of the first assault. That error was compounded when, in planning the second attack, Wellesley selected an assault team to show the 5th how, with proper dash, the job could be done. He created despair, the feeling among the men that no one cared about what happened to them. The second assault was little more than a bad copy of the first. The butcher's bill would again be high. The troops, filled with anxiety and anger, nonetheless battled through the defenses and into the town's streets. At that point, leadership failed once more. So many officers were killed and wounded in the attack that the men were left unsupervised. Despair, anger, and anxiety turned to violence as the soldiers broke into shops and houses, looting, burning, and, by some reports, raping and murdering. The few officers still alive who tried to restore order were either threatened or ignored. Only after the men were satiated with drink and plunder did they become soldiers again.

In all fairness, a defense of the Schnee Eifel, predicated on poor intelligence and staff work, and given the inexperienced troops and their obscenely thin deployment, would have taxed the best leaders. When the German offensive exploded across the American front, General Jones responded with confusion and denial. He did not make sound tactical decisions, transmitting orders that were obsolete by the time his field officers received them. He stayed in his headquarters, a captive of events and his own timorous staff, oblivious to the realities engulfing his command. Colonels Cavender and Descheneaux, commanding the most threatened regiments, were swamped by the German attack. Communications having failed, they never clearly grasped the situation. Tactical responses were frequently made by battalion, company, and even platoon leaders. Many fought valiantly. In the end, both colonels surrendered their regiments despite the eagerness of many junior officers to keep fighting. Walking into captivity, those men felt betrayed.

The massacres at Sand Creek and My Lai represent soldiers operating without leadership at the moment when they needed it the most: at the inception of the attacks. The on-site leadership, Chivington and Medina, brought their commands to emotional peaks before the engagements, led them to the battles, then did nothing as the military operations turned to butchery and wanton murder. The subalterns participated in the barbarous acts. A few men remained aloof, refusing to do anything, the quiescent observers.

Even though the specifics of leadership failure varied with each example, I offer two generalizations. First, men of very different character failed. Old General Hewitt was nearly senile, and Carmichael-Smyth was an unimaginative fool. Joffre was reclusive and phlegmatic. Wellesley led with an aristocratic hauteur. Jones was a professional plodder who gave his life to the Army but knew nothing about battle. Neither Cavender nor Descheneaux knew anything about leading men in combat. Chivington was a bully, a liar, and a jumped-up Bible thumper who had no business holding a commission. Medina, operating under the incompetent Barker, tried to keep authority in his hands alone and lost it in crisis.

The second generalization supports the first: communications broke down in each command. The British and the sepoys talked past one another, the social and cultural distance between them confounding communications, the British substituting what they wanted to believe about the sepoys for reality. Within the French Army, both social and physical distance separated the men in the trenches from the generals who plotted their death in chateaux far from the trenches. Battlefield communications usually broke down under German bombardment, adding confusion to already badly confused situations. At San Sebastian, on the Schnee Eifel, at Sand Creek, and at My Lai, clear communications were impeded. Sometimes the messages were the wrong ones, such as Wellesley's chastisement of the 5th Division for their failure, or the French generals blaming the troops for failing to crack the German lines. At the Schnee Eifel, poor communications also resulted from faulty intelligence and incorrect assumptions, impossible promises of help on the way and, to be sure, inadequate communications equipment. Sand Creek and My Lai were both cloaked in official obtuseness, mendacity, and cover-ups.

The Collapse of Primary Groups

Millions know the ritual: Attention! Stand at ease! Strip that weapon. Left, right, left, right. Rise and shine. Eat, run, march, hurry, hurry, eat, go to sleep, rise and shine—the never-ending cadence that peels away the layers of civilian life; the unhesitating obedience to orders. Day after day, week after week, recruits learn to be soldiers, absorbing military ideology and learning to function as a dedicated, aggressive team. This is the formal military system of indoctrination and in most instances it works.

The formal system also provides the organizational context for the development of informal relationships, primary group relationships, that emerge from intimate, daily, face-to-face interactions. "We groups" and "in-groups" are synonymous phrases. Outside the military, such groups are classically exemplified by families, play groups, friendships, some work groups, and old neighborhoods. Within the military, such groups are the squads, platoons, companies, and, in the very particular example of the British Army, battalions (traditionally designated by the peculiarities of their logic as regiments) that John Keegan characterized as closed societies.[1] Primary group relationships develop their own statuses irrespective of formal rank. A private who earns the respect of his comrades may have higher primary group status than a corporal or sergeant. The army might define that person as a natural leader, but the private may not accept higher rank because the status he enjoys in the group could be withdrawn if he accepted. Primary groups also define roles, the expectations of one's behavior by the group, sorting out who is one's buddy and who are the surrogate big brothers, the jokers, the fools, and the regular guys. That web of primary group relationships is the social catalyst of a unit.

The connection between primary groups and social disintegration was recognized by Morris Janowitz and Edward Shils in their study of the German *Wehrmacht* during World War II.[2] Central to their concerns was why some units kept fighting and others collapsed under nearly the same battle conditions. They found that disintegration followed the disruption of primary groups, be it within a company, platoon, or squad. Appeals to political ideology, to German Army traditions, and patriotism became meaningless when faced with group extinction. Feeling the group's survival was threatened, the individual soldier could easily conclude that his personal survival was in doubt. That doubt was enhanced by the belief that the group was isolated—that no one cared about them anymore—and by anxieties concerning the army's inability to provide adequate food, clothing, and medical aid, and worries about the safety of their families in Germany. Those stresses moved the soldiers beyond the social controls of both the military and their primary groups, creating new values and beliefs related to personal survival. The collapse of primary groups as an integral process in the disintegration of *Wehrmacht* units is an idea easily transferable to the examples used in this study.

In both the Indian and French mutinies, old normative relations were fractured as some men mutinied and others did not, or, having mutinied, some walked away, defecting from the defectors. Battalions and companies were shredded as the men rejected formal leadership for informal leaders emerging from within their ranks. New roles replaced old ones, and new values and beliefs were created in crisis, replacing those formed from the bonds of group stability. In both India and France, the new associations emerging from the old were born as crowds, and crowds they remained.

At San Sebastian, on the Schnee Eifel, at Sand Creek and My Lai, formal military unit integrity broke under the strain of crises. The informal social controls implicit to primary groups soon followed. For in each example, the units became diffuse. At San Sebastian, lacking restraints, the men formed street mobs. On the Schnee Eifel, the two isolated regiments of the 106th Division cracked under the German assault, leaving American companies and platoons scattered about the battle zone, and all wondering whether or not they would survive. At Sand Creek and My Lai the units turned into lynch mobs cast beyond the interior controls of the primary groups, much less the formal military, their malevolent leadership encouraging the emergent values that condoned massacre.

What appears common in all these examples, however relative the degree, is that as the formal military units collapsed, so too did the primary groups. This seems dangerously tautological until we understand that the military formation and the primary group relations formed within it are twin-born. Each army had its rules and regulations, but the same men, forming intimate bonds within those formations, created their own value and belief systems. When in crises, the primary group systems became vulnerable to the extent that the formal systems failed. The primary groups continued to disintegrate because they lacked the means of responding to the crises. Then, in each example, new associations developed that took the direction of crowd behavior.

Alienation

Alienation is essential to understanding the foundations of military disintegration. Thus far, however, beyond dropping the word on occasion, the concept has received little attention from military historians. One reason for this absence is the apparent conflict between the concept of alienation and the process of social disintegration. Alienation, the concept, as in Melvin Seeman's important explication of meanings,[3] is often studied from the standpoint of individual expectations. Military disintegration, in contrast, is a group process. The social psychologist Tamotsu Shibutani made the theoretical connection between alienation and social disintegration as well as anyone when he stated that under conditions of social change difficulties in "attaining reasonable gratifications lead to alienation from old meanings and an increasing sensitivity to new possibilities."4 Group disintegration is a profound social change. Hope is lost, nothing seems to work anymore, and the old values, beliefs, and meanings do not deliver with any certainty—with any gratification—the messages they once delivered. As Seeman points out, individuals define crisis situations in relation to various forms of alienation: powerlessness, normlessness, meaninglessness, and isolation. Those individual definitions are easily shared, especially within primary groups where they become part of the group ethos.

Alienation contributes to social disintegration at the point where individuals within primary groups are suddenly confused as to what they ought to believe, and that they can no longer predict the outcomes of their behavior. This is meaninglessness, the result of failed formal values and beliefs. The French soldiers in 1917, exemplified by those in Jolinon's *mémoire de la guerre*, felt betrayed by all they were taught to believe. They discovered there was no glory in dying, and they were convinced the government, and probably France at large, did not give a damn whether they lived or died. They were confused, and they could not predict with certainty where their next move would lead them. Charley Company in Vietnam was torn between what they knew they ought to believe and the reality of what they had to believe in order to survive. As in the French example, Charley Company finally concluded that no one in the chain of command really cared about them. There seemed to be no other explanation for the long and fruitless patrols that ended with more comrades dead and wounded, and for nothing.

Once meaninglessness is established within the group, it is an easy slide into isolation, the assignment of low reward to values and beliefs usually given high rewards by the rest of society. In each example, the soldiers shed military values and beliefs, and, reshaping their groups into crowds, they invented new values and beliefs that, in four examples, opened the doors to violence. The Indian Mutiny, of all the examples, represents the clearest, almost methodical, transformation from formal units and primary groups to crowds. The mutiny was launched when the sepoys rejected the value and belief system they thought the British were imposing on them. They tried to be reasonable and patient with their British masters and sought orderly redress of their grievances, but were constantly ignored or rebuffed. To preserve their own culture, they rejected that of the British, including the military values of loyalty, duty, and regimental tradition. Out of that rejection was born a belief in the efficacy of revenge and destruction. Overt violence followed.

Powerlessness, again, is the expectation that no matter what the soldiers in a particular situation do, they cannot influence the outcomes of their behavior. Normlessness is the expectation that only socially unapproved behaviors will alter the situation. The sepoys, unable to ameliorate their grievances by approved means, mutinied, butchered, and burned. Many French mutineers refused to obey orders, throwing aside their weapons and shouting revolutionary slogans. Most would man the trenches but refused to attack the Germans. These were radical solutions to their defined crisis. Even though punishment was forthcoming, so too were reforms. At San Sebastian, the men ran amok through the streets, seeking a kind of escape through violent, normless behavior from what they perceived to be the intolerable expectations of an uncaring commander, a situation they were powerless to change. The portrait of alienation in the 106th Division is uneven. Individually and in cut-off units, men felt despair, isolation, and meaninglessness. Many surrendered, powerless to do anything else. Many others wanted to continue the fight. Interestingly, the most pronounced expressions of powerlessness and normlessness toward the Army and their own leaders was felt by those men who marched into German prisoner-of-war camps. Discipline became a major problem, morale plummeted, sharp and rude accusations were made against Cavender and Descheneaux, and many men crawled into self-imposed isolation, opting out of anything remotely military.

The 3rd Colorado Volunteers demonstrate another slight variation on the theme of alienation. The 3rd never was a military unit. It was a lynch mob waiting to happen. Consequently there was little military ideology or behavior to reject. Instead the men brought into their hundred-days' enlistment profound distrust of a government that had failed to protect them as civilians on the frontier, and the feeling that nothing they did as civilians could rectify the situation. In the regiment, by contrast, they became the avenging hand of all those who were victims of Indian depredations and, simultaneously, found the means to escape the intolerable situation they believed the Indians imposed on their lives. The situation at Sand Creek was hand tailored for a leader like Chivington who preyed on the men's hatred to complete his own agenda.

My Lai was not much different from Sand Creek. The men of Charley Company were powerless to alter their circumstances as they hunted VC in Quang Ngai. The only escape was through socially unapproved behavior directed at the Vietnamese, the defined source of their collective misery. Thus the enemy was everywhere. No one was to be trusted. The soldiers soon discovered that rape, torture, murder, and looting could be perpetrated without much fear of punishment. They reinvented values and beliefs confirmed by their experiences. Sand Creek and My Lai did not just happen; indeed, they were metaphors of their preexisting violent subcultures.

Desperation

A military unit undergoing disintegration will ultimately reach a point of desperation, a "loss of hope for their future and faith in themselves."[5] Desperation will arise when the primary group determines that there is no possibility of improving their condition within the parameters of the formal system. It is the final judgment that the group is faced with great danger either morally or physically and that, on the edge of powerlessness, there is nothing the group can do to alter circumstances.

Leaders, as the examples discussed demonstrate, may not recognize that crisis is upon them or, recognizing crisis, may choose to ignore it. The leaders' responses may be inappropriate or impotent. Or the leaders may be less interested in averting crisis than they are in maintaining the military status quo at any cost because of their own career investment in the institution; consequently they foster the crisis.

The time it takes for a unit to reach desperation varies with circumstances. A slow burn of discontent that lasted for decades preceded the violent outbreak of the Indian Mutiny. The French soldiers kept faith with their leaders through three years of butchery. But the British soldiers at San Sebastian reached desperation only at the end of the siege when they realized that the second assault was a copy of the disastrous first attempt to break the defenses. Charley Company reached desperation after only a few weeks of abysmal patrols. Generalizations about the two American regiments surrounded on the Schnee Eifel are difficult to make. Some men obviously reached a point of desperation within a few hours or, at most, a few days. Because the situation was so diffuse and varied in intensity, some men never experienced desperation and many others did not reach that point until they were made prisoners of war.

A variety of events, feelings, and perceptions can bring a group to despair. But among the examples discussed in this study, there was one complex factor that stood out: the feeling within the various groupings that no one cared about them, that no one listened, that they were somehow cut off, alone both physically and socially in a violent world. Almost any concession, however slight, by the military or governmental leaders would have been "sufficient to revive the hope of the discontented and to postpone the growth of desperation."[6] That did not happen in any of the historical examples. Discontent grew into desperation, taking the soldiers beyond the norms of their defined groups, both formal and informal, toward rebellious and even violent behavior.

THE ELEMENTS OF COLLECTIVE BEHAVIOR: CROWD FORMATION

To grasp the nature of military disintegration fully, it is necessary to restate the principle that a military unit is not just battalions, companies, platoons, and squads. As Janowitz and Shils pointed out in their study of the *Wehrmacht*, and as Samuel Stouffer and his colleagues demonstrated in their study *The American Soldier*, military units are simultaneously informal groups—primary groups—that maintain the units' cohesion. Formal and informal groupings are two layers of military association. Disintegration of both those layers reveals a third that lurks in the shadows of military life. These are the collective behaviors that emerge when disintegration becomes a *fait accompli*. Collective behavior, such as the crowds and mobs to which I have alluded, is a spontaneous emergence of new, alternate organizational forms, values, and beliefs. The duration of any collective behavior, such as a crowd, is only as long as the crisis in which it arises.[7]

Participation in a crowd or mob—the two words are frequently used synonymously—is seldom by selection. The soldiers must obviously all be in the unit experiencing stress, discontent, desperation, and finally aliena-tion. Moreover, the soldiers must be proximate to the events leading to crowd or mob behavior. For example, of all the troops attacking San Sebastian, only those who actually made it into the town participated in the drunken-ness, looting, and burning that followed. At Sand Creek, Captain Silas Soule kept his men out of the battle, following the course of the massacre from the opposite creek bank. At My Lai some soldiers opted to literally stand apart from the massacre. Men who participated in these crowds did so because they really believed their actions would make a difference, although they would have been hard pressed to say what that difference was, or because they believed participating was the expedient thing to do.

The emergence of crowds presumes that all the foundations of disinte-gration have been at work on the formal and informal systems. This means that leadership has failed, the primary groups are in disarray, alienation in its various forms is working its way through the men, and a pervasive feeling of desperation has taken hold.

What brings these conditions and feelings together into the collective action of a crowd has been given different labels: milling; social contagion; interactional amplification. These phrases all denote the process by which the interaction between individuals intensifies, creating new levels of aware-ness of others and what they are doing. Jolinon's would-be mutineers talking about their options was a marvelous example of the milling process. They were subjected to rumors about those units already mutinous, which were going to mutiny, the general staff, and what was happening in train stations. Some rumors were discarded and others were believed, but all was grist for the argumentation that shaped an arena for more intense interactions. At Meerut, for example, following the arrest of the sepoys who refused the greased cartridges, there was much overt desperation among the remaining troops. They talked with each another, shouted, argued, cajoled, and finally took the step to violent action. The situation at San Sebastian is more difficult to understand because the mob actions were the real flash point of action. Although there is little documentation that describes in any detail what went on, I think it is safe to say that the interactional amplification must have taken place spontaneously as the men ran through the streets inciting one another to aberrant conduct. At the other end of the historical spectrum, the men at My Lai needed little amplification. As one of them said, they already lived in an environment of violence, the predisposition toward atrocities against noncombatants etched in the company's history. The Army simply transported a ready-made mob to the battle, and Medina pointed them in the desired direction. The expectation of battle, provoking high anxiety, easily brought the company to violence.

Milling or amplification builds upon itself, beginning with a few soldiers talking over the problem. As Ralph Turner and Lewis Killian point out in their book *Collective Behavior*, this stirs others to join. Anticipation builds. Excitement builds. Intensity increases. From that intensity a common mood develops, "a collective definition of the appropriate reaction to [the] novel situation."[8]

Imitation and rivalry enhance interactional amplification. Someone shouts, "Let's get 'em!" or "*À bas l'armée*." These abrupt, evocative directions and slogans are easily imitated by others until the whole crowd is chanting in unison. The broad participation results from individuals wanting to be part of the crowd in which they invest their hope. Others imitate the shouts but add volume or some words of their own. "Down with the government!" That is rivalry. The motivation is not so much self-aggran-dizement as a willing and satisfying participation in the collective process.

Shouting and chanting can move a crowd to action. But the persons who initiated the shouting likely did not think of themselves as leaders; never-theless, in the context of crowd behavior, they were leaders, fortuitous at best but leaders. This type of leadership confounds the purposes of more determined, usually professional leaders, such as speechmakers. As noted in the French mutinies, speechmakers, however inflammatory, seldom if ever move a crowd to actions those leaders want. Everyone cheers, and the messages sound grand, but the real leaders are the anonymous voices shouting "Let's get 'em!" And that call can take the crowd in directions unanticipated by the speechmakers.

Four of the six principal historical examples developed in this study—the Indian Mutiny, San Sebastian, Sand Creek, and My Lai—turned violent. As Richard La Piere noted in his work *Collective Behavior*, violent conduct does not occur without an incident, any incident, that focuses the despair of those in crisis. The arrest and humiliation of the sepoys at Meerut intensified interactions among their comrades, focusing their attention on that single incident. Wellesley's humiliation of the 5th Division galvanized existing discontent, the interactions between the men becoming more intense as the second attack drew near. "Remember the Hungates," Chivington shouted just before his men opened fire at Sand Creek. The Hungate atrocity and the subsequent public display of their mutilated bodies focused attention, fear, and the hatred felt by many settlers, including the hastily organized 3rd Colorado Volunteers. Before My Lai, Charley Company held a memorial service for a popular sergeant. That was one casualty too many for the abused and forgotten men.

An essential ingredient of the mythology about crowds is that violence is directed toward random targets, as if destroying anyone or anything will satisfy the crowd's rage. But things are not so random.

First, crowds identify someone, some class of persons, or something they think responsible for the focusing incident, for all other such incidents, and for their collective misery. The identification process can begin early in the formal military and primary group experience. The sepoys were aware for decades of a British cultural invasion. The men in Charley Company, during training in Hawaii, learned to assume that the Vietnamese at large were their enemy. Combat experience merely confirmed the assumption. Second, who or what is selected may or may not have any relationship to the incident that sparks the violence and, in fact, may be far removed from the real causes of misery. Of the four violent examples, only the Indian mutineers initially attacked targets, the British, who were demonstrably responsible for the incident that provoked the violence—Carmichael-Smyth's firing-parade—and for incursions upon their native culture. At San Sebastian, Sand Creek, and My Lai, violence was perpetrated against scapegoats. The Spanish townspeople, the Cheyenne and Arapahoes, and the Vietnamese villages were not directly responsible for poor leadership and bad policy. Third, the chosen targets shared common characteristics necessary for the eruption of crowd violence: they were tangible and accessible. The sepoys could not attack Britain or British imperial policy, the British 5th Division could not attack Wellesley, the 3rd Colorado and Charley Company never thought of attacking the United States government. Consequently inaccessibility of those actually responsible necessitated a direction of energy toward what was available. Of course, this presumes that an appropriate level of demonizing and dehumanizing of the target has already taken place within the crowd, providing rationales for the ensuing violence.

The historical examples demonstrate that different kinds of crowds develop from disintegration. Sociologists have classified crowds in a variety of ways. Even though such classifications are important, the results are sometimes verbose and overly complex. But, with due respect to those efforts, drawing from them where necessary, and letting the evidence guide my selection and modifications of those classifications, I think that the examples represent three kinds of crowds (at the same time realizing that other examples might very well yield different kinds of crowds). The first is the diffuse-passive unfocused crowd, the second is the diffuse-hostile unfocused crowd, and the third is the solidaristic-hostile focused crowd.

Whether passive or hostile, a diffuse crowd, a class developed by Turner and Killian, usually has a core or compact crowd, as it were, a nucleus of crowd behavior. Because of its intense interactions, the compact crowd draws to it clusters—Turner and Killian call them knots—of like-minded people at their periphery, thus expanding the compact crowd's sphere of influence. The possibility exists that these peripheral clusters, interacting with each other or moving in independent directions, can themselves develop into compact crowds, attracting the energies of still newer clusters.

The French mutinies emerged as a lot of diffuse clusters looking for a nonexistent core. Men gathered together, trying to decide what to do. Some battalions or even regiments crossed the line to overt mutiny by creating pseudo-revolutionary enclaves within the Zone of the Army. Other units opted for a slowdown, much like unionists in a work-to-rule action. Others obeyed orders but left their weapons aside. Still others just talked and talked and did nothing. Many more took to drink and were punished by nothing more than aching heads.

The French mutineers in their diffuse clusters not only vainly sought a compact crowd to which they could attach their interests, but they often could not find each other. Communications between the clusters was poor to nonexistent, the pawns of rumor rather than information. Moreover, the army was spread out over several miles, and any attempts to make physical contact were thwarted by the ever-present military police and cavalry. The mutinies were also spread out in time. One unit might begin and end its mutiny in May and another, quite independently, would repeat the process in June. No coordination of activity existed anywhere. Thus, for all the shouting, clenched fists, red banners, and singing of the *Internationale*, the mutinies remained passive. They lacked an accessible unifying target against which to vent their desperation and anger.

The 106th Division at first seems like a diffuse crowd, men spatially scattered across the Schnee Eifel, clusters looking for a core, all wondering what to do. Unlike the French examples, the 106th was determined to fight, to get into the war. However, with many officers killed, wounded, or captured, lacking clear direction from regimental and especially divisional leadership, the men remained in diffuse clusters, many of which approximated their formal military organization. The 106th, fractured by the German assault, by despair, and by the confusion of their leaders' responses, teetered on becoming a diffuse crowd but did not. The division consequently forms an exception to the examples presented here. Unfortunately a clear explanation of that failure to become a crowd of any sort resides in the prisoner-of-war camps where the real disintegration took place, the afterword of the division's story that has never been fully told.

The Indian Mutiny contained all the ingredients of a classic diffuse crowd. Each garrison within the Bengal Army that mutinied developed a compact crowd from among the sepoys. Similar to the Meerut firing-parade, there was usually in each place a precipitous event that galvanized long-felt desperation. Peripheral clusters of like-minded people emerged from other military units and from the civilian populations. As at Meerut and Delhi, troublemakers from the local bazaars excited the sepoys and civilians. However, like the cavalryman riding into Meerut shouting that the British troops were coming, fortuitous leaders actually led the crowds into violent action.

At that point, the Indian Mutiny went in a different direction from the French. Instead of remaining passive, the sepoys became many hostile cluster crowds.[9] At first they directed their hostility against British officers, shooting and hacking many to death. Then the families of the officers became targets. Soon, as at Cawnpore, any Briton became a target. Having killed, burned out, or chased away the British populations, the mutineers and their supporters turned rapaciously on their own people, killing, burning, looting, and forcing the survivors to flee.

San Sebastian is another example of diffuse crowds directing hostility toward unfocused targets. Unit integrity was lost as the men dispersed through the town's streets, forming small, fortuitously organized clusters. As in France, these clusters remained diffuse. There never was a compact crowd; furthermore, the clusters were not inclined to develop one. As in India, the hostility turned rapacious, the targets as diffuse as the crowds.

Changing targets and wanton destruction gave these hostile crowds a commonly attributed fickle character. As with many popular beliefs about crowd behavior, this generalization is wrong. The crowds lacked fixed internal organizational leadership and social controls. The sepoys might agree that the British had to be killed. However, running out of targets, but revenge not satisfied, with temptations and greed surfacing, and the intensity of interaction building on itself, the crowds easily moved to the next level by targeting Indians who worked for the British, such as the civil service, those who converted to Christianity, and Indian-run English language newspapers, banks, schools, and churches. If some ordinary Indian citizens and their houses and shops stood in the way of the rapacity, that was too bad. Hence the Indian Mutiny began as so many diffuse crowds that turned hostile with unfocused objectives or targets. The San Sebastian crowds knew what they wanted, but the location of the wine, loot, and women determined the order of the attacks.

Nor was the shifting from one objective or target to another in India and at San Sebastian the consequence of a so-called mob mentality, some frenzied black hole that absorbed the individualities within the crowds. As Neil Smelser points out, such shifting of objectives occurs when the crowd, making a commitment to violent actions, draws to itself "many deviant and destructive persons in the population."[10] Because diverse motivations propelled the crowds—desire for drink, loot, women, the sheer catharsis of destruction—different objectives were attacked, sometimes serially as the Indian Mutiny evidence suggests, and sometimes simultaneously, as suggested by events in San Sebastian. Smelser is correct only to a point. For the socially unapproved behavior of crowds is not just the creation of socially deviant individuals. Perfectly decent people become violent and rapacious.

The common denominator in the examples that allowed nice people and horrid people to commit the same atrocities is that such behavior was often the flash point of crowd behavior. Social controls were nonexistent, and the opportunity to take or to do whatever one wanted with impunity, together with the ecstasy engendered by even temporary release from crisis, was a once-in-a-lifetime experience. Individuals adapted new behavioral expectations—new social roles—that were different from normal expectations. The differences in expectations created inner conflict called role strain.[11] To resolve the strain one way or another, the individuals available to join the crowds made judgments, probably quite spontaneously, about the relative rewards and punishments participation promised. Necessarily, individuals also assessed their relationships with the crowd. To the degree that rewards outstripped punishment, to the extent that individuals felt some union with the crowd, they willingly joined even though reprehensible behaviors followed. Other men made judgments that led them to stand aloof.

The massacres at Sand Creek and My Lai exemplify the third type of crowd: solidaristic-hostile with focused objectives or targets. Solidaristic crowds are characterized by the focus they direct toward a given objective or target. Because no single individual can achieve the objective or hit the target, a total crowd effort is required.[12] The ensuing organization of hostility, indeed violence, as Neil Smelser noted, will "correspond to the degree of pre-existing organization."[13] At Sand Creek and My Lai, the formal leaders—Chivington and Medina—did not care that their orders to kill were beyond the parameters of military norms because they did not impose on their units unwanted behavior. Rather, they played to preexisting sentiments and beliefs. The focused objective of both examples was the annihilation of the respective villagers. No one in the 3rd Colorado needed to be told that he should hate Indians and want to kill them. The men in Charley Company, suspicious of the Vietnamese from the outset, wanted to revenge their fallen comrades and given a good bash to the designated cause of their collective misery. Thus the inherent complicity between leaders and followers allowed both the 3rd Colorado and Charley Company to form cluster crowds that approximated their formal organization. Then, unified by their focused objective, they methodically murdered their victims. Any other depredations such as torture, rape, and mutilation simply made the final act more satisfying.

Role strain at Sand Creek and My Lai was resolved for most of the men through their participation in violent behavior. For them, that was the right choice. However, there is clear evidence in these two examples that some men did not participate, having made the judgment that violent behavior indeed went too far. Thus crowd formation does not necessarily lead to complete social absorption of those available.

FINAL THOUGHTS

An army, in the interests of national security, is an extension of state power invested with a virtual monopoly on the use of armed force. The usual rationale is that the army is the society's institutionalized response to possible crisis such as invasion by a foreign power. In many societies, the military is actually used to quell domestic disorder, acting to preserve the status quo. In that role, the army may function as a self-declared carrier of social virtues, an arbiter of patriotism, an invincible shield against all enemies, real and imagined. Thus besmirching the army is to insult the whole society. Armies, perforce, tend to be conservative institutions.

Disintegration of an army or of some unit within it reveals chinks in the military armor. All is not right: poor training; poor morale; poor leadership; too many incorrigible men; subversive elements at work. Disintegration is an embarrassment the army wishes would go away. But not to worry. The army will get to the bottom of things. Investigations will be made. Responsibility will be fixed. Heads will roll. Those are the ritual promises.

Sometimes, as with the Indian Mutiny, the disintegration and ensuing collective behaviors assume such magnitude that they will not go away. The Indian Mutiny turned into a generalized war fought vigorously by both sides for three years across northern India. The impact was profound. Queen Victoria took the title Empress of India, bringing that great land closer to the crown and firmly within the ample folds of British imperial policy. The East India Company and its army were disbanded. A new Indian Army was formed, one more controlled by the British regular army with the result that India after the reforms was more British than before. But never again did the Indians and British claim mutual trust.

Broad consequences of disintegration, like those in India, are rare. The process tends to be short-lived, episodic, with few if any long-range military or social implications. Yet when disintegration does occur, the military must find ways to ameliorate the situation.

Disintegration and the crowds it spawns can be minimized, even trivialized, by viewing the crisis as a minor and isolated event, a group catharsis through which built-up tensions are released, or a momentary breach of discipline caused by soldiers of bad character leading the innocent astray. This last is what William Gomm would have us believe about San Sebastian, and what Smelser would have us believe about hostile crowds in general. Disintegration can also be trivialized by burying it under more important events. The 106th Division fell apart. Unfortunate. Poor Jones. Poor Cavender and poor Descheneaux. And pity the poor men marched into prison camps. How much more uplifting and patriotic to remember the valiant Bastogne defense and George Patton's electrifying maneuver when he turned around his Third Army and raced to help rescue the beleaguered 101st Airborne. And there was a lot of war to fight: the Rhine River still had to be crossed and Germany invaded. The disintegration of the 106th warranted scant attention. Trivialization also surrounded the Sand Creek massacre. The army made inquiries. The U.S. House of Representatives and Senate made inquiries. Nothing of any consequence happened. Few people east of the Mississippi River really cared that the Army killed a bunch of Indians. For all anyone knew, they deserved their fate. There was a war to fight, a war to preserve the Union. In that context, massacring some Indians could not possibly compare to what happened at Antietam and Gettysburg.

Military disintegration and subsequent depredations can be denied. Sergeant David Mitchell, a member of Charley Company, concluded about My Lai: "It is my opinion that what they say happened did not really happen. Period."[14] Denial haunted the My Lai massacre during the following year. Gradually the press and the government brought the true dimension of the horror to the American public, *Life* magazine publishing the grim photos of the massacre taken by an army Public Relations cameraman who accompanied the operation. Congress asked questions, and the Army investigated, resulting in the Peers Report. Enlisted men and officers were indicted on a host of charges. Most of the indictments were dismissed, and Lieutenant Calley, the only man convicted of murder, was pardoned. With that act, the denial was complete and the Army's wish fulfilled as My Lai, after a suitable period of beatifically wrapping Calley in the flag and making him a paper hero, conveniently shuffled into obscurity.

The denial surrounding My Lai was small stuff compared to that cloaking the French Army mutinies. Little information appeared in the French press, and much of that in radical newspapers whose veracity could be denied. Jolinon's *mémoire* of the Coeuvres mutiny appeared in the *Mercure de France*, a journal with more limited circulation than newspapers. Government bureaus remained unapproachable and their files sealed. Pétain, having rescued the situation with common sense, discipline, and compassion, reaped justifiable rewards, but he never discussed the mutinies with anyone. Nor did anyone else in authority. Full public disclosure, officials reasoned, might have compromised the war effort by making the general staff look inhumane and incompetent. The government itself was in jeopardy, not only from opposition parties in the National Assembly but also from revolutionary groups. The needs of national security demanded silence. This was denial on a massive scale.

Trivialization, cover-up, and denial often work to disguise the true dimensions of military disintegration, and can be dismissed as minor impediments to an army's mission. Also, mutinies are rare in western democracies. Soldiers may still loot but seldom on a wholesale basis. Surrender is harder to rationalize but is often seen as individual choice. Rape and murder are viewed as individual crimes rather than expressions of collective behavior. The military can also count on public apathy and wait for interest to shift as new events compete for attention. When all else fails, a senior officer or two can be sacrificed for the good of the service, forced into retirement rather than endure a court-martial where public disclosures are a risk.

The most foolish action the military can take is to close ranks around the person on whom responsibility is fixed, feeling that blaming the one condemns all. A military mantra usually follows: "When Colonel so-and-so was charged, we were all hurt. We closed ranks around him. We're family, you know." Codes of silence are suddenly invented. Whistle blowers are ostracized. Patriotism is invoked. Self-interest is confused with national interest. The blameworthy undergo public image transformations to heroes. A fortress mentality takes over. Thus the first task of an army is to survive, both in battle and in the field of public relations.

Disintegration forces on the military a moral dilemma. They can continue to trivialize, deny, and cover up, hoping the horrors will disappear. Or they can tell the truth, openly land frankly, risking exposure of its failures, even admitting that the crowd behaviors were not the actions of bad guys in the ranks or a group catharsis but, to borrow an idea from Turner and Killian,[15] a testing by soldiers in certain situations of the military's normative value system. The French Army mutinies, for example, created temporary disorder. From that, despite the secrecy drawn around the soldiers' actions, there emerged a new high-level change of attitudes and a greater stability at the front.

The first choice exposes the military to charges of protectionism and self-interest. The second diminishes the military's aura of invincibility. This moral dilemma will be carried by any army into the future because the possibility of disintegration remains a fact of group life.

Notes

CHAPTER 1

1. For good introductions see William Moore, *The Thin Yellow Line* (New York: St. Martin's, 1975); Trevor Dupuy, *Understanding Defeat* (New York: Paragon, 1990); and John Keegan, *The Face of Battle* (New York: Viking, 1976).

2. For a recent study see David Daiches, *The Last Stuart* (New York: Putnam's Sons, 1973).

3. The sizes of the rebel and royal forces constantly changed. For details see R. R. Jarvis, *Collected Papers on the Jacobite Risings*, vol. 1 (New York: Barnes and Noble, 1971), chaps. 1 and 2; and Katherine Tomasson and Francis Buist, *Battles of the '45* (New York: Macmillan, 1963), chaps. 2–3.

4. Kerr later denied making the remark. Tomasson and Buist, *Battles of the '45*, p. 78.

5. See Christopher Hibbert, *Corunna* (New York: Macmillan, 1961); and D. W. Davies, *Sir John Moore's Peninsular Campaign, 1808–1809* (The Hague, Netherlands: Martinus Nijoff, 1974).

6. "Recollections of Rifleman Harris," in T. McGuffie, ed., *Rank and File* (New York: St. Martin's, 1964), p. 99.

7. Steven Runciman, *The First Crusade*, vol. 1, *A History of the Crusades*, rev. ed. (Cambridge: Cambridge University Press, 1962), pp. 336–341.

8. Ibid.

9. *Arab Historians of the Crusades*, ed. F. Gabrieli, tr. E. Costello (Berkeley: University of California Press, 1969), p. 11.

10. Fulcher of Chartres, *A History of the Expedition to Jerusalem*, ed. H. Fink, tr. F. Ryan (Knoxville: University of Tennessee Press, 1969), p. 122.

CHAPTER 2

1. See Richard La Piere, *Collective Behavior* (New York: McGraw-Hill, 1938), chap. 6.

2. For the volunteer-conscript debate, see Eliot Cohen, *Citizen Soldiers: The Dilemmas of Military Service* (Ithaca, NY: Cornell University Press, 1985); and *Conscripts and Volunteers*, ed. Robert Fullinwider (Totowa, NJ: Rowman and Allanheld, 1983).

3. *Historical Records of the Twenty-First Regiment of Foot* (London: Parker, 1848), p. xvii.

4. H. de Watteville, *The British Soldier*, 2nd ed. (New York: Putnam's Sons, 1955), p. 16.

5. George Mosse, *Fallen Soldiers* (New York: Oxford University Press, 1990), pp. 26–28, 53–69, and 165–166.

6. John Baynes, *Morale* (Garden City Park, NY: Avery, 1988), pp. 43–50.

7. For U.S. Army and Marine Corps training during World War II, see Samuel Stouffer et al., *The American Soldier*, vol. 1 (Princeton, NJ: Princeton University Press, 1949), esp. chap. 2; and Eugene Sledge, *With the Old Breed* (Novato, CA: Presidio Press, 1981), chaps. 1–2.

8. R. P. Reeder, ed., *Fighting on Guadalcanal* (Washington, DC: Government Printing Office, 1943), p. 47.

9. John Keegan, "Britain and America," *Times Literary Supplement* [London], 17 May 1985, p. 544. See also Ardant du Picq, *Battle Studies*, p. 137, in *Roots of Strategy*, Book 2, tr. J. Greely and R. Cotton (Harrisburg, PA: Stackpole, 1987), p. 137.

10. Ward Just, *Military Men* (New York: Knopf, 1970), p. 9.

11. Cohen, *Citizen Soldiers*, p. 76.

12. Sledge, *With the Old Breed*, pp. 40–41.

13. *Wartime: Understanding Behavior in the Second World War* (New York: Oxford University Press), chap. 7.

14. Barrie Pitt, *The Crucible of War: Western Desert, 1941* (New York: Paragon, 1989), pp. 285–286.

15. Bruce Allen Watson, *The Great Indian Mutiny: Colin Campbell and the Campaign at Lucknow* (New York: Praeger, 1991), pp. 91 and 112–113.

CHAPTER 3

1. See Christopher Hibbert, *The Great Mutiny* (New York: Viking, 1978), containing an extensive bibliography. For military perspectives see Bruce Allen Watson, *The Great Indian Mutiny: Colin Campbell and the Campaign at Lucknow*

(New York: Praeger, 1991); also Michael Edwardes, *Battles of the Indian Mutiny* (London: Batsford, 1963). For an Indian perspective see Seyed Haq, *The Great Revolution of 1857* (Karachi, Pakistan: Pakistan Historical Society, 1968).

2. Watson, *The Great Indian Mutiny*, p. 60. For the Delhi rising see James Leasor, *The Red Fort* (New York: Reynal, 1957), and Hibbert, *The Great Mutiny*, pp. 91–119.

3. Leasor, *The Red Fort*, p. 75.

4. Hibbert, *The Great Mutiny*, pp. 126–127.

5. For the Cawnpore mutiny see P. G. Gupta, *Nana Sahib and the Rising at Cawnpore* (Oxford: Clarendon Press, 1963), and Hibbert, *The Great Mutiny*, chap. 9.

6. Gupta, *Nana Sahib*, pp. 66–70.

7. Hibbert, *The Great Mutiny*, p. 218.

8. Ibid., pp. 237–238.

9. See Rudrangshu Mukerjee, *Awad in Revolt, 1857–1858: A Study in Popular Resistance* (New Delhi, India: Oxford University Press, 1984); also Watson, *The Great Indian Mutiny*, pp. 68–71.

10. William Howard Russell, *My India Mutiny Diary*, ed. Michael Edwardes (London: Cassell, 1957), p. 97.

11. *Suppression of Mutiny* (Ludhiana, India: Sirjana Press, reissue 1974), p. 25.

12. Leasor, *The Red Fort*, p. 130.

13. Lawrence Shadwell, *The Life of Colin Campbell, Lord Clyde*, vol. 2 (London: Blackwood, 1881), p. 88.

14. Richard La Piere, *Collective Behavior* (New York: McGraw-Hill, 1938), p. 519.

15. Melvin Seeman, "On the Meaning of Alienation," *American Sociological Review* 24 (December 1959), pp. 783–791.

CHAPTER 4

1. For a recent and well-written history of the war, see Martin Gilbert, *The First World War* (New York: Holt, 1994).

2. *The Great War and Modern Memory* (New York: Oxford University Press, 1975), pp. 36–37.

3. Gilbert, *The First World War*, p. 541.

4. *Dare Call It Treason* (New York: Simon and Schuster, 1963), p. 91.

5. *The Fall of the Dynasties* (Garden City, NY: Doubleday, 1963), p. 230.

6. For Verdun see Alistair Horne, *The Price of Glory, Verdun 1916* (New York: Macmillan, 1962); also Gilbert, *The First World War*, pp. 230–235 and 299–300.

7. Georges Bond, *Verdun*, tr. F. Frenage (New York: Macmillan, 1961), p. 16.

8. See Henri Gallichet, *L'offensive française de 1917* (Paris: Garnier, 1919).

9. All numbers are from Gilbert, *The First World War*, p. 323.

10. Watt, *Dare Call It Treason*, pp. 177–179.

11. Ibid., p. 183.

12. Joseph Jolinon, "La mutinerie de Coeuvres," *Mercure de France* 142 (15 August 1920), pp. 70–96.

13. Watt, *Dare Call It Treason*, pp. 192–195.

14. Ibid., p. 235. For Pétain's responses to mutiny see chaps. 13–14.

15. George Adam, *Treason and Tragedy* (London: Jonathan Cape, 1929), p. 97.

16. Melvin Seeman, "On the Meaning of Alienation," *American Sociological Review* 24 (December 1959), pp. 783–791.

17. George Mosse, *Fallen Soldiers* (New York: Oxford University Press, 1990), p. 5.

18. Richard La Piere, *Collective Behavior* (New York: McGraw-Hill, 1938), p. 549, note 19.

CHAPTER 5

1. Good surveys of the campaign include Michael Glover, *Wellington's Peninsular Victories* (New York: Macmillan, 1963), chaps. 1–3; and David Gates, *The Spanish Ulcer* (New York: Norton, 1986), chap. 15. For an evaluation of Masséna's leadership of the French in the campaign, see Eric Niderost, "One Campaign Too Many," *Military History* 8 (June 1991), pp. 42–49.

2. Glover, *Wellington's Peninsular Victories*, pp. 107–108, and Gates, *Spanish Ulcer*, p. 386.

3. Glover, *Wellington's Peninsular Victories*, p. 313.

4. Lawrence Shadwell, *The Life of Colin Campbell, Lord Clyde*, vol. 1 (London: Blackwood, 1881), p. 15.

5. See Frederick Myatt, *British Sieges of the Peninsular War* (New York: Hippocrene, 1987), chaps. 9–10; Charles Oman, *A History of the Peninsular War*, vol. 6 (Oxford: Clarendon Press, 1930), pp. 557–586, and vol. 7, chaps. 1–2; also Gates, *Spanish Ulcer*, pp. 392–396 and 422–426.

6. John Fortescue, *History of the British Army*, vol. 9 (London: Macmillan, 1920), p. 187.

7. *Letters and Journals of Field Marshal Sir William Gomm, 1799–1815*, ed. F. Carr-Gomm (London: Murray, 1881), p. 311.

8. Shadwell, *Life of Colin Campbell*, vol. 1, pp. 25–26.

9. *Letters and Journals of William Gomm*, p. 319.

10. William Napier, *History of the War in the Peninsula and the South of France*, vol. 5 (London: Cavendish, 1886), pp. 277–278.

11. *Britain and Her Army, 1509–1970* (New York: Morrow, 1970), p. 242. For the siege at Badajoz see David Patten, "Iron Duke's Sad Victory," *Military History* 8 (February 1992), pp. 50–56.

12. *Wellington's Army, 1809–1814* (London: Arnold, 1912), p. 291. For a recent study see Philip J. Haythornthwaite, *The Armies of Wellington* (London: Arms and Armour, 1994).

13. H. de Watteville, *The British Soldier*, 2nd ed. (New York: Putnam's Sons, 1955), p. 109.

14. *Collective Behavior* (New York: McGraw-Hill, 1938), pp. 442–443.

15. Elizabeth Longford, *Wellington: Years of the Sword* (New York: Harper and Row, 1969), p. 332. See G. R. Gleig, *The Subaltern* (Edinburgh, Scotland: Blackwell, 1874), p. 34.

16. Melvin Seeman, "On the Meaning of Alienation," *American Sociological Review* 24 (December 1959), pp. 783–791.

17. Longford, *Wellington: Years of the Sword*, p. 332.

CHAPTER 6

1. All numbers are from John Keegan, *The Second World War* (New York: Viking, 1990), p. 410. Jacques Nobécourt notes the Germans lost 240,000 killed and wounded. See *Hitler's Last Gamble*, tr. R. Barry (New York: Schocken, 1967), p. 27.

2. Charles MacDonald, *A Time for Trumpets* (New York: Morrow, 1985), p. 11.

3. Hugh Cole, *The Ardennes: Battle of the Bulge* (Washington, DC: Office of the Department of Military History, U.S. Army, 1965), p. 137.

4. See MacDonald, *A Time for Trumpets*, pp. 644–655, for the complete German order of battle, with comments on unit strength and viability. See also pp. 630–644 for British and American orders of battle.

5. Ibid., p. 116.

6. Cole, *The Ardennes*, p. 149.

7. MacDonald, *A Time for Trumpets*, pp. 128–129.

8. Cole, *The Ardennes*, p. 154.

9. MacDonald, *A Time for Trumpets*, p. 327.

10. Ibid., p. 341–342.

11. Charles Whiting, *Death of a Division* (New York: Stein and Day, 1981), p. 92; see also R. E. Dupuy, *St. Vith: Lion in the Way* (Washington, DC: Infantry Journal Press, 1949). For a personal recollection see Al Hemingway, "Ghost Front Attack," *Military History* 9 (August 1992), pp. 50–57.

12. Whiting, *Death of a Division*, p. 127.

13. Cole, *The Ardennes*, p. 170.

14. Gay Hammerman, "Losing Battles: The Experience of the Combat Soldier," in *Understanding Defeat*, ed. Trevor Dupuy (New York: Paragon, 1990), pp. 25–48, and fig. 3.1.

15. *The Art of Maneuver* (Novato, CA: Presidio Press, 1991), pp. 73–76; see also John Keegan and Richard Holmes, with J. Gau, *Soldiers: A History of Men in Battle* (New York: Viking, 1989), pp. 41–42; and John Keegan, *The Face of Battle* (New York: Viking, 1976), pp. 269–279.

16. "Losing Battles," pp. 28–29.

17. Whiting, *Death of a Division*, p. 147.

18. Melvin Seeman, "On the Meaning of Alienation," *American Sociological Review* 24 (December 1959), pp. 786–788.

CHAPTER 7

1. David Lavender, *Bent's Fort* (Garden City, NY: Doubleday, 1954), pp. 337–340.

2. Stan Hoig, *The Sand Creek Massacre* (Norman: University of Oklahoma Press, 1961), p. 17.

3. Duane Schultz, *Month of the Freezing Moon: The Sand Creek Massacre* (New York: St. Martin's, 1990), pp. 59–61.

4. Hoig, *The Sand Creek Massacre*, p. 35.

5. George Grinnell, *The Fighting Cheyennes* (Norman: University of Oklahoma Press, 1963), p. 138.

6. Schultz, *Month of the Freezing Moon*, p. 73.

7. Grinnell, *The Fighting Cheyennes*, p. 152.

8. See Schultz, *Month of the Freezing Moon*, pp. 80–81, and Hoig, *The Sand Creek Massacre*, pp. 58–59.

9. Schultz, *Month of the Freezing Moon*, p. 89.

10. Hoig, *The Sand Creek Massacre*, p. 99.

11. Grinnell, *The Fighting Cheyennes*, p. 160, note 3.

12. Ibid., p. 167.

13. United States Senate, "Sand Creek Massacre," *Report of the Secretary of War*, Senate Document No. 26, 39th Congress, 2nd Session (Washington, DC: Government Printing Office, 1867), pp. 25 and 47.

14. Schultz, *Month of the Freezing Moon*, p. 134; and Hoig, *The Sand Creek Massacre*, p. 147.

15. Grinnell, *The Fighting Cheyennes*, pp. 176–180.

16. United States House of Representatives, "Massacre of the Cheyenne Indians," *Report on the Conduct of the War*, 38th Congress, 2nd Session (Washington, DC: Government Printing Office, 1865), pp. v and 104. See Hoig, *The Sand Creek Massacre*, chap. 10, for a narrative of the investigations.

17. Schultz, *Month of the Freezing Moon*, p. 137.

18. Richard La Piere, *Collective Behavior* (New York: McGraw-Hill, 1938), p. 519.

CHAPTER 8

1. William Peers, *The My Lai Inquiry* (New York: Norton, 1979), p. 130.

2. Michael Bilton and Kevin Sim, *Four Hours in My Lai* (New York: Viking, 1992), p. 33. See also Joseph Goldstein, Burke Marshall, and Jack Schwarz, *The My Lai Massacre: Beyond the Reach of Law?* (New York: Free Press, 1976), chap. 9. This publication reproduces the entire Peers Report, the Army's official inquiry, and will be noted hereafter as the Peers Report.

3. Bilton and Sim, *Four Hours in My Lai*, pp. 39–41, and the Peers Report, pp. 194–195.

4. Philip Caputo, *A Rumor of War* (New York: Holt, Rinehart, and Winston, 1977), pp. 228–229.

5. Bilton and Sim, *Four Hours in My Lai*, pp. 34–41.

6. Ibid., chap. 3. The Peers Report, chap. 4, gives details of the unit's organization and training.

7. The Peers Report, p. 201.

8. *Four Hours in My Lai*, pp. 73–74.

9. Ibid., p. 68.

10. Jonathan Schell, "The Military Half," in *The Real War* (New York: Pantheon, 1987), pp. 198 and 235.

11. Bilton and Sim, *Four Hours in My Lai*, p. 70.

12. Seymour Hersh, *My Lai 4: A Report on the Massacre and Its Aftermath* (New York: Random House, 1970), p. 34.

13. Bilton and Sim, *Four Hours in My Lai*, pp. 98–101.

14. Hersh, *My Lai 4*, p. 50; see also Bilton and Sim, *Four Hours in My Lai*, pp. 119–120.

15. The Peers Report, p. 135.

16. Hersh, *My Lai 4*, p. 75. See also Bilton and Sim, *Four Hours in My Lai*, p. 134.

17. Melvin Seeman, "On the Meaning of Alienation," *American Sociological Review* 24 (December 1959), pp. 783–791.

18. The Peers Report, p. 213.

19. Bilton and Sim, *Four Hours in My Lai*, pp. 92–93, 367–368.

CHAPTER 9

1. John Keegan, "Regimental Ideology," in *War, Economy, and the Military Mind*, ed. G. Best and A. Wheathead (Totowa, NJ: Rowan and Littlefield, 1976), p. 17; see also John Baynes, *Morale* (Garden City Park, NY: Avery, 1988), p. 102–108, and chap. 7; Samuel Stouffer et al., *The American Soldier*, vol. 2

(Princeton, NJ: Princeton University Press, 1949), p. 105; and David Marlowe, "The Manning of the Force and the Structure of Battle: Part I—The AVF and the Draft," in *Conscripts and Volunteers*, ed. Robert Fullinwider (Totawa, NJ: Rowman and Allanheld, 1983), p. 53.

2. "Cohesion and Disintegration in the *Wehrmacht* in World War II," in *Military Conflict*, ed. Morris Janowitz (Beverley Hills, CA: Sage, 1975), pp. 177–220; see also Morris Janowitz and Roger Little, *Sociology and the Military Establishment*, 3rd ed. (Beverley Hills, CA: Sage, 1974), pp. 103–109; see also Omer Bartov, *Hitler's Army* (Oxford: Oxford University Press, 1991), esp. chap. 3.

3. "On the Meaning of Alienation," *American Sociological Review* 24 (December 1959), pp. 783–791. Seeman also discussed self-estrangement, but its application to this study was of dubious value. For more recent literature see Melvin Seeman, "Alienation Studies," *Annual Review of Sociology* 1 (1975), pp. 91–123; also R. Felix Geyer and David Schweitzer, eds., *Alienation: Problems of Meaning, Theory and Method* (London: Routledge and Kegan Paul, 1981).

4. *Society and Personality* (Englewood Cliffs, NJ: Prentice-Hall, 1961), p. 569.

5. Richard La Piere, *Collective Behavior* (New York: McGraw-Hill, 1938), pp. 520–521.

6. Ibid.

7. Ibid., pp. 3–4; also Ralph Turner and Louis Killian, *Collective Behavior* (Englewood Cliffs, NJ: Prentice-Hall, 1957), pp. 3–4; and Neil Smelser, *A Theory of Collective Behavior* (New York: Free Press, 1963), pp. 8–9.

8. Turner and Killian, *Collective Behavior*, p. 61.

9. For a complex discussion of crowd hostility, see Smelser, *A Theory of Collective Behavior*, pp. 101–109.

10. Ibid., pp. 260–261.

11. W. J. Goode, "A Theory of Role Strain," *American Sociological Review* 25 (August 1960), pp. 438–496.

12. Turner and Killian, *Collective Behavior*, pp. 84–85 and 100.

13. Smelser, *A Theory of Collective Behavior*, p. 255.

14. *Newsweek*, 22 December 1969.

15. Turner and Killian, *Collective Behavior*, p. 529.

Selected Bibliography

Babington, Anthony. *For the Sake of Example: Courts-Martial 1914–1920*. London: Leo Cooper, 1983.

Barnett, Correlli. *Britain and Her Army, 1509–1970*. New York: Morrow, 1970.

Bartov, Omer. *Hitler's Army*. Oxford: Oxford University Press, 1991.

Baynes, John. *Morale*. Garden City Park, NY: Avery, 1988.

Bhargava, Moti Lal. *Architects of Indian Freedom Struggle*. New Delhi, India: Deep and Deep, 1981.

Bilton, Michael, and Kevin Sim. *Four Days in My Lai*. New York: Viking, 1992.

Brissett, Dennis. "Collective Behavior: The Sense of a Rubric." *American Journal of Sociology* 74 (July 1968), pp. 70–78.

Cannon, Richard. *Historical Record of the Ninth Regiment of Foot*. London: Parker, 1848.

Cole, Hugh. *The Ardennes: Battle of the Bulge*. Washington, DC: Office of the Department of Military History, U.S. Army, 1965.

Daiches, David. *The Last Stuart*. New York: Putnam's Sons, 1973.

David, Saul. *The Salerno Mutiny*. New York: Brassey's, 1995.

Davies, D. W. *Sir John Moore's Peninsular Campaign, 1808–1809*. The Hague, Netherlands: Martinus Nijoff, 1974.

Dorset, Phyllis. *The New El Dorado*. New York: Macmillan, 1970.

Dupuy, R. E. *St. Vith: Lion in the Way*. Washington, DC: Infantry Journal Press, 1949.

Dupuy, Trevor. *Understanding Defeat*. New York: Paragon, 1990.

Edwardes, Michael. *Red Year: The Indian Mutiny of 1857*. London: Hamilton, 1973.

————. *Battles of the Indian Mutiny*. London: Batsford, 1963.

Falls, Cyril. *The Battle of Caparetto*. New York: Lippincott, 1966.

Fortescue, John. *Six British Soldiers*. London: Williams and Norgate, 1928.

Fulcher of Chartres. *A History of the Expedition to Jerusalem, 1095–1127*. Ed. H. Fink; tr. F. Ryan. Knoxville: University of Tennessee Press, 1969.

Fullinwider, Robert, ed. *Conscripts and Volunteers*. Totowa, NJ: Rowman and Allanheld, 1983.

Gallichet, Henri. *L'offensive française de 1917*. Paris: Garnier, 1919.

Gates, David. *The Spanish Ulcer*. New York: Norton, 1986.

Glover, Michael. *Wellington's Peninsular Victories*. New York: Macmillan, 1963.

Glover, Richard. *Peninsular Preparation: The Reform of the British Army, 1795–1809*. Cambridge: Cambridge University Press, 1963.

Goldstein, Joseph, Burke Marshall, and Jack Schwartz. *The My Lai Massacre and Its Cover-Up: Beyond the Reach of Law?* [The Peers Report]. New York: Free Press, 1976.

Gomm, William. *Letters and Journals of Field Marshal Sir William Gomm, 1799–1815*. Ed. F. Carr-Gomm. London, Murray, 1881.

Grinker, R. G., and J. P. Spiegel. *Men Under Stress*. New York: McGraw-Hill, 1963.

Grinnell, George. *The Fighting Cheyennes*. Norman: University of Oklahoma Press, 1963.

Gupta, P. C. *Nana Sahib and the Rising at Cawnpore*. Oxford: Clarendon Press, 1963.

Haq, Syed. *The Great Revolution of 1857*. Karachi, Pakistan: Pakistan Historical Society, 1968.

Heathcote, T. A. *The Indian Army: The Garrison of British India, 1822–1922*. New York: Hippocrene, 1974.

Hersh, Seymour. *My Lai 4: A Report on the Massacre and Its Aftermath*. New York: Random House, 1970.

Hibbert, Christopher. *The Great Mutiny, 1857*. New York: Viking, 1978.

————. *Corunna*. New York: Macmillan, 1961.

Hicken, Victor. *The American Fighting Man*. London: Collier-Macmillan, 1969.

Hill, J., and L. Hill. *Raymond IV, Count of Toulouse*. Syracuse, NY: Syracuse University Press, 1962.

Hoig, Stan. *The Sand Hills Massacre*. Norman: University of Oklahoma Press, 1961.

Horne, Alistair. *The Price of Glory, Verdun 1916*. New York: Macmillan, 1962.

Janowitz, Morris, ed. *Military Conflict*. Beverley Hills, CA: Sage, 1975.

Janowitz, Morris, and Roger Little. *Sociology and the Military Establishment*. 3rd ed. Beverley Hills, CA: Sage, 1974.

Jolinon, Joseph. "La mutinerie de Coeuvres." *Mercure de France* 142 (15 August 1920), pp. 70–96.

Kahan Commission. *The Beirut Massacre*. New York: Karz-Cohl, 1983.

Keegan, John. *The Second World War*. New York: Viking, 1990.

———. *The Face of Battle*. New York: Viking, 1976.

———. "Regimental Ideology," in *War, Economy, and the Military Mind*, pp. 3–18. Ed. G. Best and A. Wheathead. Totowa, NJ: Rowan and Littlefield, 1976.

Kohn, Richard. "The Social History of the American Soldier: A Review and Prospectus of Research." *American Historical Review* 86 (1981), pp. 553–567.

Krey, A. C., ed. *The First Crusade: The Accounts of Eye-Witnesses and Participants*. Gloucester, MA: Peter Smith, 1958.

La Piere, Richard. *Collective Behavior*. New York: McGraw-Hill, 1938.

Lavender, David. *Bent's Fort*. Garden City, NY: Doubleday, 1954.

Lunt, James, ed. *From Sepoy to Subedar: Being the Life and Adventures of Subedar Sita Ram*. Tr. (1873) Lt. Colonel Norgate. London: Routledge and Keegan Paul, 1970.

MacDonald, Charles. *A Time for Trumpets*. New York: Morrow, 1985.

Manteuffel, Hasso von. "The Battle of the Ardennes," in *Decisive Battles of World War II: The German View*, pp. 391–418. Ed. H. Jacobsen and J. Rohwer; tr. E. Fitzgerald. New York: Putnam's Sons, 1965.

Marshall, S.L.A. *Men Against Fire*. New York: Morrow, 1957.

Millar, Ronald. *Death of an Army: The Siege of Kut, 1915–1916*. Boston: Houghton Mifflin, 1970.

Moore, William, *The Thin Yellow Line*. New York: St. Martin's, 1975.

Moran, Lord. *The Anatomy of Courage*. 2nd ed. London: Constable, 1966.

Moyse-Bartlett, H. "The British Army in 1850." *Journal of the Society of Army Historical Research* 52 (1974), pp. 221–237.

Myatt, Frederick. *British Sieges of the Peninsular War*. New York: Hippocrene, 1987.

Nobécourt, Jacques. *Hitler's Last Gamble*. Tr. R. Barry. New York: Schocken, 1967.

Oman, Charles. *A History of the Peninsular War*. Vols. 6 and 7. Oxford: Clarendon Press, 1930.

———. *Wellington's Army, 1809–1814*. London: Arnold, 1912.

Peers, William, *The My Lai Inquiry*. New York: Norton, 1979.

Picq, A. du. *Battle Studies*, in *Roots of Strategy*, Book 2, pp. 27–299. Tr. J. Greely and R. Cotton. Harrisburg, PA: Stackpole, 1987.

Reeves, R. A. *The Shooting at Sharpeville*. Boston: Houghton Mifflin, 1961.

Runciman, Steven. *The First Crusade*. Vol. 1. *A History of the Crusades*. Rev. ed. Cambridge: Cambridge University Press, 1962.

Russell, William Howard. *My India Mutiny Diary*. Ed. Michael Edwardes. London: Cassell, 1957.

Schell, Jonathan. *The Real War*. New York: Pantheon, 1987.

Schultz, Duane. *Month of the Freezing Moon: The Sand Creek Massacre*. New York: St. Martin's, 1990.

Seeman, Melvin. "On the Meaning of Alienation." *American Sociological Review* 24 (December 1959), pp. 783–791.

Sledge, Eugene. *With the Old Breed*. Novato, CA: Presidio Press, 1981.

Smelser, Neil. *A Theory of Collective Behavior*. New York: Free Press, 1963.

Stouffer, Samuel, et al. *The American Soldier*. 2 vols. Princeton, NJ: Princeton University Press, 1949.

Toland, John. *The Battle of the Bulge*. New York: Random House, 1959.

Tomasson, Katherine, and Francis Buist. *Battles of the '45*. New York: Macmillan, 1962.

Turner, Ralph, and Louis Killian. *Collective Behavior*. Englewood Cliffs, NJ: Prentice-Hall, 1957.

Ward, Andrew. *Our Bones Are Scattered: The Cawnpore Massacre and the Indian Mutiny of 1857*. New York: Holt, 1996.

Ward, S. P. "Some Fresh Insights into the Corunna Campaign." *Journal of the Society of Army Historical Research* 28 (Autumn 1950), pp. 107–126.

Watson, Bruce Allen. *Sieges: A Comparative Study*. Westport, CT: Praeger, 1993.

————. *The Great Indian Mutiny: Colin Campbell and the Campaign at Lucknow*. New York: Praeger, 1991.

Watt, Richard. *Dare Call It Treason*. New York: Simon and Schuster, 1963.

Whiting, Charles. *Death of a Division*. New York: Stein and Day, 1981.

Index

Aisne River, French offensive along. *See* French Army in World War I; French Army mutinies of 1917; Nivelle, Robert

Alienation, 26; bases of, 160–61; in Charley Company, 152–53; forms of, 161–63; in French Army mutinies, 62–64; in Indian Mutiny, 45–46; and military disintegration, 161; at siege of San Sebastian, 85–87; in 3rd Colorado Volunteers, 129; in U.S. Army 106th Infantry Division, 109. *See also* Isolation; Meaninglessness; Military disintegration; Normlessness; Powerlessness

Anthony, Major Scott, 117; duplicity of, 123, 124; at Fort Lyon, 122; at Sand Creek, 125, 127

Arapaho Indians, 112; chiefs in Washington, D.C., 118; depredations against, 125–26, 166; and Hungates, 119, 120, 121, 122; join Sioux in raids, 118–19; reservation for, 113; at Sand Creek, 123, 125; settlers' attitudes toward, 113, 116, 117. *See also* Chivington, John; Sand Creek massacre; Third (3rd) Colorado Volunteers

Army of the East India Company (Indian Army): and British officers in, 42; Cawnpore garrison mutiny, 322–34; and Christian evangelism, 44; Delhi garrison mutiny, 30–31; in the Delhi siege, 38–40; and forms of alienation, 45–46; Lucknow garrison mutiny, 35–38; Meerut garrison mutiny, 27–30, 44; perceptions of British Army, 41–42. *See also* Cawnpore; Delhi; Lucknow

Barker, Lieutenant Colonel Frank: death of, 149, 151, 158; plan to attack My Lai, 145–46; Task Force Barker, 142

Bent, George, 121; account of Sand Creek massacre, 125–26

About the Author

BRUCE ALLEN WATSON is Professor Emeritus of Art History and past chairman of the Division of Applied and Fine Arts at Diablo Valley College. In addition to books and articles on sociology and art history, he has written three books on military history: *The Great Indian Mutiny: Colin Campbell and the Campaign at Lucknow* (Praeger, 1991); *Sieges: A Comparative Study* (Praeger, 1993); and *Desert Battle: Comparative Perspectives* (Praeger, 1995).

ISBN 0-275-95223-1

90000>

9 780275 952235

HARDCOVER BAR CODE